Challenging Prophetic Metaphor

Challenging Prophetic Metaphor

Theology and Ideology in the Prophets

Julia M. O'Brien

Westminster John Knox Press
LOUISVILLE • LONDON

Book design by Sharon Adams
Cover design by Lisa Buckley
Cover art courtesy of Getty Images/Stockbyte

First edition
Published by Westminster John Knox Press
Louisville, Kentucky

This book is printed on acid-free paper that meets the American National Standards Institute Z39.48 standard. ♾

PRINTED IN THE UNITED STATES OF AMERICA

08 09 10 11 12 13 14 15 16 17—10 9 8 7 6 5 4 3 2 1

Library of Congress Cataloging-in-Publication Data

O'Brien, Julia M.
  Challenging prophetic metaphor : theology and ideology in the prophets / Julia M. O'Brien. — 1st ed.
    p. cm.
  Includes bibliographical references and indexes.
  ISBN 978-0-664-22964-1 (alk. paper)
  1. Bible. O.T. Prophets—Criticism, interpretation, etc.   2. Bible. O.T. Prophets—Feminist criticism.   3. Metaphor in the Bible.   I. Title.
  BS1505.52.O27   2008
  224'.06—dc22   2008008476

Contents

Acknowledgments

*I*n *The Writing Life*, Annie Dillard describes how a work in progress easily grows into a beast. Every night it gains strength and stature, and every day the writer must take up chair and whip to master it again: "Simba!"[1]

I am grateful to those who gave me the resources, the encouragement, and the courage to stay in the ring. My colleagues at Lancaster Theological Seminary offered much. Anabel Proffitt and David Mellott made sure that I did not forget the joy of writing, and Anne Thayer and Greg Carey made necessary corrections to my historical overview. Chuck Melchert and the students in his Doctor of Ministry seminar shared with me the wisdom of their experience. My friends and colleagues at nearby Elizabethtown College, Chris Bucher and Erika Fitz, read earlier versions of my attempts to wrestle with prophetic metaphors and offered insightful feedback. I appreciate the ways in which all of these friends listened to and commiserated with my struggle to say what I needed to say.

Through it all, my husband David has been my partner, ever aware of my need both for "a room of my own" and for loving companionship. And even as she begins to furnish a room of her own, my daughter, Anna, continues to remind me of why and for what I keep shouting, "Simba!"

I am grateful for all of these people in my life.

I thank, too, my editor, Jon Berquist, for helping the book take its current shape, and all the helpful staff at WJK Press.

Julia M. O'Brien
January 30, 2008

Bible Translations Used

ASV   American Standard Version, 1901

KJV   King James Version, 1611/1769

NIV   New International Version, 1984

NRSV   New Revised Standard Version, 1989

RSV   Revised Standard Version, 1952

TNK   Tanakh translation, Jewish Publication Society, 1985

Introduction

As someone who spends much of her life teaching and writing about the Old Testament, I have two primary goals in regard to these texts. One is to help people value, even enjoy, the Old Testament and move beyond negative stereotypes of this collection as difficult, nasty, or just plain boring. I long for readers to quit saying, "Why do I have to read the Old Testament, anyway?" and to experience for themselves the fascination and power of these texts.

My other goal is to challenge readers to acknowledge the violence, sexism, and other "problems" of the Old Testament and of the Bible as a whole. I want them to see—really see—how much all parts of the Bible are shaped by assumptions about people and about the world that many of us spend our energies and our money to combat.

As you might imagine, these goals often rub up against each other. Asking students or church members to see that there is even more sexism and violence in the Old Testament than they may have noticed usually makes the text less (not more) likable, or it at least confirms all the negative impressions of the Old Testament that they already have. Once, after a class devoted to naming the assumptions about children and women that run through the Genesis account of Abraham's near sacrifice of Isaac, a student asked me why I study the Old Testament, since, she claimed, "You don't seem to like it very much."

Valuing the Old Testament and taking its ethical difficulties seriously: is it possible to do both?

The Current Stalemate

Looking at how folks respond to the Prophetic Books of the Old Testament, the answer would seem to be "no." Both in the academy and on the pew, interpreters tend to choose one option at the expense of the other: people love or hate the Prophetic Books with equivalent passion. As I will trace in the next chapter, the Christian church has long praised the Prophetic Books as the pinnacle of ethics and value in the Old Testament. Interpreters in the nineteenth century heralded the individual prophets as the champions of "ethical monotheism," lone voices against the corruption of Israel's neighbors and of its own religious hierarchy. More recently, the well-respected Old Testament scholar Walter Brueggemann has insisted that the prophets, through the power of their speech, denounced deadly "royal ideology"—Brueggemann's term for systems of domination that deny the sovereignty of God.[1] Beyond the academic sphere, Christian social activists rally behind Micah's insistence that what God requires of mortals is "to do justice, and to love kindness, / and to walk humbly with your God" (Mic. 6:8). Not only Martin Luther King Jr. but also current denominational slogans echo Amos's rousing cry to "let justice roll down like waters, / and righteousness like an everflowing stream" (Amos 5:24). Such readers locate within the Prophetic Books all that is most true of Christian teaching.

And yet, a thorough reading of all that Micah and Amos and the rest of the Prophets have to say has raised an outcry from those who see just how ethically problematic these "liberating" texts are. Most challenging of all, feminist interpreters of the Prophets have insisted, repeatedly and convincingly, that these texts are misogynistic. Throughout the Prophetic Books, the nation and/or the city are called "whores," the punishment for which is described in graphic language that can only be described as rape. Some of the language is so sexually explicit and voyeuristic that feminist interpreters such as Athalya Brenner label it "pornoprophetic."[2]

Other aspects of these books should raise concerns as well. While the Prophetic Books do criticize people for their violence, they also call for God to be violent in response. In Isaiah 63, for example, God is envisioned as a warrior returning from battle dripping in blood, and Habakkuk 3 pleads for the Divine Warrior to march again. Those who read from psychological perspectives see the Prophets' insistence that national defeat is the punishment for wrongdoing as perpetuating dangerous patterns of blame and guilt. Other readers have shown how prophetic texts reinforce nationalism and social stratification. Reasons to dislike the Prophetic Books present themselves all too readily.

These two very different perspectives on prophetic literature are usually pitted against one another as incompatible. Chapter 3 provides examples of this "either/or" thinking. On the one hand, commentators who wish to embrace the ethical value of the Prophets tend to ignore feminist critique, dismiss it as "unchristian," or strategically relegate it to footnotes. On the other hand, those incensed by the prophetic treatment of women explain why these books cannot be accepted as authoritative, or even fruitfully read, in public or private contexts. To be fair, some attempts have been made to bridge these two perspectives. As I will explain, however, most of these attempts remain unconvincing because, after struggling with the tension between the two options, they ultimately choose one at the expense of the other.

And so the dilemma remains. Is it possible to take seriously the sexism and violence of the Prophetic Books and still find value in them, to refuse to pit appreciation against critique? Is there a way to do theology after critique, to let critique inform theological reflection rather than stand as its opponent?

Prophetic Metaphors as a Case Study

As a way to approach such big and important questions, I have chosen to focus on one aspect of the Prophetic Books: the metaphors that they use to describe Yahweh, God of Israel, and cities or countries. The Prophetic Books are filled with such images, explicit and implicit. Many are familiar, such as God as a father or king and Jerusalem as daughter. Others are perhaps more surprising: Yahweh is "a garland of glory, / and a diadem of beauty" (Isa. 28:5–6) and "will be like the dew to Israel; / he shall blossom like the lily" (Hos. 14:5); Zion is "like a shelter in a cucumber field" (Isa. 1:8).

In my judgment, the Prophetic Books provide some of the Bible's most challenging metaphors. Christians who pray the God images of the Psalms, meditating on God as a gentle shepherd or strong fortress, may find more strange and jarring Hosea's comparison of Yahweh to maggots (5:12), to a bear robbed of her cubs, and to a lion and a leopard—all ready to devour the people (Hos. 13:7–8). As I will explore in the following chapters, Hosea casts God as an abusing spouse. In Nahum, Yahweh threatens rape. Even metaphors for God that appear elsewhere in the Bible in contexts of comfort and care, such as God as father, also take on a harsher tone in the Prophets. Similarly, while the images of Jerusalem as a daughter and the nation of Edom as a brother seem benign, even tender, they too are intertwined with problematic ways of thinking about others.

These metaphors, clearly, provide fertile ground for the question of how contemporary people might respond to the messiness of the prophetic texts. If the Prophets present us with worldviews that we consider problematic, even dangerous, should we continue to read them? If so, in what way?

Reading Prophetic Books

The Prophetic Books can be—and are—studied in a wide variety of ways. Over centuries of interpretation, attention has ranged from how the Prophets predict Jesus, to how they inform church doctrine, to the method of their composition, to their literary style. In the current climate, scholars investigate ancient Near Eastern parallels, rhetorical style, the phenomenon of prophetic ecstasy, and the shaping of materials into a canon. Given all of these options, I attempt to describe my own approach to reading the Prophetic Books and the understandings that will guide this project.

The Prophets as Books, Not People

Many readers of the Bible attempt to understand what the prophets were like as individuals—how they received their messages, what kinds of lives they led, or what their personalities were like. Interpreters, for example, have devoted a great deal of energy to reconstructing the home life of Hosea, the emotional profile of Jeremiah, and the psychological history of Ezekiel. Throughout the generations, these reconstructed prophets have been understood in different ways—as champions of ethics over ritual, as social activists, as ecstatic mystics, as bearers of tradition. All of these understandings, however, share the view that the prophets were important individuals who faithfully delivered God's message in specific times and places.

In contrast to these approaches, this study does not consider the prophets as people but instead focuses on the books that bear their names. It does so for several reasons. The first is that the books themselves devote little interest in the personality of the prophet. As a general rule they provide scant biographical information about the one whose words are recorded: rarely do we know the age of the prophet at the beginning of his career, his genealogy, or details of his personal life. Many of the books (such as Nahum, Obadiah, and Malachi) reveal so little about the prophet as to be functionally anonymous. The books' relative lack of interest in the biography of the prophets is reflected, too, in the way the Prophetic Books are organized. Few progress chronologically, and most are apparently organized by the themes of speeches. Even those books with frequent date markers, such as Haggai and Zechariah, leave large blocks of time unaccounted for, leaving the reader to wonder what prophets did before and after delivering their messages. Other factors also suggest that the individuality of prophets was unimportant to those who composed their books. The books are similar in vocabulary and theme, often borrowing from one another. The vision that Isa. 2:2–4 offers of the future appears as well in Mic. 4:1–3, and Obad. 1–9 is nearly identical to Jer. 49:7–22. The book of Zephaniah echoes the themes and vocabulary of other Prophetic Books, reading like a prophetic primer.

A second reason for focusing on the book rather than the "historical prophet" is that I have not been persuaded by the claims of some scholars that they can reconstruct the actual words of the prophets from the writings that we have. In the early twentieth century, scholars such as Hermann Gunkel developed a method called "form criticism," which they claimed could help readers distinguish between the original words of the prophet and the contributions of their editors. According to this approach, certain literary styles distinguish authentic prophetic speech from later additions. A prophet's oracle of salvation or oracle of judgment has a particular pattern; when that pattern is disturbed or verses seem to reflect a time period later than that of the prophet's lifetime, we reasonably can conclude that those verses are the work of a redactor.

I see numerous problems with such form-critical approaches. As others have well argued, the conclusions of early form critics were strongly shaped by their prior presuppositions, such that any note of hope in a preexilic prophet must be a later addition. I also share with many contemporary scholars of the Prophets the belief that many if not all of these books were crafted long after the dates listed in their superscriptions, some as late as the Persian period (fifth–fourth centuries BCE). For example, I have argued elsewhere that Hosea-Zephaniah may have been shaped into their current form in order to conform to the picture of the "former prophets" frequently mentioned in the book of Zechariah.[3]

The third and perhaps strongest reason that I focus on the Prophetic Books rather than prophets as individuals is because the books are what we have. The Prophetic Books, not prophets, constitute the canon and confront the modern reader with challenges. I do at times speak of the "author" of the Prophetic Book as the agent behind its current shape, not to deny that the books have a complex history but to stress that a human writer (perhaps many human writers) has chosen particular words and images for a larger purpose.

Prophetic Books As Documents Written by Humans

Since the late seventeenth century, scholars of the Bible have increasingly focused on its human authors. The legacy of "historical criticism," as described in the next chapter, is a concern with the way that biblical writings reflect the concerns of specific, historically grounded communities.

Although (with the exception of the last chapter) this volume does not devote significant attention to the specifics of dating the Prophetic Books or to the specific social and political situations in which each was written, it is informed by the assumption that these writings are not "God's words" in a simplistic way. These books, I contend, are not verbatim transcripts of God's prepared speeches. Rather, they are intentionally crafted pieces of literature.

To read the content of the biblical books as human creations admittedly rubs against the way the Prophetic Books present themselves. The brief statements of historical setting that open the books (called superscriptions) name what follows as the prophet's report of what God spoke to him or showed him in a vision. The words of the prophets are marked with "messenger speech" ("thus says the LORD"), and prophets like Jeremiah complain that God gave them no choice but to deliver the divine message. Some translations even put God's speech to the prophet in quotation marks, although biblical Hebrew itself does not have such markings.

Rather than taking this presentation of the prophet at face value, readers instead may understand it as part of the rhetorical style in which the authors of the book chose to portray the prophet. The writers of the Prophetic Books not only decided how to organize the books but also when to mark a saying with "thus says the LORD." By including messenger speech in the writing of the book, the authors instruct the reader to grant what is said divine authority, to read as if the prophet's personality did not affect his message, and to "forget" that there is a writer who has presented what that prophet said in a particular way.

To understand "thus says the LORD" as the style of the writing rather than evidence that God spoke these words verbatim to the prophet does not rule out the very real and important possibility that the Prophetic Books do faithfully speak for God. It does, however, mean that I proceed from the conviction that it is impossible to speak of God outside the realities of human language and culture. When humans talk about, think about, and experience God, they do so in ways that are shaped by their language, their culture, and their worldviews. That is true of God-language today and of God-language in the Bible. The language of the Prophets, just as much as the Wisdom literature of the Old Testament, reflects human attempts to understand the divine and the divine's expectations for human thought and behavior.

The Prophetic Books as Persuasion

I work from the conviction that the Prophetic Books are persuasive literature. They seek to move readers to see the world in a particular way in order to change their thinking, feeling, and, ultimately, their behavior. That is, the Prophetic Books constitute creative theology—the efforts of those who composed this literature to communicate their understandings of God and God's relation to humanity.

Metaphor is one key technique that the Prophets use to persuade. Along with other rhetorical devices such as hyperbole, puns, alphabetic sequences, poetic meter, and repetition of words and phrases, the authors use comparison to convince readers to see reality in a new way. According to the story line of the book of Jeremiah, when leading politicians in the sixth century BCE argued that making alliances with Egypt and Babylonia was good military strategy, Jeremiah ridiculed the policy by calling his nation a "lusting wild ass at home in the wilderness, in her heat sniffing the wind!" (Jer. 2:24). Against the implied setting of the powerful Assyrian Empire, the book of Nahum portrays Nineveh, the Assyrian capital, as a whore stripped and sexually violated for her crimes. Providing a new mental picture for the current situation, creating a necessary fiction in which to think, prophetic language attempts to change behavior by changing perception.

The shock value of these latter metaphors is likely their intended purpose. If powerful enough, a shocking comparison provokes an emotional response—and leads to change. In the case of metaphors for God, comparing God with something or someone who is not obviously godlike shocks ancient and modern readers into seeing God in new ways. Given the strong theme of judgment in the Prophets, it is little surprise that these metaphors do not portray a warm and fuzzy deity.

The Prophetic Books Read Ideologically

Because they self-consciously draw on human relationships to describe God and communities, prophetic metaphors invite consideration of the *human* origins and *human* consequences of this language. That is, they invite ideological critique. In general terms, *ideology* refers to a worldview or set of beliefs shared by members of a group. That worldview is so obvious to those members that it most often remains invisible: it is treated as common sense or "the way things are."

Ideologies, however, are rarely if ever innocuous. They reflect ways of thinking about privilege and power. According to Marxist thinkers, those who have power impose their ideologies on everyone, making what really only benefits a few appear as if it benefits all. Language and texts both reflect the ideologies of those who produce them and reinforce those ideologies by making them seem normal and right. For example, calling the death of civilians "collateral damage" or the bombing of an enemy's home a "surgical strike" or "air support" benefits military interests by making the actions sound supportive, medically necessary, and unrelated to human lives. Similarly, while racism can be supported by hate speech and acts of violence, it is also supported in more subtle ways through the use of the language: as in labeling "ethnic" only people who are nonwhite or non-European, or food not recognized as "American." Language is one way in which systems of power are silently, subtly, but strongly kept in place. According to Toni Morrison, an ideology such as racism is an invisible fishbowl, "the structure that transparently (and invisibly) permits the life it contains to exist in the larger world."[4]

In the case of the Prophetic Books, then, comparisons used for God and communities do not just tell us about God and communities. They also tell us something about how ancient Israel thought about the relationships to which they are compared. When the Prophetic Books call God King, Father, and Husband, they reveal the privilege granted to human kings, fathers and husbands, privilege quite different from that of human queens, mothers, and wives. In a loop of cause and effect, the human roles in which God is depicted also take on greater power. According to the famous words of Mary Daly, "When God is male, male is God."

But not only writers have ideologies. So do readers and particular ways of reading. We believe certain things about the world that carry over into the way that we read. We have commitments to certain values and ideas that govern our understandings of a text.

On the one hand, those ideologies are shaped by individual experience. Readers' understandings of and reaction to texts that describe God as father are affected by their experience (or lack of experience) of their own father, though a positive or negative experience does not guarantee any particular reaction. Not all people will have had the same experiences of their fathers, so that what may be a powerful positive image to me may be the one most meaningless or even horrific to the person sitting beside me on the bus.

As ideological critics insist, my thinking about fathers is also affected by how my culture has taught me to think about fathers and their roles. My image of a father is shaped not only by my childhood but also by the TV programs I watch, the Father's Day cards I read, the newsletter of the local PTA. Similarly, when in modern America I imagine God as a king, I draw not on my personal experience of kings but from my education in European and world history as well as my memories of fairy tales.

Stephen Fowl has argued that distributions of power are found *only* in readers: "Texts don't have ideologies."[5] According to Fowl, the fact that a single text can be pressed into the service of multiple, competing ideologies (such that diverse stances can appeal to the same biblical passage) indicates that ideologies are in readers and in their communities—not in texts. While Fowl is right that texts can be used to empower different groups, I believe he under-estimates how patterns found within texts influence (though do not determine) power dynamics. Especially when the world in which the text was produced shares similar ideologies to the culture that reads it, the text comes across as speaking directly to the reader because it is able to tap into and participate in power dynamics within the reader's culture. For example, as I will discuss below, ancient Israel and many modern cultures share common thinking about male dominance and family hierarchy. When modern people who believe in male dominance read texts that assume male dominance, the ideology of male dominance is reinforced. Even the most reader-centered interpreters agree that while the text can mean a lot of things, it cannot mean all things. Some features within the text guide the reading process.

Naming Commitments

Ideological analysis of biblical texts can be descriptive only, seeking to unmask the worldviews and thinking of ancient writers. Most frequently, however, ideological critique speaks from a position of advocacy. Since ideologies are not themselves value neutral, neither is engaging those ideologies in the contemporary world. For example, feminist critique of the Prophets (which I consider a subset of ideological concerns) does not simply attempt to name what was going on in the ancient world for women; rather, it seeks to help contemporary women by unmasking the damaging thinking found in and supported by these texts.

In the discussions that follow, my own commitments will be evident, but I name them from the outset. While no one likes to be reduced to labels, I proudly claim the designation "feminist." I share with feminism the commitment to mak-ing women's lives better and to challenging patriarchy in all its forms. I also share with bell hooks the conviction that patriarchy harms all people, including men.[6] The particular brand of feminism that interests me is "gender theory," a perspective that focuses more on the way gender roles are determined by cul-ture than on any definition of women or men in biological terms. In considering the ideologies of the Prophets, I am interested in how cultural understandings of femininity and masculinity—both in the past and in the present—shape and limit the prophetic claims about humans and about God. In order to pay close atten-tion to gender assignments, I often quote the biblical text from the Revised Stan-dard Version or give my own translation. The New Revised Standard Version, though an excellent translation in other ways, tries so hard to be gender inclu-sive that it often masks the extent to which the texts are male biased.

My thinking and my commitments also have been profoundly shaped by post-Holocaust theology. I insist on a theology that takes human suffering seriously, one that is concerned not only with explicit violence but also with the mentalities that perpetuate and normalize it. For me that means a perspective that not only resists sexism but more importantly resists the attempt to make into a god any human institution—the state, the family, or anything else. In reading the Prophets, I ask whether their ideologies feed or mitigate violence—in the world and in the family. I challenge any description of God that trivializes human pain or offers simplistic solutions to trauma. While Irving Greenberg's famous quote has been criticized as too dramatic, too paralyzing, it nonetheless informs my understanding of my work: "No statement, theological or otherwise, should be made that would not be credible in the presence of burning children."[7]

Post-Holocaust Christian theology also insists that Christians find ways of articulating their faith that do not demonize or seek to replace Judaism. In the case of biblical studies, such an approach refuses to find only the bad in the Old Testament and only the good in the New Testament or to suggest that only the Old Testament raises difficulties for readers. While my focus here is not on the New Testament, I would remind Christian readers that many of the issues that I raise in the Prophets surface in the New Testament texts as well: the image of God as father and king, the assumption that good sons are obedient to their fathers, the use of the term *daughter* to reinforce the vulnerability of women, the image of God as an angry warrior. To be honest about the Bible means reading both testaments with the same appreciative-yet-critical eye.

A post-Holocaust perspective cautions as well against any suggestion that ancient Israel invented patriarchy or that it was particularly patriarchal. Based on her comparison of biblical laws with those of Assyria, Tikva Frymer-Kensky has argued that ancient Israel does not reflect patriarchy at its worst.[8] I focus on the Old Testament not because of its uniqueness in the past but because it holds a particular status in the present. As canon for Jews and for Christians, this collection of texts is granted authority; it matters to people in ways that most ancient documents do not.

In light of my post-Holocaust commitments, my choice to continue to call this collection the Old Testament calls for explanation. Many understand this label as inherently anti-Jewish, reflecting and perpetuating a view that these writings and Judaism itself are outdated, superseded by the superior revelation of the New Testament and Christianity. I am sympathetic to this argument against the term. Not only do modern ears hear the term "old" as inferior to "new," but these labels for the two testaments were actually coined by church leaders who understood Christianity as replacing Judaism in God's plan of salvation. I have, however, found no other term for this collection that solves the problem without creating others. The common alternate label "the Hebrew Scriptures" implies either that these books belong only to the Hebrew people or that they are all written in the Hebrew language, neither of which is accurate. These books are Christian Scripture as well as Jewish, and the Bible of Roman Catholic Christians contains material originally written in Greek. I acknowledge the problem of the term but have no alternative to offer, other than to challenge anti-Judaism directly.

The Task Ahead

No reasoned argument will convince readers to share my commitments. For those who do share them, who look at life in similar ways, I hope that my experiment in theological engagement with the Prophetic Books might serve helpful. Even if they do not affirm my conclusions, I invite readers sympathetic to these concerns to bring to their reading of the Bible the same commitments that they bring to all of life and to let those convictions matter. For readers who do not share my commitments, I offer at the very least an opportunity to learn that some of us who struggle with the Bible do so not out of disrespect but out of the conviction that what lies closest to our hearts also touches the heart of the divine.

I believe it is important, even ethically mandatory, to recognize and resist dangerous thinking wherever it occurs, including and perhaps especially in the Bible. To be faithful, I believe, demands recognizing the problems of biblical texts, how they participate in a web of power relations that are toxic. As long as the Bible is canon or even a "classic," as long as it carries weight in the church and in the culture, I believe it has to be read responsibly, with eyes wide open. To attempt to "fix" the problems of the Old Testament by reading it selectively or making excuses for it is, in my understanding, not only dishonest but also dangerous.

But I also maintain that these books should be read, that they have value for the life well lived. As I will explain, wrestling with these books as led me into deep reflection on intimate relationships, parenting, anger, violence, politics, the power of language, and the responsibility that Christians have for the way that they think and talk about the divine.

To those accustomed to viewing the Bible as "the rule of faith and practice" or the "rulebook for life," my approach offers an alternative perspective. It suggests that the Bible can be engaged rather than simply obeyed. As with people, I do not have to agree with everything the Bible says in order to be challenged by it, to respect it, and to learn from it. The Old Testament makes for valuable reading even when readers do not—or should not—like what it says. That is good news, I believe, not only for those who read the Bible within the context of religious communities but also for those outside the church who seek to experience some of what this powerful text can offer. The Old Testament can be a resource for our lives, even when we cannot or will not submit to its claims.

The volume proceeds as follows. The first two chapters explain the origin of the current "assent or dissent" stalemate. Chapter 1, through a selective overview of the history of Christian interpretation of the Prophetic Books, outlines the strong tradition of assent. Chapter 2 explains the nature and severity of feminist challenge to this tradition and shows, theoretically and by examples, the resulting polarization of attitudes toward the Prophetic Books. After explaining my own approach in chapter 3, I turn in the remainder of the volume to the task of doing theology with key prophetic metaphors.

In each case, I consider how the metaphor functions rhetorically and what ideologies it reflects and supports. My goal is to suggest how careful attention to both the metaphor and its critique can invite readers into deeper reflection on human society and their language for the divine. I hope to model a way that readers can be challenged by and benefit from the power of the Bible without ignoring or perpetuating its problematic ideologies—a way to like the Old Testament while reading it with eyes wide open.

Chapter 1

Prophetic Theology

A Brief History of Interpretation

As a way of explaining the origins of the current stalemate in theological approaches to the Prophets, I offer an overview of the history of this enterprise: how have the Prophetic Books been read for theological meaning in the Christian church? Of course, such a survey cannot be exhaustive or objective; my goal is to explain how I trace broad contours and themes.

The overview takes a chronological shape, suggesting that dominant modes of interpretation characterize particular periods of history. Admittedly, chronology is not the only, or even necessarily the best, way to tell the story of Christian theological interpretation of the Prophets. Approaches could be mapped thematically, geographically, or along the lines of race, class, and gender. Moreover, no single "age" is monolithic: diversity is nothing new within the Christian church. The advantage of a chronological scheme, however, is that it calls attention to an important aspect of the history of interpretation: the way in which Christians interpret the Prophetic Books, and the Bible as a whole, is always in conversation with the larger philosophical and social debates of an era. The history of biblical interpretation is, to some degree, also a history of reigning worldviews.

One question facing those who write the history of biblical interpretation is whether to focus on the interpretations of those in some position of authority—church officials, academics, those who wrote books; or to attempt to uncover something of popular piety—the ways that average Christians understood the traditions of their faith. Despite a wish to be more egalitarian, I focus here on academics and church leaders for several reasons. One is their greater accessibility: the perspectives of those who left written documents are easier to reclaim than those of ones who did not. More important, perhaps, is that the official writings of bishops and academics have left an impact on the church, even if in polarizing ways. The current stalemate that I see in theological approaches to the Prophets has much to do with the legacy (for good and for ill) of these men in power.

This selective survey will attend to the "spirit of interpretation" in each age and suggest how that "spirit" aligns with the "spirit of the age." It also will trace threads of continuity between the periods and their legacy for the present situation.

Theological Interpretation of the Prophetic Books before the Enlightenment

The earliest available examples of interpreting the Prophets might broadly be termed "predictive" readings, the understanding that the prophetic word was an inspired utterance that revealed historical events in advance. This tendency appears long before the birth of Christianity. For example, the prophecy of Jer. 25:11–12 that the exile will last seventy years is applied by the writer of Dan. 9:2 to his own time period, understood by most scholars to be that of the Hellenistic persecutions that led to the Maccabean revolt in 167 BCE. In the hands of the writer of Daniel, Jeremiah's prophecy confirms that his community's own calamity will last seventy *weeks* (Dan. 9:24), as opposed to Jeremiah's seventy *years*. Several biblical commentaries among the Dead Sea Scrolls treat the Prophetic Books in the same way. Commentaries on Habakkuk and Nahum employ the style of the *pesher*, which in almost interlinear style directly applies prophetic writings to the current situation of the turn-of-the-era Qumran community.

The New Testament

The New Testament turns this predictive approach to a distinctively Christian end, attempting to show that Jesus' birth, life, death, and resurrection were all as God "spoke through the mouth of his holy prophets from of old" (Luke 1:70). According to 1 Pet. 1:10–11, "the prophets who prophesied of the grace that was to be yours . . . testified in advance to the sufferings destined for Christ and the subsequent glory."

New Testament writers, however, employ the prophecy-fulfillment reading strategy in different ways. The Gospel of Matthew applies the scheme rather woodenly. Within the first two chapters of the Gospel, the writer quotes five times from the Prophets, in each case showing how a particular feature of Jesus' birth was anticipated. While the writer of Luke uses "fulfillment" language as well, such as when Jesus reads from the book of Isaiah in his hometown synagogue in Luke 4, this writer portrays Jesus more as fulfilling the hopes and aspirations of the prophets rather than as living into a script written long before his earthly incarnation. The Magnificat of Luke 2, for example, sees in the dawning of the new age the "spirit" of what earlier biblical voices had longed for.

Richard Hays's extensive exploration of the "echoes" of the Old Testament in the writings of Paul stresses that Paul's use of the Old Testament (in the form of the Septuagint) reflects not simple proof-texting but rather an artful reinterpretation of earlier Scripture in light of the Christ event.[1] While Paul occasionally employs the *pesher* style (see Hays's explanation of the use of Deut. 30:14 in Rom. 10:8–9),[2] his general approach to the Old Testament is more holistic:

> [Romans] is most fruitfully understood when it is read as an intertextual conversation between Paul and the voice of [OT] Scripture. . . . Paul, groping to give voice to his gospel, finds in Scripture the language to say what must be said, and labors to win the blessing of Moses and the prophets. . . . [For Paul,] the gospel must be understood as the fulfillment of the ancient promise that God's righteousness would be revealed in an act of deliverance for the Jews first and also for the Gentiles.[3]

According to Paul, Jesus embodies the purposes—indeed the very being—of the God of the Old Testament.

John Sawyer and Brevard Childs have masterfully shown that the book of Isaiah took pride of place in the New Testament's appeal to Scripture: the New Testament quotes, paraphrases, or alludes to Isaiah over four hundred times.[4] And yet, despite this focus on Isaiah, for New Testament writers "prophets" and "prophecy" were not limited to the books included in the Prophets section of the canon. Quotations from Psalms and Genesis are also treated as "prophecy"; David and Abraham are credited with "prophetic" utterances; and references to "the prophets" do not delineate a particular list of books.

> For *whatever was written in former days* was written for our instruction, so that by steadfastness and by the encouragement of the scriptures we might have hope. (Rom. 15:4; my italcs)

Almost exclusively, New Testament authors locate the primary meaning of the Scripture as a whole in how it testifies to and illuminates Jesus.

Patristic and Medieval Periods (100–1300 CE)

Christological interpretation of the Prophetic Books in particular and of Scripture in general flourished in the patristic period. As Sawyer suggests, while

New Testament writers appealed to the Old to defend their claims about Jesus, for the church fathers the Old Testament became revelation in its own right.[5] The Prophets (and Psalms) spoke directly to the church, independently of their appropriation by New Testament writers.

The church fathers approached all Scripture convinced that it bears multiple levels of meaning. Following the philosophy of Plato, they insisted that all narratives reveal not only surface-level, earthly truths (called the literal or historical sense) but also, and far more important, higher spiritual mysteries. When read in the spiritual sense, the Old Testament speaks not only about the past but also about the individual soul and the church's governance, doctrine, and eschatology.

While early Christian interpreters followed the New Testament writers in devoting much attention to the book of Isaiah, their use of allegory allowed them to discover far more treasures in Isaiah than had their predecessors. Patristic writers drew proof texts from both the literal and the spiritual senses of the book, such that in the first three centuries Isaiah was read as bearing witness to the Immaculate Conception of Mary, baptism, the Eucharist, and the ordination of bishops and deacons. In the words of Jerome in the fourth century, Isaiah is the Fifth Gospel, an independent source for Christian practice:

> Isaiah contains all the mysteries of Christ: . . . born of a virgin, worker of famous deeds and signs, who died and was buried and rose again from hell, the Savior of all nations.[6]

Along with Isaiah, other prophets attested to God's intention for the emerging shape of the Christian church. Justin (*Dial.* 117.28, 41) quotes Mal. 1:11 as proof that Gentiles are the people of God, and the *Didache* (a second-century writing) finds in the same passage justification for the Eucharist (14.3).[7]

Even when the church fathers did consider the literal, "historical" sense of Scripture, they found testimony to the Christ event. Childs highlights, for example, that while Jerome claimed to prioritize the historical/literal sense of Scripture, for Jerome the "literal" sense of the Old Testament is predictive of the New:

> Although he insists on first focusing on the historical background of the Old Testament when dealing with a prophetic text, he assumes, as if by reflex, that the full context is only recognized when the New Testament is included. Hebrew prophecy always flows in some fashion, directly or indirectly, into New Testament fulfillment.[8]

Clearly, "historical" or "literal" did not refer specifically to the ancient context of a biblical passage but rather to its more simple meaning as defined by patristic assumptions.

Not all patristic interpreters lauded the superiority of the allegorical method. For example, while the school of Antioch did not reject allegory completely, it did attempt to place controls on the application of allegory to the biblical text. Theodore of Mopsuestia set the Prophets within their own time and place and resisted reading them as predictive of Jesus. Theodore insisted that Old Testament prophets testified only to what they knew and did not foresee the coming and divinity of Christ; their chief role was as messengers of monotheism. Julian of Aeclanum's commentaries on Hosea, Joel, and Amos similarly argued for the priority of the literal sense of the Prophetic Books.

Even "historical" interpreters such as Theodore, however, did not break with the view that the Prophets predicted the future. While Theodore argued that the Prophets did not predict the details of Jesus' birth, life, death, and resurrection, he did claim that the Prophets predicted events yet to come: for example, prophets in the eighth century predicted events to take place in the postexilic and Maccabean periods.[9] Jerome, justifiably recognized for his insistence on "historical" matters, such as the importance of reading the Old Testament in Hebrew rather than in Greek and of understanding Hebrew language and tradition, nonetheless read for the spiritual sense as well. Jerome, Augustine, and others, despite all their interest in the historical sense, read Scripture in ways that did not pose significant challenge to the church's understanding of the Old Testament as witness to Christ.

In many ways, the interpretation of the Prophets in the Middle Ages continued and built on patristic exegesis. Medieval interpreters continued to find vast christological treasures in the Prophets and continued to search out the multiple senses of Scripture. Proof-texting continued as well: for example, in the twelfth century Robert of Rheims read the promise of Isa. 60:9 that "I will bring my sons from afar" as a prophecy that the Franks would defeat the Saracens in the First Crusade.[10]

Medieval interpreters, however, demonstrated an attention to the language, grammar, and text of the Old Testament beyond that of patristic interests. Following the lead of Jerome, they recognized the importance of the Hebrew language and consulted Jewish scholars for instruction. Increasingly, commentators appealed to the historical sense of Scripture, as seen in the work of the Victorines, scholars attached to the Abbey of St. Victor in Paris.

In the twelfth century, Hugh of St. Victor insisted that interpretation must begin with geography and history and only then move to allegory. He ridiculed those who did not ground their allegorical interpretation in a solid understanding of the text's literal sense:

The mystical sense is only gathered from what the letter says, in the first place. I wonder how people have the face to boast themselves teachers of allegory, when they do not know the primary meaning of the letter.[11]

Hugh did not limit Scripture's meaning to the literal, but in interpreting the Prophets he often located its primary meaning in the past. For example, while his contemporaries quickly allegorized the prediction in Isa. 4:1 that "in that day, seven women shall take hold of one man," Hugh argued that the literal meaning of the passage relates to the time period of the prophet. Consistently, he sought interpretations that would integrate true historical inquiry and the life of faith:

It is one thing not to discern what the writer intended, another to err against piety. If both are avoided, the fruit of reading is perfect.[12]

Hugh's disciple, Andrew of St. Victor, advocated even more adamantly for the literal sense of Scripture. In his extensive commentary on the Prophets, he expounded on the distinctiveness of individual prophets, highlighting Daniel's wisdom and Isaiah's royal bearing, as well the details of Isaiah's death. In Andrew's hands, Isaiah became less of the Fifth Gospel and more of a prophetic word to an ancient audience. One of the first interpreters who refused to read "the rod of Jesse" in Isa. 11:1 christologically, he also reported Jewish objections to understanding Isa. 7:14 as a prediction of Jesus without any comment of his own.[13] In his treatment of the "man of sorrows" (Suffering Servant) in Isa. 53, Andrew did not even mention christological interpretation.

Hugh and Andrew were striking in their challenge to the dominant interpretative tradition of the Middle Ages:

No western commentator before [Hugh] had set out to give a purely literal interpretation of the Old Testament, though many had attempted a purely spiritual one.[14]

The priority placed on the "literal sense" by the Victorines was continued by Thomas Aquinas, often considered the greatest of the medieval theologians. Aquinas's extensive study of the philosophical works of Aristotle, along with his training in other classics, allowed him to consider Scripture as both human and divine:

Thomas could speak emphatically of God or the Holy Spirit as author of the Bible; he could with equal enthusiasm probe the literary intentions of authors such as Isaiah and Jeremiah.[15]

Particularly in matters of theology, Aquinas stressed the primacy of the literal sense of Scripture. Aquinas considered the text's literal sense as closest to its true meaning.

Importantly, however, the medieval definition of the "literal" or "historical" sense of Scripture does not match the way in which most contemporary scholars and Christians use the term. For these interpreters, "literal" refers less to the setting of ancient Israel and more to the "plain sense" of Scripture, one that rarely strayed from traditional christological readings. For example, while Aquinas found the virgin birth in Jer. 31:22 and Ezek. 44:2 by reading allegorically, he maintained that Isa. 7, 9, and 11 refer to Christ in the literal sense.[16] His blending of the historical and the spiritual is evident in his treatment of Isa. 44, 45, and 49, in which Cyrus is both a historical figure and a type of Christ.[17] Similarly, while Aquinas identified the "servant" in Isa. 42 and 49 as Israel, he understood the "man of sorrows" in Isa. 53 as Christ.[18]

Summary of General Trends

As seen in this overview, the dominant trend in Christian interpretation of the Prophets through the Middle Ages was to see their message as supporting claims about Jesus. The Prophets lent their authority not only to the church's claims about Jesus' divinity but also to the emerging institutional and doctrinal shape of the faith.

This way of reading the Prophets clearly spoke to the perceived needs of early Christianity. Books like Isaiah could transcend their antiquity to testify to God's clear intention to embrace Gentiles and reject the Jews.[19] Unlike Marcion, who rejected these old Jewish documents on the grounds that they portray an angry, even demonic, deity, the church fathers aided by allegory could affirm the enduring spiritual truths of these texts. Ancient writings could become the "Old Testament" logically followed by a "New Testament," which formed a unified Bible, all equally revelation and all equally testifying to the truth claims of the emerging orthodox movement, as well as to a particular shape of the new Christian canon.

Importantly, this reading strategy also allowed learned interpreters to integrate the study of Scripture with the academic standards of their day. When the dominant intellectual school was that of Platonic philosophy and its privileging of the spiritual realm over the realm of matter, patristic and medieval writers could demonstrate how Scripture revealed the spiritual. Reading allegorically allowed Origen the Christian to remain Origen the Platonist, to integrate non-Christian scholarship with his own strong convictions about Jesus. When during the later Middle Ages attention turned to the "historical sense" of Scripture and to Aristotelian philosophy, writers such as Aquinas found the literal sense itself to witness to Christ.

The new attention placed on the Hebrew text of the Old Testament in the Middle Ages and the increased willingness of Christian academics to consult Jewish scholars brought additional complexities not only to Jewish-Christian relations but also to easy assumptions that the Old Testament spoke plainly about Jesus. Christian scholars who accepted the authority of Jewish scholars on what Hebrew words meant and believed that Jews were a continuation of their Old Testament counterparts often struggled to reject those authoritative Jewish readings when they conflicted with Christian doctrine. The tension between the spiritual and literal senses of Scripture (often identified with Jewish readings) appears already in the Middle Ages.

Nonetheless, it would be fair to claim that through these periods, the "rule of faith" as articulated by church leaders placed boundaries on biblical interpretation. Interpreters like Thomas Aquinas did not dismiss christological readings or challenge most traditional church teachings. Such a strategy precludes the finding of anything "problematic" in Scripture. A passage that may appear difficult, odd, or even immoral on first reading proves otherwise when read allegorically. The allegorical method wedded with Christian commitment ensures that all Scripture reveals the perfect truth of God, which in turn undergirds the church and the individual soul. For interpreters like Origen, not to see the perfect spiritual realm in the Bible is to misread it.

Of key importance for our overview is the recognition that the interpretation of the New Testament, patristic, and medieval periods did not treat the Prophets as a distinctive witness. In marked contrast to later periods, these writers did not speak of a "prophetic consciousness" or a "prophetic witness," much less a "prophetic personality." In turn, they did not see the Prophetic Books as advancing a theology any different from the rest of Scripture: the Bible was a consistent voice of divine revelation. These writers did appeal to Isaiah and the other prophets but not in a manner recognizably different from the way they appealed to other Scripture: they read all Scripture christologically, with Genesis and Psalms pointing to Jesus just as much as Isaiah. In patristic and medieval interpretation, the Prophetic Books do not simply predict the coming of the Christ; along with the rest of Scripture, they testify to it.

The Rise of Humanism and the Protestant Reformation

The Victorine emphasis on the literal sense of Scripture might be seen as a precursor to humanism, the intellectual movement that began to shape Euro-

pean thought in the late fourteenth century. This movement defined the previous period as a Dark Age, one that had fallen far from the grand achieve-
ments of classical Greece and Rome and one from which humanity must be
"reborn." Scholars such as Erasmus sought to recapture the treasures of
ancient art, literature, and learning, burning off the superstitious dross over-
laid on ancient texts by medieval commentary. In biblical interpretation,
humanists endeavored to reconstruct as much as possible the "original" state
of the Bible. New attention turned to textual criticism and languages, and in
1311 the Council of Vienna established chairs of Greek and Hebrew. Church
tradition, particularly the legacy of medieval scholars, held far less authority
for the fourteenth through seventeenth centuries than reasoned arguments
based on careful study of primary sources.

Humanism strongly influenced the Protestant Reformers Martin Luther and
John Calvin. Luther insisted on translating the Old Testament directly from
Hebrew, refusing to accommodate his translation to the Septuagint, as Jerome
had done, or to the now-normative Latin Vulgate. Luther criticized allegory
as employed by patristic and medieval interpreters as "blunting the full force
of scripture as plain speech"[20] and argued the necessity of searching out the
historical sense of Scripture.

Despite his interests in their "original" meaning, however, Luther continued to find in the Prophets a witness to Christ. In his reading of Isaiah, Luther
agreed with humanist interpreters that, based on careful study of Hebrew,
'almâ in Isa. 7:14 means "young woman," so that the church's traditional
translation "a virgin shall conceive" is inaccurate. But Luther also argued that
for the event to have been a miracle the "young woman" must have been a
virgin. Indeed, he found multiple messianic prophecies within the Old Testament: Luther states that the basic meaning of all Scripture is that which concerns Christ.[21]

Even more directly than Luther, John Calvin attempted to avoid the use of
allegory by equating the spiritual and literal senses of Scripture:

> Calvin's notion of the literal sense is deep enough not to need another tex-
> tual level to carry a spiritual meaning by means of allegory. Rather, the lit-
> eral sense is the true and genuine meaning of scripture.[22]

While Calvin insisted that the interpreter must use every tool at his disposal
to translate and understand accurately the words of the human prophet, the
real author of Scripture remains the Holy Spirit. When the "original" meaning of a prophetic text is not evidently christological, Calvin insisted that a
passage can have different *literal* meanings for the past, the present, and the
future. He claimed, for example, that the "sons of Levi" in Mal. 3 refers to the

time of Ezra and Nehemiah, *and* to the coming of Christ, *and* to the corrupt leadership of his own time. In the case of future promises in Malachi, however, the meaning can only apply to the coming of Christ.[23] The same approach can be seen in his treatment of Isaiah:

> Calvin's interpretation of Isaiah paid great attention to the task of determining the prophet's own intention and the original historical context, he meticulously avoided the language of allegory and typology, but at the same time believed that it was essential to ensure that every interpretation was both christocentric and relevant to the contemporary Church.[24]

Even more so than with Luther, Calvin's exegesis of the Old Testament led directly to doctrine:

> In sum, the human and the divine intention are virtually identical, and in no instance is one played against the other in his interpretation. Nor is the integrity of the prophet's words ever denigrated or relativized.[25]

The discussion so far reveals both the continuity and discontinuity between the Protestant Reformers and the prior interpretative tradition. On the one hand, the Reformers embraced more humanistic principles of interpretation than had earlier writers, but they also followed the tradition of the church in understanding the Prophets as informing the Christian about Jesus.

The Reformers did, however, develop distinctive themes in their interpretation of the Prophetic Books. Luther and Calvin identified a primary message of the prophets as criticism of idolatry, an idolatry that they located within the established church. According to the Swiss reformer Ulrich Zwingli,

> As to ceremonies, we must constantly bear in mind . . . that these ceremonies had been scorned and rejected out of the mouth of God even before Christ, as is clear from Isa 1:11–17; Jer 6:20; Ezek 20:25; Amos 5:21.[26]

The Reformers also found prophetic warrant for locating all authority for the Christian in the Bible alone: Luther identified "the word of the LORD" that "remains forever" in Isa. 40:8 with Scripture itself. This passage remained a key verse for the Reformers, one that attested to the authority and durability of Scripture.

Observations

The methods of biblical interpretation employed in the fourteenth to seventeenth centuries, as in other periods, accommodated to the era's philosophical and intellectual milieu. While the patristic writers once conversed with and attempted to justify their interpretation of the Bible to Platonists by showing how the Prophets speak of ideal truth, the sixteenth-century Reformers conversed with and attempted to justify their interpretation of the Bible to humanists by appealing to primary sources and human reason.

Sawyer notes, too, that while patristic writers turned the polemics of the prophets against the Jewish community of their day the Reformers applied the prophets' harangues to the established church.[27] Although interpreters in both periods underscored the role of prophetic challenge, the distinctiveness of the prophetic voice becomes clearer in readings guided by humanistic assumptions. The humanist insistence on the historical sense of Scripture also found an easy home in Luther's dictum of *sola scriptura*: if Scripture speaks directly to the believer, unmediated by church tradition, then its meaning must not be esoteric but clear.

For all the innovations of humanist and Reformation interpreters, however, they continued to understand Scripture as witnessing to the incarnation and as authorizing Christian doctrine. Indeed, by denying the authority of church tradition and hierarchy to determine the rule of faith, the Reformers gave Scripture a new importance. It became the believer's rule, authority, and guide. And the Prophets, who confirm that "the word of the LORD stands forever," bear witness to that truth.

The Enlightenment and Historical Criticism

Humanism laid the groundwork for the European and New World philosophical movement known as the Enlightenment. Even more than the humanists before them, Enlightenment thinkers valued the power of human reason. Impressed by Sir Isaac Newton's discovery of universal, predictable forces of nature, the intellectuals of the seventeenth and eighteenth centuries aspired to discover all the laws and logic that governed the universe. They believed that through observation of their own experience, they could learn how the world works and, ultimately, how to control and improve it.

This supreme confidence in science, progress, and human reason led many Enlightenment thinkers to challenge religious institutions and teachings while embracing views of God as the Supreme Scientist, sometimes imagined as the Great Clockmaker who had engineered the world and then left it to run its natural course. In the late 1600s, the Jewish philosopher and scientist Baruch Spinoza argued that the Bible should be read via an empirical method, which would discern the intention of its (human) authors. Spinoza challenged the veracity of Scripture when it failed to be internally consistent. He concluded, for example, that because 1 Samuel, Jeremiah, and Joel disagree about whether God can repent, the Prophets cannot be trusted to inform the reader about God's true nature:

> We have now more than sufficiently proved our position, that God adapted revelations to the understanding and opinions of the prophets, and that in matters of theory without bearing on charity and morality the prophets could be, and, in fact, were, ignorant, and held conflicting opinions. It therefore follows that we must by no means go to the prophets for knowledge, either of natural or spiritual phenomena.[28]

Spinoza likewise explained biblical passages that contradict the dictates of reason, such as Joshua's account that the sun stood still, as the result of ancient misconceptions or apologetics: in this case, the biblical writer "related the occurrence as something quite different from what really happened."[29]

Spinoza's assumptions, especially his insistence on reading the Bible in light of reason, soon dominated the philosophical and intellectual circles of Europe and the newly formed United States. By the late eighteenth century, intellectuals employed an approach to Scripture given various names: the scientific study of the Bible, historical criticism, critical study, and, when referring to the specific task of setting passages within their ancient context, Higher Criticism. These interpreters stressed that the Bible was written, transmitted, and read by humans and should be read in the same way as any other human book. The reader can assume that human nature and the natural world itself have operated consistently over time, and that knowledge allows one to judge which parts of Scripture are indeed "true." In Spinoza's words,

> Recognizing the kinship of men, and their subjection to the same general laws, we realise that under similar conditions they will think and act similarly.[30]

Early historical critics of the Old Testament explained variation within the Bible as the result of chronological development. Differences in style and in teaching revealed that different passages were written by different authors in different time periods. Historical critics looked behind the Bible as well, attempting to discern the development of Israelite religion and institutions.

The historical method had profound significance for the study of the Prophets. Historical critics downplayed the predictive elements of prophecy, preferring natural explanations over supernatural ones, and exhibited far more concern about what the Prophetic Books could reveal about the ancient world than what they proved about Jesus. The Prophetic Books were no longer one plank of a consistent biblical witness but rather a distinct voice within Israelite tradition, one that could be studied and its influence traced. Indeed, the individual prophets themselves were not monolithic, historical critics argued, but rather different persons articulating different, though related, understandings of religion.

Such an approach is evident in the work of the influential nineteenth-century German historical critic Heinrich Ewald. Ewald endeavored to discern what the prophets were like as individuals and how they related to their contemporaries. According to Ewald, the prophets advocated ethical monotheism over against the rituals of the Israelite cult and their Canaanite counterparts. The prophets insisted on the sole worship of Yahweh and the ethical treatment of others.[31]

Two of Ewald's students built in important ways on the work of their teacher. Julius Wellhausen integrated Ewald's identification of the prophets as ethical innovators into his theory of the development of Israelite religion. The prophets, Wellhausen maintained, had attempted to spiritualize the primitive religion of the Israelites, calling humans to rise above superstition. In the postexilic period, however, the Israelite priesthood succeeded in promoting ritual over ethics, such that the genius of the prophets was replaced by the promulgation of Law. In his influential *Prolegomena to the History of Israel* Wellhausen traced this chronological development of Israelite religion in the Pentateuch: while the earliest source, J, testifies to primitive religion, the latest source, P, reflects a legalism that Wellhausen deemed "Jewish."[32]

The other student of Ewald, Bernhard Duhm, more fully developed his teacher's understanding of prophecy itself. In *Theology of the Prophets*, Duhm argued that the prophets represented the highest advance in Israelite religion. They were

> true creative pioneers . . . inspired revolutionary spirits, who combined in their make-up both intellectual genius and irrepressible zeal for reform and spiritual renewal . . . teachers of the true religious and moral values of mankind.[33]

Ewald, Wellhausen, and Duhm envisioned prophets quite differently than had pre-Enlightenment thinkers. By the nineteenth century, prophets had become important not for their predictions of Jesus but for their articulation of a Christian ethic. Prophets were those who challenged religious ritual and the priests who presided over it. Courageously, they stood against religious establishment to call Israel to moral living.

In the early twentieth century, attention turned to an additional dimension of the "prophetic personality"—the ecstatic, mystical nature of the prophet's experience of revelation. While Duhm acknowledged this aspect of prophecy in the first edition of his Isaiah commentary, later thinkers developed this line of thought. Gustav Holscher, for example, devoted much of this study to mantic aspects of Israelite prophecy.[34]

The ecstatic experience of the prophet was also the starting point of the influential work of Herman Gunkel.[35] Gunkel claimed that the originating event of prophecy was the prophet's reception of a short, predictive vision. The prophet, in turn, reported on that vision in short speeches. Over time, the prophets' words and even his later expansions of his experience were collected and edited by a series of later interpreters. The Prophetic Books are the result of this process of addition and expansion.

For Gunkel, the original saying of the prophet was the true kernel of revelation and thus needed to be extracted from later additions. In good Enlightenment optimism, Gunkel believed that human reason could sift through the layers of editing to reconstruct the original sayings of the prophets. The method he developed, "form criticism," looked for written clues to the "forms" in which these short sayings had been delivered. Gunkel's conviction was that certain linguistic features left traces of how and where and to whom prophetic oracles were first given. Just as stories beginning with "Once upon a time" conjure ideas of childhood and nurseries, so Gunkel believed that formulas like "Woe to you" indicated a particular kind of speech and a particular setting.

The Legacies of Historical Criticism

Historical critics through the early twentieth century crafted a new and highly influential portrait of the prophets. First and foremost, they turned focus away from the prophetic text itself to the individual prophetic genius to which the text testifies. The personalities of Amos and Hosea, not necessarily the books that bear their names, took on ultimate theological significance. Indeed, many form critics dismissed later additions to the words of these great men not only as inauthentic to the book but also as irrelevant to their religious message.

In the hands of historical critics, prophets also became teachers/preachers of morality. Prophets challenged the religious establishment, both of the neighboring Canaanites and also of Israelite religion itself. Promoting the spiritual and moral rather than the legalistic and ritualistic, prophets towered like moral giants over their contemporaries and over the rest of the Old Testament canon.

Although these critics claimed that their methods were scientific, objective, value free, and unfettered by confessional constraints, they no less than interpreters before them reflected the spirit of their own intellectual, philosophical, and political environments. Much has been written about the many biases of historical critics, and only a few of these critiques receive attention here. Michael Dick outlines how Ewald, Wellhausen, and Duhm were strongly shaped by Lutheran pietism in Germany, which prioritized not only "spirit" over "law" but also the individual's mystic encounter with God. Dick points, too, to the influence on nineteenth-century scholars of the Romantic movement: just as Wordsworth and Coleridge valued the "rugged individualist," the hero who stands against his culture, so too historical critics of this era valued prophets for their heroic individualism.[36] As widely discussed, anti-Jewish assumptions undergird Wellhausen's insistence that the Law was late in Israel's history and that it marks a devolving of pure Israelite religion into "Judaism."

Historical criticism affected Christian interpretation of the Bible as a whole by shifting the locus of authority from traditional church teachings to the intention of the ancient author. Gone was the assumption that any part of the Bible would necessarily support Christian doctrine. In the case of the Pentateuch, Wellhausen argued against the tradition of Mosaic authorship of the Pentateuch. In the case of the Prophetic Books, his work and that of other critics challenged the long history of reading the Prophets as predictions of Jesus. Yet in the hands of historical critics the Prophets took on an unprecedented theological importance. The prophetic figures themselves became the pinnacle of Israelite religion; they were proto-Christians and ethical geniuses. By the mid-twentieth century, they had even become models for contemporary Protestant clergy. According to the 1942 publication titled *Preaching from the Prophets*,

> the Old Testament prophets were preachers who had color, courage and dynamic qualities. Twentieth century preachers can learn much from them.[37]

By the mid-century, most of these historical-critical understandings of the Prophets had become axiomatic within academic circles. The core of the prophetic message was identified as an ecstatic experience originally uttered orally and only later committed to writing and subjected to editing; the primary contribution of the individual prophets was seen as the articulation of ethical monotheism; and the prophets were seen to have challenged both Canaanite religion and also the Israelite cult itself.

Mid-Twentieth Century

Theological treatments of the Prophets through the end of the century challenged some of these themes and integrated others into new configurations. One point of disagreement was the degree to which the prophets had been innovators. In marked contrast to Ewald, Wellhausen, and Duhm, for example,

Sigmund Mowinckel and Alfred Haldar stressed the strong ties between the prophets and the Israelite religious cult. They insisted that some prophets operated within the temple itself and that the forms of prophetic speech were closely related to liturgical forms in the book of Psalms. Mowinckel and Haldar portrayed the theology of the prophets not as unique but rather as a creative synthesis of earlier tradition.[38]

The work of Walther Eichrodt and Gerhard von Rad, two highly influential Old Testament theologians of the mid-twentieth century, took up the debate about the uniqueness of the Prophets and also advanced new perspectives. Like earlier historical critics, both Eichrodt and von Rad strongly insisted on the ecstatic nature of the prophets' experience as well as the prophets' stance against non-Israelite religious practices, but each offered distinctive contributions to the understanding of prophetic theology.

Walther Eichrodt

In his major work *Theology of the Old Testament*, published in German in 1933 and translated into English in 1961–67, Eichrodt defined the central organizing principle of Israelite theology as "covenant"—Israel's conviction that it was bound to an exclusive relationship with Yahweh. This theme runs throughout the Old Testament, including the Prophetic Books. According to Eichrodt, the prophets advanced Israel's understanding of the covenant by confronting it with the sovereignty of Yahweh, the radicality of Yahweh's claims on the nation and on the individual.

Like previous interpreters, Eichrodt emphasized the individual prophet's ecstatic religious experience. God broke in upon the prophets with "inconceivable otherness," "numinous terribleness";[39] the prophets experienced

the reality of God as something numinous and terrible, definable in terms of personality and great to a degree that allows no competitor.[40]

This numinous experience underscored the total power and radical freedom of Yahweh. Everything that Israel considered holy—state, monarchy, war, and wealth—was eclipsed by the reality of God.[41]

Eichrodt's focus on divine sovereignty led him to challenge many earlier understandings of the prophets. He sharply criticized those such as Ewald and Duhm who attributed to the prophets a distinctive set of ethics, including "ethical monotheism":

The new divine reality, whose irruption the prophets experience, is not to be expressed in terms of any ethical common denominator.[42]

The prophets *did* contribute to Israel's ethics but not by advancing general ethical norms or any sense of what is "naturally" good. Rather, they insisted on the individual dimension of covenantal obligations: each individual must surrender totally to what the sovereign God commands. The prophets called for compassion, gentleness, and concern for the poor, but only in response to requirements of the God who embodies these characteristics. "Social aid and concern" were not universal humanistic principles; their importance derives solely from "the unity and universality of the morality required by God, which is binding on all who bear the face of Man."[43]

Eichrodt's prioritization of divine sovereignty also led him to downplay the degree to which the prophets opposed Israel's religious cult. Even though he described a "degeneration of cultic life in the prophetic period,"[44] he insisted that the prophets only attacked the cult when, like any other institution or belief system, it challenged God's power or freedom. While the cult had allowed humans to remain focused on the outward appearances, the prophets called for a deeper allegiance to divine claims—"the law written on the heart."[45]

Gerhard von Rad

Like Eichrodt, von Rad joined earlier interpreters in underscoring the core importance of the prophet's experience of divine revelation. In *The Message of the Prophets*, he described the word of God as coming to the prophet unannounced and without prior preparation. This experience was so overpowering, so monumental, that von Rad insisted that the "call narratives" of the prophets must not only describe the originating event of the individual prophet's mission but also mark the first "form" of prophetic speech. "The call commissioned the prophet."[46]

Like Eichrodt, von Rad traced continuities between the prophets' message and Israel's earlier convictions. But, while Eichrodt portrayed the prophets as contributing to the overarching Old Testament theme of "covenant," von Rad set the prophets within his own, different, understanding of Old Testament theology: that of salvation history.[47] According to von Rad, the Old Testament is the record of the sovereign God's saving acts on Israel's behalf, a continual reappropriation and reunderstanding of the core memory preserved in Deut. 26:5b–9:

> "A wandering Aramean was my ancestor; he went down into Egypt and lived there as an alien, few in number, and there he became a great nation, mighty and populous. When the Egyptians treated us harshly and afflicted us, by imposing hard labor on us, we cried to the LORD, the God of our

ancestors; the LORD heard our voice and saw our affliction, our toil, and our oppression. The LORD brought us out of Egypt with a mighty hand and an outstretched arm, with a terrifying display of power, and with signs and wonders; and he brought us into this place and gave us this land, a land flowing with milk and honey."

For von Rad, reconstructing the theology of the Old Testament did not require a "history of religions" (the reconstruction of the developmental stages of ancient Israelite faith) but rather "tradition history" (the tracing of Israel's preservation and repeated reconfiguration of its historical memories).

The prophets, claimed von Rad, appealed to Israel's memory of God's saving works—the traditions associated with the exodus, wilderness, David, Zion, and so on. These memories served both as reminders of the past and also as precedent for Israel to believe that God again would act in sovereign freedom in the future. The prophets' reminder that Yahweh is the God Who Acts challenged both Canaanite religion, which according to von Rad treated time as cyclical, and also priestly theology, whose rituals von Rad portrays as guaranteeing the dependability, even predictability of divine response.

Reflections on Eichrodt and von Rad

Scholars often starkly juxtapose Eichrodt's and von Rad's approaches to Old Testament theology. The former traces a single organizing principle while the latter discerns the history of continual reinterpretation. For one, theology is found in the constancy of the divine-human relationship; for the other, theology becomes the recital of God's actions on humanity's behalf. Walter Brueggemann's assessment of the legacy of these two great theologians sees the tension between them as one between underscoring the coherence of the Old Testament vs. acknowledging its diversity. This tension, Brueggemann suggests, is ultimately irresolvable.[48]

Despite their differences, however, these two approaches to the theology of the Prophets in particular and the Old Testament in general have much in common, especially when viewed from the vantage point of later developments in the field. In the case of the Prophets, both insist that prophecy originates in the individual prophet's direct experience of the divine. Like the generation before them, Eichrodt and Von Rad accepted the prophetic call narratives as historical "proof" that the prophet had experienced God directly, unmediated through institutions or culture.

Both supplemented the focus on the individual experience of the prophet with new appreciation for the continuity between the prophetic message and earlier Israelite tradition. Although Eichrodt and von Rad defined the nature of Israelite faith as a whole differently (covenant vs. a recital of great acts), neither viewed the prophets as innovative. Both challenged the claim of Ewald and his disciples that the prophets taught ethics, and both treated Israel's priesthood and religious cult more respectfully than had the previous generation. For neither, however, did this irenic spirit extend to non-Israelite cultures. Eichrodt and von Rad both emphasized the radical disjunction between Israelite faith and that of its Canaanite neighbors.

In emphasizing the radical demands of a sovereign God, these theologians isolated Israelite faith from its larger ancient Near Eastern cultural background. They left little room for sociological analysis, for the possibility that the culture in which the prophets lived influenced them. The prophets spoke the divine decree and explained to others their experiences, but they did not reflect the ideologies of their culture.

Both Eichrodt and von Rad attempted to define their work as distinctly theological, in contrast with the "history of religions" approach that had long dominated the field of Old Testament study. Yet for both the task of theology remained one of historical retrieval. Eichrodt and von Rad equated Old Testament theology with reconstructing the contours and impulses of ancient Israelite faith. They trusted historical inquiry to illumine this faith, as well as the experience of the historical prophet; both assumed the resulting reconstruction to be normative for Christian believers. They found in the Prophets a faith to be embraced.

Just as much as earlier interpreters, the claims of Eichrodt and von Rad clearly resonated with and against the theological and political settings in which they lived. Theologically, both wrote in the wake of the "Barthian revolution," the widespread acceptance of Christian theologian Karl Barth's insistence on the radical uniqueness of the biblical message and the Christ event. Walter Brueggemann explains that, along with Eichrodt, von Rad "took up Barth's demand that Old Testament interpretation should be not only descriptive, but also normative."[49] Eichrodt's identification of "covenant" as the unifying theme of the Old Testament also fit well within the Reformed church to which he belonged, one that had long explained the Bible in light of "covenant theology."

Perhaps even more obviously, Eichrodt and von Rad (along with Barth) asserted the demands of a sovereign God while facing the hegemony of National Socialism in Germany. Eichrodt's mature work was written in the 1930s, during the rise of Nazism. Slightly younger, von Rad took a position at the university at Jena two years after the Barmen Declaration, the 1934 statement of the Confessing Church opposing the accommodation of the German church to reigning Nazi ideology:

8.23 We reject the false doctrine, as though the State, over and beyond its special commission, should and could become the single and totalitarian order of human life, thus fulfilling the Church's vocation as well.

8.24 We reject the false doctrine, as though the Church, over and beyond its special commission, should and could appropriate the characteristics, the tasks, and the dignity of the State, thus itself becoming an organ of the State.[50]

Von Rad taught and preached in Confessing Churches, who would have found his insistence that ancient Israel's ancient creed challenged its Canaanite neighbors strikingly contemporary:

Von Rad imagined an Israelite community that was, not unlike German churches (the confessing church), seeking to find standing ground against a formidable theological alternative. In Israel's case, the challenge was of "Canaanite religion"; in the case of the German church, it was the blood-and-soil ideology of the National Socialist regime.[51]

For Eichrodt and von Rad, the prophetic word required the church to resist all challenges to the total freedom of God.

Late Twentieth Century

The closer our discussion draws to the present, the more obviously subjective any choice of "key" commentators appears. While hindsight allows some measure by which to suggest the legacies of earlier interpreters, the immediacy of contemporary concerns allows no such distance.

To describe developments within the past fifty years, I focus on two interpreters. Brevard Childs and Walter Brueggemann are widely recognized as major voices in current theological approaches to the Old Testament and to Christian readings of the Prophets.

Brevard Childs

An American, Childs completed his doctoral studies under Eichrodt in Basel in the years after World War II. While in Basel, he attended lectures by Barth at nearby Heidelberg University. Both theologians left their clear stamp on his thinking: Eichrodt's insistence on reading the Old Testament as a unified whole, and Barth's insistence on the normative, distinctive claims of the Christian gospel.

Consistently from the 1970s until his death in 2007, Childs insisted that the Old Testament must be read in accordance with the shape and the intention of the larger canon. Emphasizing his difference from von Rad, he defined Old Testament theology not as the reconstruction and adoption of the faith of ancient Israel but rather as the appreciation and acceptance of the way that Scripture (Old and New Testaments) constitutes an intentional and coherent whole.

Childs contravened the assumptions that had driven historical-critical scholarship for over three hundred years. He denied historical criticism's assumption that the intention of the text's author(s) determines its meaning; he valorized the final form of the text, not its original forms or sources; and, perhaps most important, he affirmed that the Bible must be interpreted in light of and for the sake of the faith communities that created it. A "canonical approach" (Childs preferred this label over "canonical criticism") interprets

the biblical text in relation to a community of faith and practice for whom it served a particular theological role as possessing divine authority.[52]

Childs stressed this theme consistently in all of his works, though he is perhaps best known for his magnum opus *Introduction to the Old Testament as Scripture*, published in 1979.

Child's program of reading canonically, *with* rather than *against* the tradition of the church, bears significantly on interpretation of the Prophetic Books. Not surprisingly, he wrote frequently and passionately on Isaiah, a book that, as we have seen, the early church read as the Fifth Gospel but that historical criticism fought valiantly to place in historical context. Childs challenged five hundred years of the Enlightenment-inspired focus on the author(s) of the book to provide a way in which Isaiah again could be seen as a Christian book. In his *Introduction*, he argued that that historical-critical approaches to the "Servant Songs" in Isa. 40–55 leave the identity of the "servant" profoundly ambiguous: Is the servant Israel and/or an individual? Historical study of the book itself, then, cannot resolve this key issue; rather, readers must turn to other parts of the canon. Although Childs does not explicitly claim that the Servant Songs are to be interpreted in the light of their New Testament application to Jesus, he does say,

The diversity within the witness could not be resolved in terms of Israel's past experience; rather the past would have to receive its meaning from the future.[53]

For Childs, that future is the Christ event.

Reflections on Childs

Childs brought to the field of Old Testament scholarship a new respectability to reading the Old Testament in light of the confessions of the Christian church. Reading according to the contours of the canon offered a means by which twentieth-century interpreters could read the Bible as a consistent witness to Jesus Christ, one that would fit postmodern sensibilities rather than premodern ones.

Although he took a polemical stance against historical criticism, Childs continued to rely on its method of inquiry. Historical-critical investigation dominates his *Introduction*; curiously, although he claims the normative status of the Christian canon, Childs organized the *Introduction* according to the canonical shape of the *Jewish* Bible. These observations suggest that Childs accepted historical criticism as a tool of study but resisted historical interpretation as the sole determinant of a text's meaning. Historical-critical findings provide insight, but the true meaning of the text lies within its interrelatedness with the rest of the canon.

Clearly, then, Childs's confessional readings of the Old Testament did not mark a simple return to the church's earliest interpretative traditions. Childs did not read Isaiah the same way that Augustine did: for Childs, the historical Isaiah may not have predicted Jesus, but the canon instructs the Christian reader to see the connection between the canon's words about Isaiah and its words about Jesus. His approach did, however, embolden Christian scholars to talk *in the academy* about the Old Testament as a document of the church. Students from Childs's long legacy of teaching at Yale continue his project, presenting papers on canonical readings of Scripture at academic conferences, holding teaching positions at major research universities, and continuing to raise up new disciples.

Walter Brueggemann

A prolific writer and speaker, Walter Brueggemann perhaps comes the closest to anyone that Christian Old Testament scholarship might call a "celebrity." No other contemporary Old Testament scholar has written and worked more directly for the sake of the church or influenced more strongly the way that academics, pastors, and church leaders think about the Old Testament.

Still very much actively thinking and writing, Brueggemann cannot be categorized too easily. His topics have ranged widely, and his ideas have developed over time. Here, I focus on his legacy thus far for the interpretation of the Old Testament in general and the Prophets in particular. To do so I focus on two of his many works: first, his influential *The Prophetic Imagination*, published first in 1978 and then in a second, revised edition in 2001 (quoted here); and second, his magnum opus, *Theology of the Old Testament: Testimony, Dispute, Advocacy*, published in 1997.

In *The Prophetic Imagination*, Brueggemann articulates the understanding of prophecy that runs throughout all of his work. He presents the prophets of ancient Israel as challenging "royal ideology," Brueggemann's label not only for the monarchy but, even more so, for all mentalities in the dominant culture (in ancient Israel and in the present) that deify wealth, status, and stability. Because royal ideology required citizens to be passive and accept social inequities, the prophets could only challenge such thinking by shocking hearers into imagining the possibility of an alternative reality: a world in which God alone rules. In continuity with God's work in Moses to liberate Israel from the bondage of Pharaoh, the prophets sought to illumine the death inherent in the current situation and to energize the people for change.

In the endeavors of the prophets, pathos played a key role. The prophets lamented Israel's dire situation and called the people to do the same, says Brueggemann:

> I believe that grief and mourning, that crying in pathos, is the ultimate form of criticism, for it announces the sure end of the whole royal arrangement.[54]

The prophets were not direct social reformers but rather those who called Israel to accept and understand the reasons for its impending death in order that a new, alternative life might be possible.

For Brueggemann, prophecy not only is an ancient phenomenon; it also remains an ongoing goal of the Christian church. His description of prophecy does not stop with ancient Israel but moves forward to describe the prophetic imagination of Jesus of Nazareth, who challenged the status quo and whose resurrection energizes his followers to hope for an alternative, and then to suggest what a contemporary "prophetic ministry" entails. Like ancient Israelite prophecy, modern prophetic ministry laments the morbidity of the current situation and calls forth an alternative community—one committed to responding to the claims of a sovereign God and one that denies the hegemony of wealth and power. The postscript to the revised edition gives examples of such prophetic ministry: churches involved in the care of Alzheimer's patients, in urban ministries, and in other forms of social justice; and individuals who have challenged the injustices of the dominant culture, such as Martin Luther King Jr., Dietrich Bonhoeffer, and Jimmy Carter.

Brueggemann's *Theology of the Old Testament* advances and nuances these earlier ideas. Here he explains his approach to the theology of the Old Testament as an attempt to move beyond the impasse of the contrary legacies of Eichrodt and von Rad. While Eichrodt emphasized the coherence of the Old Testament message and von Rad stressed its plurality, that is, the way in which the acts of God were continually reinterpreted, Brueggemann identifies both (1) Israel's core testimony, its consistent claims about Yahweh's character, and (2) its countertestimony, its acknowledgements of Yahweh's hiddenness, ambiguity, and negativity. Testimony, however, also leads to (3) advocacy, the insistence that "a Yahweh-version of reality"[55] challenges dominant structures and ideologies. Throughout, Brueggemann resists any attempt to integrate the parts of the Old Testament into a single, consistent whole yet claims that the Old Testament reveals key, life-altering truths about God.

Within this framework, the Prophetic Books provide both testimony and countertestimony. For example, Hosea affirms Yahweh's commitment to the covenantal relationship[56] and the power of divine pathos[57] but also the possibility that Yahweh can deceive.[58]

While references to the prophets appear throughout the volume, the chapter on "The Prophet as Mediator" outlines most clearly Brueggemann's understanding of prophecy. Here, he reiterates and expands the themes advanced in *The Prophetic Imagination*, claiming that prophets endeavored "to disrupt the 'safe' construals of reality."[59] Like scholars before him, Brueggemann stresses the importance of the individual prophet's experience of the divine and the "newness" of the message:

> These originary are odd individuals and cannot be explained by any antecedent. In that regard the older notion of "lonely geniuses" has an element of truth in it.[60]

Yet Brueggemann also underscores that culture and traditions inform the prophetic imagination: prior memories and institutions influenced their thought. He acknowledges both the individual and communal dimensions of prophecy but argues that, ultimately, the prophets remain unexplainable apart from their individual encounter with Yahweh.

In both of these volumes, Brueggemann embodies his message. Mirroring his portrait of the prophetic texts, his own writing laments the current situation of the world and seeks to energize readers for change. Brueggemann does not simply describe the prophetic message but also takes up the prophetic mantle himself, fostering the prophetic imagination and spurring readers to lament and to hope.

Reflections on Brueggemann

In the interpretation Brueggemann offers in these two volumes, the experience of the individual prophet remains the "originating event" of prophecy. While Brueggemann acknowledges far more than most previous scholars the influence of Israelite society and tradition on the Prophetic Books, he retains the focus on the individual prophetic experience that has dominated prophetic scholarship since the nineteenth century. Following a long tradition, he views the prophet as one who experienced an odd, unprecedented encounter with God; this experience alone propelled the prophet to speak.

Like Eichrodt and von Rad before him, Brueggemann identifies the message given to the prophet as proclaiming the implications of divine sovereignty: prophets confronted Israel with its failure to acknowledge that Yahweh alone is God. For Eichrodt and von Rad, the sovereignty of God challenged Canaanite religion and static forces within Israel; for Brueggemann, God's sovereignty primarily challenges the "royal consciousness"—oppressive social practices within Israel itself that numbed it to God's reality. The focus on divine sovereignty also aligns Brueggemann with Eichrodt and von Rad in challenging the claim of Ewald, Duhm, and Wellhausen that the prophets were primarily teachers of ethical monotheism. For Brueggemann, the countercultural nature of the prophetic message was not its primary intent but rather the result of its insistence on the sovereignty of God. The prophets were concerned with ethics only because God's radical freedom deprioritizes all human institutions and constructs.

Like other Christian scholars since the nineteenth century, Brueggemann views the Prophets as the tradition of the Old Testament most closely aligned with Jesus; Jesus' ministry was prophetic, as the contemporary Christian's should be. But, unlike Ewald and his students, Brueggemann refuses to denigrate in toto the rest of the Old Testament. Rather, contemporary communities of faith need (selected) dimensions of each part of the Old Testament story: the Torah's commands on purity and debt cancellation; the monarchy's "practice of power for well-being"; the prophets' disruptive challenge to the status quo; the priestly tradition's insistence on the sacramental nature of all of life; and the wisdom tradition's embrace of daily life.[61]

Particularly in contrast to Eichrodt, but also even more than von Rad, Brueggemann insists on the plurality and diversity of the Old Testament. He resists at all turns any approach to the Old Testament that discerns a single, unifying message. Indeed, one of his major criticisms of Childs is that a canonical reading of the Bible "flattens" its diversity and blunts its radical claims. The text should challenge the church rather than allow the church to determine the text's interpretation. But, along with Childs, Brueggemann insists that Old Testament theology cannot remain a descriptive enterprise. It must actively and passionately evaluate the text's claims to truth. Using language more appreciative of the academy than does Childs, Brueggemann entrusts Old Testament theology to the church, *as long as* the church remains in conversation with criticism, plurality, and the Jewish community.

No more and no less than earlier commentators, Brueggemann explicitly and implicitly works within his own political, intellectual, and ecclesial contexts. In an early chapter of his *Theology of the Old Testament*, he explicitly attributes his focus on pluralism to the intellectual climate of postmodernism and echoes the postmodern insistence that "there is no interest-free interpretation, no interpretation that is not in the service of some interest and in some sense advocacy."[62]

But like von Rad before him, Brueggemann does not truly break with the reigning historical-critical paradigm. Unlike a true postmodern critic, he does not name his own interests or acknowledge how his own social location factors into his reading of the Old Testament text. He presents his readings as if they are objectively in the text itself: in Brueggemann's rhetoric, the text has a voice, a stance, a claim, one that stands over against its readers. His close attention to the details of the text and the breadth of his coverage help create the impression that he is *discerning* the biblical message rather than crafting a particular interpretation of it. While no commentator bears full responsibility for how he or she is understood by others, the following review of his *Theology of the Old Testament* points to how Brueggemann's style allows him to be read as "objective":

> [Brueggemann] has unearthed a profound and empirically grounded conception of what the Old Testament is all about. . . . This is probably the reason why I like Brueggemann so much: his honesty with himself and the text. He is willing to let the chips fall where they may because he is committed to something higher and more compelling than passing fancies and theological fads.[63]

Brueggemann's claim to postmodernism while speaking in an "objective" style, as I will argue further in a later chapter, is but one of several instances in which he "tips" his hat to a competing claim without considering adequately the challenge it poses to his own perspective.

While not explicitly mentioned in these volumes, Brueggemann's own location within the United Church of Christ also provides an unseen conversation partner in his discussion. Although he shares with the UCC a strong commitment to plurality and diversity, he has been quite vocal in calling the denomination to greater emphasis on the Bible. In his insistence that the prophets were not social activists in the mold defined by liberal Christianity, he challenges the way in which official documents of the UCC have invoked the prophets. By stressing the prophets' reliance on the sovereignty of God rather than on culturally defined notions of justice, he offers to the UCC. and other Christians a "biblical" way to talk about social justice. Although Brueggemann differs from Childs, both read for the sake of the church.

Concluding Observations

This survey (which I acknowledge to be selective and cursory) demonstrates, on the one hand, how Christian interpretation of the Prophets has changed over time. While the premodern period read the Prophetic Books as but one part of the Bible's consistent witness to Jesus Christ, historical critics of the nineteenth century isolated the prophetic voice from the rest of the Old Testament and portrayed prophets as teachers of newly formulated ethical norms. While earlier periods placed priority on the christological significance of the Prophetic Books, later writers underscored the importance of the individual prophet and his encounter with God. The prophets have been seen to fully articulate the Christian message, to mark a particular stage in its development, and to anticipate its core convictions about God and society.

For all these differences, however, every interpreter surveyed here has judged the prophetic message consistent with Christian teaching. While numerous interpreters have denigrated priestly materials or other parts of the canon, none has challenged the Prophets. Whatever interpreters have found in the Prophets has been normative for Christian faith and practice. The Prophetic Book, or at least the experience behind it, holds authority.

Perhaps because of the authoritative role granted prophets, few of these interpreters have traced significant points of contact between the Prophetic Books and the culture(s) in which they were written. Although von Rad and Brueggemann traced the dependence of the prophets on earlier traditions and intellectual trends, they insisted that the prophets used these earlier traditions to challenge cultural expectations.

Only with an awareness of the weight of this interpretative tradition can readers fully appreciate the radical nature of the challenge posed by ideological critics of the Prophetic Books. As the next chapter will explain, not all who read the Prophets find them quite so countercultural or quite so paradigmatic for Christian faith and practice.

Chapter 2

The Challenge of Feminist Criticism of the Prophets

*I*n the previous chapter, I suggested that the dominant trend in Christian interpretation of the Prophetic Books has been to laud the Prophets' contributions to the Christian message. Although the specifics of prophetic interpretation have changed over time, the positive role attributed to the Prophets has not.

In this chapter, I endeavor to explain what I see as a major challenge to this attitude of assent: that of feminist critique. While other voices have raised problems with the Prophets, feminism has posed the most direct and pointed challenge to the assumption that the Prophetic Books should serve as the normative model for Christian faith and practice.

Rather than follow the historical approach of the previous chapter, I instead undertake the task at hand more thematically and descriptively, attempting to explain the thoroughgoing nature of the feminist challenge. After a general discussion, I will offer the marriage metaphor of Hosea as a case study of the difference that reading as a feminist can make. The chapter concludes with examples of the resulting stalemate between feminist criticism and the dominant paradigm. Feminist critique, if taken seriously, makes traditional ways of doing theology with the Prophets extremely difficult, if not impossible.

Feminist Interpretation of the Prophets

Stated simply, feminist interpreters pay attention to the way in which the Prophetic Books describe women. In so doing, they prioritize different aspects of prophetic rhetoric than do other interpreters.

Feminists look, for example, at how prophetic literature portrays the women of the ancient world. The portrait is not a flattering one. Despite their low social status in the ancient world and their inability to own property, women receive a disproportionate amount of blame in the Prophetic Books for the nations' sins. Amos 4 calls the wealthy women of Samaria "cows of Bashan" and announces that, like cattle, they will be led to slaughter. In her entry on Amos in the *Women's Bible Commentary*, Judith Sanderson protests:

> Amos specifically condemned wealthy women for oppressing the poor (4:1) but failed specifically to champion the women among the poor. Yet both the analogy of modern times and the witness of the Bible itself strongly suggest that women were disproportionately represented among the poor in Israel. . . . As Amos singled out wealthy women—a small group—for special condemnation, a balanced analysis would also have singled out poor women—a much larger group—for special defense and a show of that solidarity of which he was so clearly capable.[1]

Isaiah 3:16–24 criticizes the daughters of Zion for wearing fine clothes and jewelry, which are cataloged at length. Cheryl Exum ponders, however, "Where did the women get this finery in the first place? From their own economic endeavors, or from their husbands and fathers?"[2] Exum highlights the willingness of the prophets and many of their male interpreters to blame the crimes of men on women's behaviors—even on women's attitudes.[3]

Women do not function as independent agents in the Prophetic Books. Numerous passages criticize women's choice of worship practices (Jer. 7; 44; Ezek. 8:14). Women are victims of rape (Zech. 14:2) and violence (Hos. 13:16). When women *are* described as self-supporting, the context is one of humiliation: Isaiah portrays the dire future ahead as a time in which

> Seven women shall take hold of one man in that day, saying,
> "We will eat our own bread and wear our own clothes;
>   just let us be called by your name;
>   take away our disgrace."
>
> (Isa. 4:1)

The Prophetic Books frequently depict women reacting to crisis: they are grieving, barren, and lamenting (Isa. 32:9–14; Jer. 9:20).

As depressing as the fate of real women in the prophetic literature may be, more striking (and of greater interest to feminists) is the prophetic use of female metaphors. Repeatedly, cities, countries, behaviors, and attitudes appear in a woman's dress. Extending far beyond the use of feminine pronouns, the Prophetic Books elaborately compare cities to daughters who are dependent on male saviors and cities/countries to whores who flaunt their sexuality and who deserve (and receive) violent punishment, often sexual in nature. In Zech. 5:5, evil itself takes the form of a woman, thrust into a basket and deported from the land.

Of the many female metaphors, some of which I will explore in later chapters, the prophetic comparison of Israel/Judah to a wife has drawn the most consistent and scathing feminist criticism. This "marriage metaphor," in which the relationship between Yahweh and the nation is compared to that between a man and a woman, runs throughout the Prophetic Books—explicitly in Isaiah, Jeremiah, Ezekiel, and Hosea, and perhaps implicitly in other books such as Malachi.[4]

Although the metaphor turns even more violent and demeaning in Ezekiel 16 and 23, feminist attention often focuses on the book of Hosea because scholars believe it reflects the earliest example of the metaphor. To demonstrate the severity of the feminist critique of prophetic metaphor, then, I offer a consideration of how Hosea 1–2 fares with feminists.

The Case of Hosea

An Overview of the Metaphor

Hosea 1 quickly establishes the "marriage metaphor." God tells the prophet to take an unfaithful woman not because he loves her or in order to turn her life around but rather to make a point: Israel, like the woman, has been unfaithful. After Hosea takes Gomer as wife, he then is instructed to act in ways toward her that mirror the way in which God acts toward Israel. The names given the children borne of their union indicate God's displeasure with Israel: they are Lo-ruhamah ("Not pitied"), Lo-Ammi ("Not my people"), and "Jezreel" (the site of a bloody coup in the time of Jehu).

The vocabulary used for Gomer/Israel's unfaithfulness is sexually loaded. She is called a "harlot" (RSV) or a "whore" (NRSV) or an "adulteress" (NIV). The Hebrew word used comes from the root *znh*, which refers literally to a prostitute, but elsewhere in the Old Testament it can function as a slur for a promiscuous woman. Its usage here might be more akin to the crass colloquial term "slut."

Hosea 2 outlines the punishment that the whoring woman deserves. God/the prophet instructs the children to warn their mother that if she does not return to her husband,

> I will strip her naked
> and expose her as in the day she was born,
> and make her like a wilderness,
> and turn her into a parched land,
> and kill her with thirst.
>
> (2:3)[5]

The children themselves will receive no pity, and the wife will find no escape from the punishment she deserves. Her many lovers offer no refuge, but her husband "will uncover her shame in the sight of her lovers" (2:10).

In 2:14, the tone of the husband turns tender. Words like "allure" and "tenderly" replace his earlier rage:

> Therefore I will allure now her,
>> and bring her into the wilderness,
>> and speak tenderly to her. . . .
> There she shall respond as in the days of her youth,
>> as at the time when she came out of the land of Egypt. . . .
> I will make you lie down in safety. And I will take you
>> for my wife forever.
>
> (2:14–19)

This "second honeymoon" witnesses the reunion of husband and wife and the father's reclaiming of the children.

In Hosea 1–2, the metaphor remains consistent. The prophet acts toward his wife as God acts toward Israel. *He* is hurt and jealous but also forgiving. *She* is unfaithful and deserving of death. The woman can credit her restoration not to her own merit but solely to *his* willingness to forgive.

The Feminist Critique

For at least twenty years feminist interpreters have argued that Hosea's marriage metaphor arises from and perpetuates patriarchy and that, in turn, it hurts women and men's attitudes toward women. Various features of the text illumine this pervasive patriarchy.

The Metaphor Equates God with Male

Feminists have long decried the dangers of depicting God in exclusively male terms. Identifying God as masculine not only limits human understanding of the divine but also reinforces the godlike nature of human males. In the (in)famous words of Mary Daly, "When God is male, male is God." When only men are allowed to imagine themselves as truly created in God's image, women suffer in social status and in self-esteem.

Hosea's marriage metaphor intensifies the male identification with God. God's masculinity is established not only by the use of masculine pronouns, but more strikingly by the comparison of God to a *particular* human male: God is like the male prophet Hosea. Hosea and God are one in action, thought, and emotion. God is like Hosea. Hosea is like God. A man is like God. By the very nature of the metaphor, Gomer remains the antonym, the other side of the equation. God is not like Gomer. Gomer is not like God. God is not like a woman. A woman is not like God.

The Metaphor Gives Divine Sanction To Male Hierarchy

In Hosea's metaphor God acts, thinks, and feels like a human *husband*, and God's relationship with Israel compares to that of a husband's relationship to his wife. Even a cursory reading of Hos. 1–2 reveals that the "marriage" in question is not an egalitarian one but instead a relationship with clear, unequal rules. The woman "owes" sexual allegiance to her husband, who retains authority over her and their children. The husband "takes" the wife, names the children, threatens the wife, and assumes the right to strip and even kill her; he decides if and when to "take" her again and what the fate of the children will be. Nowhere in Hos. 1–2 does the woman speak directly; her only words are those which the husband claims that she *will* speak. Her desire for the relationship—either before or after the marriage—is assumed, or perhaps irrelevant.

Read in ideological perspective, this inequality both gives rise to the metaphor and also remains its ongoing legacy. In the ancient context, in order to confront readers with the intensity and appropriateness of God's anger against Israel, the writer appealed to a relational hierarchy already understood: because Israel owes Yahweh the same allegiance that a woman owes her husband, Israel deserves Yahweh's punishment as much as an unfaithful wife deserves punishment by her husband. As this "evident" truth continues to be repeated in the present, the metaphor reinscribes in readers the authority of a human husband. To recast Daly's dictum, "When God is husband, husband is God."

The Metaphor Reinforces the Domestic Violence

Countless feminists have insisted that the ideology of Hos. 1–2 fits the classic pattern of domestic abuse, not only because it sanctions violence against women but also because it reflects the entire constellation of behaviors and attitudes identified by social workers as abusive. According to numerous publications from women's shelters, governmental agencies, psychologists, and counselors, the spokes in the wheel of spousal abuse include the following:

1. *Emotional and verbal abuse*: The abuser calls the victim names, manipulates situations and emotions, and seeks to humiliate the victim in public.

2. *Isolation*: The abuser exhibits extreme jealousy and insists that the victim not see her friends or family members. Some abusers prevent women from access to car keys and money, or lock women inside the home. (While men as well as women can be victims of domestic violence, research continues to find that the overwhelming majority of battered partners continue to be female.)
3. *Threats*: The abuser threatens violence against the woman, her children, and even family pets; or he threatens to kill himself if she leaves.
4. *Blaming the victim*: The abuser blames the woman for making him angry, forcing him to act in violent ways.
5. *The "honeymoon"*: In some cases of domestic abuse, the abuser follows outbursts of physical violence with a period of tenderness and lavish attention. He promises never again to be violent and behaves temporarily as an ideal husband.[6]

These patterns are disturbingly evident in Hos. 2. Throughout, the husband threatens the woman—with stripping, starvation, isolation, and death (2:3, 6, 10–13)—and announces that he will not have pity on the children (2:4). He shows extreme jealousy, accusing the woman of taking other lovers and envisioning her promiscuity (2:5, 7, 13). Her only possessions are those he provides (2:8–9). In the "happy ending" of the chapter, he isolates her in the wilderness (2:14) and promises her safety. When viewed in light of the classic pattern of spousal abuse, this new period of closeness becomes a temporary, not a permanent, cessation of violence.

In attempting to distinguish Hos. 2 from domestic abuse patterns, some stress that in Hosea the male only *threatens* the woman; he never exhibits physical violence. Threats, however, are considered by most social workers as effective as actual physical abuse in controlling behavior:

> The existence of emotional and verbal abuse, attempts to isolate, and threats and intimidation within a relationship may be an indication that physical abuse is to follow. Even if they are not accompanied by physical abuse, the effect of these incidents must not be minimized.[7]

Reading Hos. 2 with the awareness of the realities of domestic violence transforms it into a "text of terror." Sympathy shifts away from the prophet/God to the woman. Outrage turns away from the woman to the one who holds her in the cycle of abuse.

The Metaphor Is "Pornographic"

One of the earliest feminist critiques of Hosea lambastes the book in yet stronger terms. In 1985, Drorah Setel made the case for labeling Hos. 1–2 as "pornography." She first summarizes previous feminist analysis of pornography and then names the following characteristics of the genre:

> (1) Female sexuality is depicted as negative in relationship to a positive and neutral male standard; (2) women are degraded and publicly humiliated; and (3) female sexuality is portrayed as an object of male possession and control, which includes the depiction of women as analogous to nature in general and the land in particular, especially with regard to the imagery of conquest and domination.[8]

Setel then proceeds to identify all three elements of pornography in Hos. 1–2. First, the book clearly portrays female sexuality as negative by calling the woman a whore, by assigning the male prophet the role of God and the woman the role of promiscuous Israel, and by fantasizing about the woman's relations with lovers. Second, the husband threatens Gomer/Israel with public humiliation in 2:10, described in the sexually loaded term "uncovering." Finally, throughout Hos. 1–2, the woman/Israel remains under the control of the prophet/Yahweh. Especially in Hos. 2, the woman's identity fuses with that of the land. The threat that the prophet/God will "make her like a wilderness, and turn her into a parched land" fits not only Israel as a nation but also the woman as a "creature of nature."

According to Setel, the degree to which this prophetic pornography objectifies women exceeds all earlier precedents. The prophets did not simply parrot cultural assumptions but helped to create a new form of misogyny, making these books uniquely problematic for women readers of the Bible. While Setel does not explicitly offer her own response to these texts, she does acknowledge that readers would be justified in concluding that

> the "pornographic" nature of female objectification may demand that such texts not be declared "the word of God" in a public setting.[9]

For Setel, because Hosea is pornographic, women assent to its authority only to their peril.

Other feminists have followed Setel in deeming not only Hosea but indeed a wide range of prophetic materials "pornographic," tracing even further connections between prophetic materials and pornography. The acceptance of this feminist insight has given birth to the catchy and damning label "pornoprophetics." Since its appearance in Athalya Brenner's comparison of the book of Jeremiah with *The Story of O*, a French pornographic novel,[10] the label has become part of the standard vocabulary by which feminists describe the sexualized violence against women that characterizes the prophetic materials.

The Significance of the Feminist Challenge

While I have focused on Hosea as a case study, feminist criticism is not limited to a few "problem passages" in the Prophetic Books. Rather, feminists have engaged the expanse—and the very core—of the prophets. For example, while the first edition of *A Feminist Companion to the Latter Prophets* (1995) focused primarily on Hosea, the second series (2001) extended feminist analysis to Isaiah, Jeremiah, Ezekiel, Zechariah, Malachi, Nahum, and Daniel.[11] Similarly, apart from articles by Beth Glazier-McDonald and Marsha White, all treatments of the Prophetic Books in *The Women's Bible Commentary* object to prophetic descriptions of women.[12] A growing number of monographs, commentaries, and articles thoughtfully and directly pose the feminist challenge.

But rather than continue to name feminist interpretations, I turn to assessing their significance for the task of doing theology with the Prophetic Books. How might feminist criticism affect Christian theological thinking about these books?

If taken seriously, feminist criticism opposes, at almost every turn, the dominant trend of Christian interpretation described in the previous chapter. It clearly opposes those who praise the Prophetic Books as the pinnacle of biblical ethics, but feminist critique also raises additional issues that deserve sustained attention.

"Reading as Male"

Feminist analysis reveals the extent to which previous critical and theological treatments of the prophets have been selective readings. Interpreters have been able to name the prophets as ethical giants only because they have focused on some parts of the prophetic message at the expense of others. Particularly, the dominant paradigm has identified (usually unconsciously) with the perspective of the male prophet and of the male God that these books describe.

Not only does "reading as male" often completely ignore the way in which women are depicted, but it also predisposes the reader to accept uncritically the perception of the male character. Seeing Yahweh as loving and kind in Hos. 1–3 requires taking the perspective of the prophet/God and seeing the situation from his vantage point. Only if the reader sympathizes with *his* plight, feels *his* pain, can the metaphor convince its audience that Israel deserves what *she* gets. "*Of course* God is angry at Israel's unfaithfulness; *I* certainly would be angry if my wife were unfaithful to *me*." The question of the woman's pain or perspective must remain unconsidered for the metaphor to function properly.

In her discussion of American literature, feminist critic Judith Fetterley has described the way that women readers, just as much as male ones, are trained to adopt this masculine perspective; and she has shown that to read as a feminist requires becoming a "resisting reader":

> Clearly, then, the first act of the feminist critic must be to become a resisting rather than an assenting reader and, by this refusal to assent, to begin the process of exorcising the male mind that has been implanted in us.[13]

Cheryl Exum, following Fetterly, has traced the same dynamics that women face in reading prophetic texts:

> Female readers are placed in a double bind. On the one hand we are asked to sympathize with God and identify with his point of view. To the extent we do so, we read these texts against our own interests. On the other hand, by definition we are identified with the object that elicits scorn and abuse. This involves acceptance if not of guilt, then at least of the indictment of our sex that these texts represent.[14]

Texts work differently when the reader identifies—or is identified by others— not with God but with the denigrated woman.

By revealing how prophetic rhetoric sounds to woman-identified readers, feminist critics have shown that the value placed on prophetic texts by earlier interpreters is less a function of the texts themselves and more a function of those readers' allegiances. Patriarchy, or at least androcentrism, in interpretation leads to the explicit or implicit acceptance of patriarchy in the text.

Patriarchal Ideology

Feminist analysis also denies the long-standing claim that prophets stood against—and ethically above—their culture. As outlined in the previous chapter, since at least the mid-nineteenth century the dominant strand of Christian interpretation has cast the prophets as men who opposed the corruption of their culture. For Ewald, Duhm, and Wellhausen, prophets were the lone voices of ethical monotheism; for Eichrodt and von Rad, they were lone voices against "naturalistic" Canaanite religion and other challenges to God's freedom; for Brueggemann, they were lone voices against royal ideology. For all of these interpreters, the prophet's message arrived, unprecedented and unbidden, from God alone.

Feminists, on the contrary, demonstrate the degree to which the prophets themselves or at least the books that bear their names remain fully ensconced within their culture's most enduring ideology: that of patriarchy. Prophetic rhetoric depends on patriarchal assumptions. Feminists disagree whether the prophets simply replicated or intensified the misogyny of their culture. As noted above, Setel has argued that by developing pornographic literary forms the prophets raised the stakes of misogyny in the ancient world. Tikva Frymer-Kensky, on the contrary, has insisted that ancient Israel did not invent or perfect patriarchy.[15] And yet, all feminists agree the prophets were not immune to, much less challenging of, patriarchal ideology. Despite the claims of earlier interpreters, the prophets cannot be seen as wholeheartedly countercultural nor as wholeheartedly committed to challenging *all* ideologies that make humans into gods.

Theological Language Is Political Language

Along with other ideological critics, feminists underscore that in the Prophetic Books as in the rest of life, language about God operates simultaneously as language about humans and the dynamics of power in those relationships. Denying the possibility of "pure theology" or of "merely descriptive" characterizations of God, feminist critique points to the political and social implications of God language. The marriage metaphor speaks about—and to—human gendered relationships, as do prophetic depictions of Jerusalem as a dependent daughter and of Nineveh as a whore deserving of rape. To the secular feminist claim that "the personal is political," Christian (and Jewish) feminists add, "and so is the theological."

Denying the possibility or even desirability of objectivity in interpretation, feminist critics unapologetically stake their claim to advocacy. They explicitly identify female experience as a key criterion for evaluating the Prophetic Books and call to task any evaluation of the Prophets that does not take into account their demeaning portrayals of women and images of violence against them. Prophets cannot be ethical giants if they are not ethical toward women.

Clearly, such a criterion leads to reevaluation not only of the Prophets but also of previous interpretation of the Prophets. Those who present overarching theories about the Prophets as mere descriptions of the text itself receive not praise from feminists but censure, as do those who treat those descriptions as revealing the "true" facts of God's nature. Cheryl Exum laments not only the way in which male interpreters reinforce the gender hierarchy of the prophetic texts but, even more, the influence that these "expert" interpreters exert on those who read their commentaries.[16] As I will explore in my discussion of God as father, at least one Jewish theologian suggests that giving theological priority to divine sovereignty derives from patriarchal thinking, a thinking that continues to paralyze Jewish theological responses to the Holocaust.[17]

Challenging Normative Authority

Feminist analysis defines the task of prophetic theology not as deriving theology *from* the Prophetic Books but as engaging theological reflection *alongside* or even *against* them. Almost to a man, the interpreters highlighted in the previous chapter found in the prophetic writings support for their own understandings of the Christian life. In the patristic and medieval periods, prophets authorized the structure and doctrine of the established church; in the Reformation, they supported the authority of the Bible; in the Enlightenment, they underscored the importance of individual genius; in the twentieth century, they insisted on the sovereignty of God against totalitarian institutions. Even when interpreters initially chafed at prophetic language, they always found reading strategies that allowed them to agree with Scripture. For example, when Origen struggled against the literal sense of Scripture, he always found the spiritual sense of the text to yield fruitful results.

Feminist criticism marks one of the first cases in prophetic interpretation in which the interpreter overtly resists at least certain aspects of the text's presentation of God. Based on the "What about women?" criterion, feminists insist that not all of what the prophets say faithfully describes the "real" nature of the divine. Feminist analysis introduces a disjunction between what the Prophets say about God and who God "really" is. In contrast to earlier interpreters for whom description of what the Prophets say *itself* constitutes theology, feminists approach the Prophetic Books as (flawed) human testimonies that must be tested for their value.

Clearly, feminist analysis challenges the normative authority of these texts. Judith Sanderson takes such a position in her reflections on Nah. 3, in which God is depicted as sexually assaulting woman Nineveh:

> No aspect of God's relationship with humankind can be represented in the modern world by an image that depends on a destructive view of women's bodied selves.[18]

Despite the claims of text and tradition, these texts cannot be embraced as clear windows through which to see God.

The Resulting Polarization of Prophetic Theology

Clearly, feminist criticism opposes the dominant way in which Christians have found theological meaning in the Prophetic Books. It does not offer minor corrections to the tradition, but rather challenges tradition at almost every turn.

Given the intensity of that challenge, contemporary Christian interpretation has struggled to integrate feminist critique of the Prophetic Books with theological reflection. Rather than integrative, discourse on the prophets tends to be polarized: most interpreters either (a) ignore, deny, or minimize the feminist critique of these books or (b) claim that, based on feminist critique, the Prophetic Books have no contemporary value. While in his *Theology of the Old Testament* Brueggemann identifies the current impasse in Old Testament theology as that between the unifying approach of Eichrodt and the pluralistic approach of von Rad, I see a more formidable impasse: one between (a) approaches that understand prophetic texts, when read properly, as faithfully witnessing to God; and (b) those that underscore the danger of prophetic texts and the need to develop alternative understandings of God. I read this polarization in academic treatments of the Prophetic Books. I hear it in sermons, in classrooms, and in churches. I listen to it in the discourse of those outside of the Christian church. Positions on the Prophets take one extreme or the other. Some positions claim to do both—to appreciate *and* critique the Prophets—but, in fact, they fail to recognize the difficulty of the task.

For examples of this polarization of assent and protest, I return to the case of Hosea. These examples drawn from academics as well as preachers show how much difficulty most Christians find in *both* valuing Hosea *and* recognizing its danger for women.

Hate It

On the "dissent" pole I point to Gerlinde Baumann's *Love and Violence*. Baumann, a German scholar and pastor, insists that Hosea and similar biblical texts damage the image of women—both in terms of women's own self-esteem and their esteem within society. "The marriage that is presented there offers no positive image for the mutual life of a woman and a man."[19] Additionally, she argues that Hosea's portrait damages the image of God, casting the holy one as a "righteous perpetrator of violence and a 'legitimator' of male violence."[20] Baumann concludes that the marriage metaphor of the prophets has no positive—or even neutral—value for contemporary believers. The metaphor is too dangerous, to women and to men, to be used: "Only permanent outrage is an adequate response to an outrageous image of God."[21] She initially concludes that we avoid all human metaphors for God: since no human metaphor is non-hierarchical or egalitarian, she claims, "the field of metaphors drawn from human social life must be abandoned."[22] But, in the closing sentences of her volume, she grants the possibility that some human images might avoid hierarchy: God as friend, lover, self-transforming clown.[23]

Love It

While other interpretations might fall further toward the extreme end of the pole, I offer Brueggemann's treatment of Hosea in his *Theology of the Old Testament* as an example of "assent." In the 750 pages of his volume, Brueggemann speaks often of Hosea, particularly Hos. 1–2, which is key to feminists. Hosea not only provides Israel's testimony that Yahweh is faithful to the covenant with Israel[24] and the countertestimony that Yahweh can be deceptive,[25] but it also reveals Yahweh's commitment to the renewal of creation.[26] For Brueggemann, the "honeymoon" stage that begins in 2:14 is the core of the chapter: "This vow [of renewed love] on the part of the husband-Yahweh to wife-Israel completely overcomes the negativity of vv. 2–13,"[27] and the behaviors in verses 10–13 that Baumann deemed "abuse" are described by Brueggemann as an "act of abandonment."[28]

At several turns, Brueggemann demonstrates his awareness of the feminist critique of Hosea. He acknowledges that feminists find Hosea's marriage metaphor problematic and mentions selected feminist writings. Yet he confines this acknowledgment, with one exception, to footnotes. In his treatment of the positive aspects of the marriage metaphor, the footnote reads:

> Obviously such imagery is profoundly problematic if it is taken as a model for sexual roles in human transactions. In my judgment, we must read this poem in its positive intention, but not with any naiveté about its ideological undercurrent.[29]

In its discussion of the punishment of the woman in Hos. 2, Brueggemann's footnote acknowledges that feminists such as Renita Weems and Gail Yee have found the image abusive,[30] and in a note to his discussion of the marriage metaphor he recognizes that it bears the inherent problems of "sexism and abusive patriarchy."[31] In neither case, however, do these acknowledgments alter the way in which Brueggemann interprets Hosea in the body of the text. For example, while his footnotes on the husband-wife metaphor acknowledge its problems, in the body of the volume itself Brueggemann claims that the prophetic presentation of Yahweh's character "requires" precisely this metaphor.[32] In the one case in which Brueggemann does discuss feminist criticism of Hosea in the body of his volume, he does so to downplay its significance:

> We are, however, alerted by feminist hermeneutical considerations to pay careful attention to the terms of the reversal (in Hos 2) now proposed by Yahweh. . . . Feminist literature notices the potential for implicit violence present in the husband imagery for Yahweh. Very likely, this is an over-statement of what is in the text.[33]

Although Brueggemann obviously knows and to some degree accepts feminist critique of Hosea, it does not affect the way in which he does theology with the Prophetic Books. He mentions the problems but does not take them seriously. Even though Brueggemann is willing to admit that the Prophetic Books portray God as "hidden" and even "deceptive," he does not admit that they are sexist.

In his failure to engage seriously feminist criticism of the prophets, Brueggemann is not alone among academics or among pastors. In the sermons collected in *Preaching the Eighth Century Prophets*, every single preacher presents the prophet's word as good news to be embraced and followed. Royce Dickinson Jr.'s sermon on Hos. 1–3, "Heartbroken for the Heartless," remains silent on feminist critique. For him, this text confronts Christians with the quandary of "How can God disclose himself to us in the disgusting imagery of steadfast love for a heartless whore?"[34] The scandal of the text is not its treatment of women, but, rather, "the real scandal of Hosea is that of a heartbroken God who absolutely refuses to stop loving a heartless people."[35]

More to the point of the polarization of prophetic theology, however, is Craig Bowman's sermon "Living in Hosea." Bowman cites feminist critics of Hosea by name—Mary Mills, Phyllis Bird, and Cheryl Exum—and describes their critique of the marriage metaphor as harsh. But for Bowman, the harshness of the critique becomes grounds for disregarding it. He claims that these critiques are too negative to be useful and explains that he "prefers" the writings of Renita Weems, Gale Yee, and Katharine Sakenfeld:

> [These] more positive constructive feminist readings of Hosea enable us to read the book as the word of God and sustain us as we move through offensive objections raised against female imagery.[36]

While one might argue with the way in which he has understood the interpreters he favors, Bowman obviously accepts only feminist interpretations that remain "positive" and allow readers to assent to biblical texts.

Not even the insights of Weems, Yee, and Sakenfeld, however, inform Bowman's presentation of the message of Hosea. In the sermon, he compares his own marriage with that of the prophet; like Hosea/God, he was able to forgive his own unfaithful wife, Patti. Through the book of Hosea, Bowman heard God tell him to forgive Patti: "Love her as I love her."[37] Clearly, despite his apparent awareness of feminist critique, Bowman embodies the very types of self-serving interpretation that feminists decry. In his application of the metaphor, *he* is like the prophet/God; *she* (his wife) is errant Gomer/Israel. The healing of the relationship comes from *his* willingness to take on the role of Hosea/God; he, not his wife, becomes the human model for God's forgiveness. Nowhere does Bowman distinguish Patti's perspective from his own: his own relationship as well as the biblical text is seen from only a male perspective.

Love *and* Hate

While on the one pole Baumann can find nothing positive to say about Hosea, on the other Brueggemann and Bowman can find nothing substantively to resist. The chasm between these poles is vast. It is a chasm between appreciation and critique, assent and dissent, acceptance and rejection.

Renita Weems's treatment of Hosea in numerous publications attempts to bridge this divide between critique and assent. In *Battered Love*, her critique anticipates that of Baumann: she claims that women read the marriage metaphor against their own interests and that this text ultimately terrorizes women.[38] But, like Brueggemann after her, Weems explains that the metaphor does provide insight: no other metaphor equals it in expressing that (1) Israel owes God allegiance and (2) even the most unfaithful might be welcomed home and loved. Weems also recognizes the popular appeal of the metaphor, especially the romanticized restoration at the end of Hos. 2. Readers like to believe in the strength of family and the power of love: that love can overcome anything and that men can be vulnerable in love.

Weems concludes that the real problem of reading the marriage metaphor is that readers have exalted Hosea's image of God as husband into a false god, forgetting that it is a metaphor.[39] What was intended to be metaphorical and poetic has been literalized and fossilized, a name for God rather than a creative comparison. The metaphor becomes especially dangerous, Weems claims, when it is the only one used for God.

The volume concludes by affirming what is good about Hosea's marriage metaphor. The comparison Hosea makes between a marriage and Israel's relationship with God insists on human responsibility—to God, to others, to the earth—and it teaches that we can risk to love again after being wounded. How does a reader hold in tension the good and bad of Hosea's language? Weems's answer is that great authors need great readers. We must talk back to texts, engage them in conversation.

By acknowledging both the good and the bad of Hosea's marriage metaphor, Weems appears to find the classic "middle ground" between ideological critique and constructive theology. She clearly takes the problems of the text seriously yet still finds the text valuable for contemporary readers. But Weems does not truly engage theology in light of feminist critique. Rather, she recognizes the problems of the text and warns readers of its danger, but she concludes that the text is so valuable that it must nonetheless continue to be read—problems and all. That is, Weems places the positive value of the marriage metaphor in one hand and its negative value in the other and weighs them against one another; theology and ideology become two separate voices that the reader/believer must negotiate. Indeed, Weems, Brueggemann, and Baumann all approach Hosea in this way, disagreeing only in the relative weight to be given theology and ideology.

In all three approaches, theology remains in tension with ideological critique. To find theological value in Hosea, the reader must deny its problematic ideology (Brueggemann) or that ideology's ultimate weight (Weems). To read ideologically, for the sake of the abused, the reader must abandon Hosea in order to do responsible theology (Baumann). In none of these commentators does theological reflection follow from ideological critique.

The Medium Is the Message

Another way to talk about Hosea's marriage metaphor and the approaches of these commentators is by using the vocabulary of metaphor theory. Scholars of metaphor often distinguish between the vehicle of a metaphor (the medium by which a message is delivered) and its tenor (the message itself). In the case of Hosea, Israelite marriage is the vehicle of the metaphor while the author's claims about God and Israel are its tenor.

The linguist George Lakoff further claims that the vehicle of a metaphor always invokes a "frame."[40] By "frame," Lakoff means the conceptual framework that undergirds the vehicle. For example, to label response to terrorist activity as a "war on terror" implies that the rules of warfare are appropriate to combating terrorism. Lakoff's definition of "frame" is similar to what I have been calling "ideology." In Hosea, patriarchy (and specifically patriarchal marriage) is the frame invoked by the comparison of God's relation to Israel to that of a man and his wife.

According to language theorists, the vehicle and the tenor of a metaphor are inseparable. To change the vehicle is to change the meaning; and if we were to try to express a different meaning, we would need a new vehicle. According to Lakoff, a comparison is never value neutral; it always invokes a frame and the ideologies that support it.

Applying this language to the commentators discussed previously reveals the differences between them, as well as why their approaches fall short of full engagement with the problems of Hosea's metaphor.

Baumann

In arguing that Hosea's metaphor continues to support the values of male privilege, Baumann shares with Lakoff the understanding that any use of this metaphor, intentionally or not, supports the frame of patriarchy. Her argument that the metaphor is unusable for those committed to gender equality logically follows from this understanding.

When, however, at the end of her book Baumann suggests that we might consider God as friend, lover, and self-transforming clown,[41] she attempts to hold on to the value of speaking of God in the language of human relationship while distancing herself from the hierarchy and violence of this particular metaphor. But, as metaphor theorists show, she simply substitutes one set of problems for another. First, the use of a new vehicle would change the tenor of Hosea's speech. To abandon the hierarchy of the image would take away Hosea's claim about Yahweh's power and change the nature of the pathos attributed to him.[42] Second, any other metaphor for God will itself invoke a new frame. Images of God as friend or lover, advanced by Baumann and by theologians such as Sallie McFague,[43] may avoid the cultural assumption of hierarchy that is built into the God-as-husband metaphor, but, like all metaphors, they are colored by human experience. Many people have been betrayed by friends or abused by lovers, and in contemporary thinking both relationships are considered optional and nonbinding. All human relationships are complicated by the dynamics of power and human failings. All carry cultural and ideological weight. None is innocent or pure.

Given the complications of human metaphors for God, one might conclude that the best solution is to use nonhuman ones instead. After all, as noted in the introduction, the prophets describe Yahweh as maggot and rock, and the book of Psalms is filled with images of God as fortress, cup, and shield. But nonhuman metaphors for God are also problematic. Understandings of "nature" and objects are no less culturally encoded than are understandings of human relationships. Ideologies construe perceptions of "nature," imposing gender (e.g., construing cats, butterflies, "ladybugs," and cars as feminine) and isolating one aspect as the "essence" of an object (e.g., focusing on the hardness of a rock but not its tendency to erode or crash down a mountain).

But, more importantly, nonhuman metaphors for God lack the intimacy, the relationality that comes with human metaphors. From infancy to death, relationships (and/or lack of relationships) profoundly shape our sense of ourselves and our world. Christian theology's affirmation of the goodness of creation, including human creation in the image of God, as well as of the incarnation—the insistence that God took on flesh and interacted with others as a human—values the divine potential of human relationships. Indeed, the presupposition of Hosea's metaphor—and indeed of much of the Bible—is that our experience of human relationships can provide glimpses of the divine.

Metaphor theory also insists that no message can be communicated without the use of some vehicle. Because we cannot describe the infinite except through our own finite and limited language, all God-language is metaphorical, even the language that we don't usually view as such. As the analytic philosophers have shown, even simple statements such as "God sees everything" or "God knows everything" rely on attributing to a nonphysical deity physical organs and senses. Saying Hosea's message in a different way would simply bring with it a new frame. That frame may be more acceptable than the one used in Hosea, but it will not communicate in the same way.

Even more significant for many readers of the Bible, Baumann's decision to "just say no" to Hosea's metaphor leaves unanswered a major question: What then do I do with the Bible? Can I simply reject anything in the Bible that I dislike? Her solution does not offer any reason to read the book of Hosea, other than to critique it.

Brueggemann (and Yee)

In the language of metaphor theory, Brueggemann focuses on the tenor of the marriage metaphor while downplaying its vehicle. For him, the message of Hosea is so important that the problems of its vehicle cannot be allowed to override the truth it conveys.

A similar conclusion is reached by Gale Yee in *Poor Banished Children of Eve*. Yee argues that Hosea's metaphor was a powerful critique of economic oppression in eighth-century Israel, one that can become lost when too much attention is placed on the vehicle of the metaphor:

> The regrettable result of employing a gendered trope for a socioeconomic critique of the *status quo* was that issues of class and colonialism became obscured by gender for later interpreters.[44]

By treating the marriage metaphor as an unfortunate choice of comparison, a case of missing the forest for the trees, both Brueggemann and Yee underestimate the power of the vehicle to invoke the frame of patriarchy. The ideology that undergirds domestic abuse is so familiar, so real, so contemporary, that to gloss over it is an obscene thing to do—equivalent to overlooking how the value systems of racism or heterosexism expose themselves in the language many people speak. While it is true that the individuals who offhandedly comment, "That's so gay" might not be consciously heterosexist, still the language only makes sense within such an ideological frame. Language matters; frames reveal our true values and reinforce them. Indeed, often the language that comes most naturally is that which is most shaped by cultural values.

Making the "honeymoon" of 2:14–20 the core of Hosea's message, such as Brueggemann does, makes the "frame" of patriarchal marriage appear sweet and romantic—even though these words reflect only the husband's perspective and even though, as domestic abuse education insists, the arrival of the honeymoon does not end violence but begins a new cycle of building tension. Unfortunately, this approach is encouraged by the Revised Common Lectionary when it lists Hos. 1:2–10 (or 1:1–11) as a reading for Year C and Hos. 2:14–20 for Year B. The Year C reading offers the establishment of Hosea's metaphor and the Year B reading the "honeymoon": missing from the lectionary is the bulk of Hos. 2, which makes the frame of domestic abuse most obvious.

When Hos. 2:14–20 is read apart from the rest of the chapter, the pathos of God masks the power of God. Such a selective reading makes the metaphor sound deceptively contemporary, even allowing a reader to imagine the marriage being described as a modern, egalitarian one rather than an ancient patriarchal one. It can even make the book appear less gender specific than it is: interpretations that focus only on unfaithfulness and hurt feelings suggest that any partner (male or female, gay or straight) could provide the image of a wounded God. As we have seen, however, altering the vehicle of the metaphor changes its message. Should the husband of Hosea become an equal partner with his wife, the book's claim of God's superiority to humans would disappear and the dangers of the violence of Hos. 2 would intensify. In Hosea's formulation, hierarchy in the marital relationship explains and normalizes violent punishment for infidelity: only if a husband can properly strip, expose, and kill his wife can the threats of chapter 2 carry weight and can the Deity's angry punishment of Israel be justified. In an egalitarian reformulation of the metaphor in which husbands and wives are equal partners, God's punishment of Israel either would lose its justification or Israel would gain equal right to jealousy and abusive behavior. On the human side of the ideological dynamic, the metaphor would normalize the violent behavior of wives as well as that of husbands. Attempting to read Hosea through the lens of egalitarian rather than patriarchal marriage would not mitigate but intensify its problematic nature.

Weems

If Baumann rejects Hosea's language because of the danger of its vehicle and if Brueggemann and Yee embrace Hosea's tenor while sidestepping its vehicle, Weems can be described as both critical of the vehicle and appreciative of the tenor. Rather than providing a synthesis of the two positions, however, she actually treats vehicle and tenor as separate, perhaps irreconcilable, aspects of Hosea's metaphor. Throughout *Battered Love*, Weems insists on how dangerous Hosea's metaphor is, but ultimately she cannot let go of it. She counsels that we accept it with caution, fully aware of what we are getting.

Weems's approach, while understandable, leaves the reader in perhaps the most dangerous position of all: compelled to remain with a metaphor that continues, every time it is used, to reinforce an abusive frame. This position is hauntingly similar to that of the battered women that Weems describes in *I Asked for Intimacy*: while in moments of clarity they can remove themselves from their abusive partners, they eventually find the appeal of their abusers irresistible and are drawn back, again and again.[45] They, or at least part of them, refuse to believe that the way that the abuser acts provides a true measure of his character: they believe that while abuse may be the vehicle of his affections, the tenor of the man is quite different.

Conclusion

This experience of feeling torn between the good and the bad of the text may feel familiar to other readers of the Bible. How can a person like the Bible and at the same time admit that at times it can be downright horrible? Is there a way to step out into the chasm between appreciation and critique without crashing on the rocks below?

Chapter 3

Another Way of Doing Theology

By devoting the previous chapter to feminist critique of the Prophets, I do not intend to imply that feminism poses the only challenge to the traditional mode of interpreting Prophetic Books or that I personally only care about women. While I do proudly call myself a feminist and share the feminist perspectives outlined in the previous chapter, I agree with bell hooks that patriarchy damages men as well.[1] I care about what texts mean for women, men, and children—as well as for folks who find the category of gender too confining or irrelevant to be useful. I also (as explained in the introduction) bring additional perspectives to my reading of the Bible. Like other ideological critics, I consider the Bible's intersections with not only gender but also race, class, and other forms of privilege. I seek to resist violence in its blatant and in its subtle forms. As I will argue, all of these issues (and more) make reading the Prophets difficult.

For me as much as for the commentators I discussed in the previous chapter, however, integrating ideological critique of the Bible with a life of faith does not come easily. Perhaps my criticism of Brueggemann, Bowman, Baumann, and Weems arises from my own disappointment that these interpreters have not answered my own burning question of how I can find meaning in the Bible while reading it ideologically. Rather than resolve my dilemma, they make it loom larger and appear even more intractable.

When in my academic and personal life I have faced an "irresolvable" problem, when I cannot find a solution that I can live with, I have learned to step back and look at the problem yet again. Especially when only two, mutually exclusive options present themselves, I consider *why* I cannot choose between them. What is it about this dilemma that paralyzes me? More important, I consider the possibility that a bigger picture has not yet come into focus. Perhaps appreciation and critique *seem* like the only options because I have been applying the wrong metaphor: what if they are not apples and oranges but rather two sides of the same coin, one that is itself but a single currency among many in the marketplace of meaning?

The Frame of Authority

Taking a step back from the "love it or hate it" approaches to the Prophetic Books outlined in the previous chapter brings into focus the overarching common assumption that they share. The larger frame of both is the *authority* of the Bible. These apparently polar approaches both assume that the Bible claims authoritative status and that in discussing prophetic texts readers take a stance on whether they *accept* or *reject* that authority.

All of the interpretations of Hosea presented in the previous chapter can be understood in this way. Despite their very real differences, all have (consciously or not) approached the text with the understanding that it makes authoritative claims. Brueggemann and Bowman, as well as the authors of other sermons in *Preaching the Eighth Century Prophets*,[2] assume that the proper posture toward Hosea is to stand behind it, to follow where it leads, to see life from its angle of vision. Baumann strives to convince readers *not* to accept the authority of this metaphor, to stand against it, to see life differently than it does. Although she does not say this directly, I suspect that Weems's ultimate decision to prioritize appreciation of Hosea over critique arises from the authority that the Bible holds for Christian communities, including her own. Generations of oppressed people have found hope and comfort in the Bible, believing that it forges the path of justice. To reject that authority, even when confronted with highly problematic passages, is not an option. Ultimately, Christians must stand behind a Bible that has stood behind them in times of crisis.

As outlined in chapter 1, the authority frame has a long history. For centuries, Christian interpreters have asserted or sometimes simply assumed that what the Prophetic Books say is the authoritative word of God. Christological readings, ethical readings, readings pointing to divine sovereignty over arrogant institutions—all presume the prophetic message to be determinative of Christian faith and practice. To be Christian means to believe what the prophets claimed or to do what the prophets did. Within the authority frame, "take it" or "leave it" become the only possible responses to the Prophetic Books. Will the reader obey their authority? Yes or no? Most say "yes" and seek what truth God might reveal through the Prophets. Feminists and other ideological critics say "no" and are left with little else to say about these books.

Perhaps the difficulty of integrating ideological critique of the Prophetic Books with theological reflection reveals not the impossibility of the task but rather the inadequacy of the frame that has governed the conversation. Perhaps abandoning the assumption that value goes hand in hand with assent will allow readers to find other forms of value in their engagement with the Prophetic Books.

The frame of authority not only constrains readers' encounters with these books, but it also can prevent them from recognizing the truth about their own reading of the Bible. Countless experiences of watching students and congregation members encounter Hos. 1–2 and other prophetic images of violence against women have convinced me that most Christian readers will go to great lengths to protect their views about the Bible. They marginalize Hosea as a "problem passage" or "an example of Old Testament thinking." No matter how many "problem passages" they encounter—biblical celebrations of war, the slaughter of innocents, even the violence of Hosea 2—many believers continue to insist that these texts are occasional blips in an otherwise steady heartbeat of a good-hearted Bible.

To them, and to readers here, I offer a two-pronged challenge. The first is to recognize that these passages are not truly exceptions; patriarchy runs throughout the Bible, even through the "good" texts. The second is to find a way to think and talk about the Bible in a way that addresses *all* of the Bible. Christians who do not accept *all the Bible* as authoritative should not affirm that they accept the authority of *the Bible*. If readers were honest, they might admit that true authority lies in their level of comfort with what they read. The authority frame "works" most of the time because most of the time Christians read the Bible as confirming their own understandings of the world. But when a reader's convictions clash with a particular text, the passage becomes an exception: "My authority is the Bible, but not *that* part of the Bible."

Indeed, one could understand the dominant trend in Christian interpretation of the Prophetic Books as that of claiming prophetic authority for one's own perspectives and convictions. The ability of the Prophets to confirm so many different approaches to life and faith over the centuries should rouse our suspicions, as should the rarity with which interpreters have called anything "prophetic" that they do not themselves value. Have interpreters accepted the authority of the texts, or have they interpreted the Prophetic Books in ways that grant authority to their own understandings?

For these reasons as well as others, I do not find the "authority of the Bible" to be a helpful frame for readers. I do not deny or reject biblical authority, but, as I have tried to explain, approaching the Bible in this way leads to theological dead ends and contributes to self-deception in interpretation.

In what follows, I experiment with other frames of thought. What happens if we ask questions about the Prophetic Books other than whether to accept or reject them?

Another Frame: The Bible as Literature

Christians have read biblical texts as instructions, as rules, as authorities to fear for so long that they often have robbed these documents of the very power that likely promoted their acceptance as canon: their power as literature. Biblical texts incite the intellect, the imagination, and the emotions, and, like other literature, they can serve as resources for readers to think about their lives, as individuals and as communities.

"Reading the Bible as literature." This phrase waves a red flag in front of most Christians because they unconsciously add the qualifier "only": "reading the Bible as *only* literature." For those accustomed to obeying the Bible, accepting it as the very words of God, even appealing to its authority in support of their own causes, such an approach may sound anemic, even demeaning, in comparison. I might be understood as suggesting that Christians abandon searching the Bible for meaning and instead content themselves with merely admiring its beauty.

Such is not my aim. I call not for passively admiring the literary features of the Bible but rather for engaging it as fully as we do other powerfully told stories, to read the Bible for all that it is worth. Annie Dillard describes the kind of rich engagement with literature I have in mind. She claims that we only read in hopes that the writer

> will magnify and dramatize our days, will illuminate and inspire us with wisdom, courage, and the possibility of meaningfulness, and will press upon our minds the deepest mysteries, so that we may feel again their majesty and power. What do we ever know that is higher than that power which, from time to time, seizes our lives, and reveals us startlingly to ourselves as creatures set down here bewildered?[3]

Dillard claims that "we still and always want waking,"[4] and that good literature sounds the alarm.

Throughout my life, entering the world of books (and their companions art, movies, and music) has helped me confront truths about myself. My problems often have come into focus while I fixed my eyes elsewhere, on an author's depiction of other people's lives. As a prelude to describing how "literature" might be a helpful frame for thinking about the Bible, I offer testimony to the power of literature in my life.

Reading a Life through the Lens of Literature

Chaim Potok's *My Name Is Asher Lev* grabbed my attention in college.[5] Weeks and months after I completed the novel, its story swirled in my mind. At the time, I struggled to understand the reason, given how greatly the world it described differed from my own. The protagonist, Asher Lev, was a young man growing up in a Hasidic Jewish community in New York; I was a twenty-year-old woman who had grown up in the United Church of Christ in the American South. Asher was consumed by a passion for creating art, a passion that placed him at odds with the teaching of his own community and strained his relationship with the parents that he so deeply loved; I was neither an artist nor at odds with my family. Yet years later I came to recognize that Asher Lev's struggles had been my own at the time. It took me longer than Asher to understand that the academic world to which I committed myself in college would distance me from my own tradition and confront me with hard choices. *My Name Is Asher Lev* worked on me long before I knew it, modeling for me the possibility of staying true to one's own nature.

Encounters with the critical interpretation of literature have also functioned in this way for me. In my early thirties at a crossroads in my life, I found myself reading and rereading Martha Nussbaum's analysis of Henry James's novel *The Golden Bowl*.[6] My interest in her analysis was not in understanding the novel better: I had not then and still have not read James's novel. My knowledge of the plot derives mostly from Nussbaum's description: Maggie Verver and her father, Adam, share such an unnaturally close bond that after her own marriage she encourages him to remarry as well. The new marriages are complicated not only by the depth of the father-daughter bond but also by the fact that their new spouses had once been lovers and eventually resume their affair. Maggie only saves both marriages by lying to her stepmother and her father and by encouraging her father to return to America with his wife. Although Maggie once had striven to be a "flawless crystal bowl, holding . . . pleasures without penalties,"[7] she comes to accept that the human condition more resembles another bowl in the novel—one flawed and eventually cracked.

What engaged me in the 1990s was not James's novel itself but rather the words Nussbaum uses to describe it. She describes the story as one of Maggie's increasing recognition that in order to love she could not be perfect, that she herself was, like the bowl, a flawed vessel. Through the character of Maggie, Nussbaum maintained, James advanced a "philosophy of life":

> This novel works out a secular analogue of the idea of original sin by show-ing a human being's relation to value in the world to be, fundamentally and of contingent necessity, one of imperfect fidelity and therefore of guilt; by showing us ourselves as precious, valuing beings who, under the strains imposed by the intertwining of our routes to value in the world, become cracked and flawed. . . . Human beings, like the golden bowl, are beautiful but not safe.[8]

Human beings, Nussbaum explained, are by nature like Maggie: "flawed crystals."

Nussbaum's description of Maggie's maturation caught my breath. In her words, I realized that I had been trying, as had Maggie, to have a flawless life, to hurt no one, never to be wrong. And I realized that, like Maggie, only sur-rendering the belief that I could be perfect would free me from the paralysis that was preventing me from taking action. Although Maggie begins the novel wanting "to be told ahead of time exactly what's right and when," she ends the story more like "an actress who finds, suddenly, that her script is not writ-ten in advance and that she must 'quite heroically' improve her role."[9] I, too, would have to give up my scripts. Two days after reading Nussbaum's chap-ter, I bought a small crystal with an obvious flaw and set it on my dresser as a reminder. Of course, as Nussbaum says, I could have learned the same les-son from reading the biblical narrative of Adam and Eve, but I suspect that the biblical story was too familiar to "blindside" me in that moment in my life. According to Richard Kearney, narrative

> provides us with a certain aesthetic distance from which to view the events unfolding. . . . It is this curious conflation of empathy and detachment which produces in us . . . the double vision necessary for a journey beyond the closed ego towards other possibilities of being."[10]

By losing myself in reading Nussbaum reading James, I learned what I needed to know about my life.

I could multiply at length examples of novels, movies, song lyrics, and even academic studies that have helped me to think more clearly about my life. I can attest, as I believe other readers can, to the ability of literature to raise big, important questions: Who am I ? What is this world? What matters? What and whom should I love?

Reading Life in Resistance to Literature's Claims

Not only literary texts themselves but also critique of those texts can function in the ways that I have been describing. While I have found it helpful to inhabit the world of a story, I also have grown by engaging in analysis of—even resistance to—what the story says about the world.

In the case of *The Golden Bowl*, Nussbaum helped me to read with the grain of the author, to hear for myself what she thought James sought to convey. In another case, it was in Nussbaum's *critique* of literature that I found meaning. In a powerful chapter of *The Therapy of the Desire*, Nussbaum studies Seneca's *Medea*, the Roman philosopher's casting of an older Greek myth into a tragic play.[11] In the original myth, Medea responds to the unfaithfulness and abandonment of her husband, Jason, with violent rage: she murders their children before his eyes, even the unborn child still in her womb, and storms away to the heavens in a chariot. Seneca, a Stoic philosopher, frames the myth as a lesson in Stoic values: the story of Medea, he insists, underscores the danger not just of jealousy and rage but indeed of all emotional attachments. By making Medea a sympathetic character, Seneca shows that she is not an evil person, but that her passionate attachment to Jason makes her fury and her murders possible—even inevitable.

Nussbaum argues that while Seneca could not change the traditional ending of the story, in which Medea triumphs, the Stoic undercuts her glory by granting to her distraught husband, Jason, the final damning word: "Where you go there are no gods."[12] The philosopher's goal is to advance his argument: to convince readers that to avoid violence and pain they must give up attachments. Nussbaum argues, however, that by making the story into a compelling tragedy, Seneca undercut his own project. By making Medea into a sympathetic character, Seneca evokes the reader's emotions rather than convincing the reader to abandon the emotional life. "In the very act of turning tragedy into a Stoic argument, Stoicism has bitten itself."[13]

In pointing to the incongruence between *what* Seneca was trying to say and *how* he was saying it, by showing the power of emotions to overtake rational arguments against them, Nussbaum helped me see something about myself. Although at the time I had been trying to resolve weighty decisions by applying rational logic, I had been feeling and speaking about the import of those decisions with overwhelming emotion. Nussbaum suggested that I might learn more about myself from listening to *how* I was telling my story than from the rational cost-benefit analysis I had been struggling to apply.

More recently, I experienced something valuable from my own resistance to a narrative. Months after listening to an audiobook of Lee Smith's *On Agate Hill,* I continued to hear the story in my head.[14] My mind constantly returned to Molly Petree, orphaned in North Carolina in the late 1860s, who struggles to maintain her independence from well-meaning but controlling benefactors. Molly initially accepts the education and the teaching career offered to her by others, though her gratitude never erases her own sense that the life chosen for her by others does not match the desires of her heart. Ultimately, Molly runs away from her respectable life with the love of her life; she chooses love over teaching, over social graces, over everything else. Molly's story does not end happily—she suffers deep loss and grief—but she remains, to the end, strong and defiant.

Early in my listening to the story, I became aware that its geographical setting and even the cadence of the tape's Southern narrator were calling me to acknowledge how much I still consider North Carolina "home." But, mostly, Molly's decision to live in the backwoods for the sake of love left me unsettled. More precisely, I was unsettled by *Smith's* choice for Molly and almost angry at her attempt to make me as a reader sympathetic to that choice. Only months later did the "obvious" occur to me, when I came to realize how much I had been struggling to value my own recent choice to forego a career opportunity for the sake of my marriage. Molly's decision left me so unsettled, I think, because I had not decided what I am and am not willing to do for love. Paying attention to the strength of my reaction to her choice became an opportunity to take more seriously my conflicted feelings about my own choices.

Neither example is truly one of ideological critique. In fact, Nussbaum has been criticized for paying too little attention to the differences that race, class, and gender make, for downplaying the differences between ancient and modern cultures in the effort to find universal human values in literature. She acknowledges, but does not make important to her interpretation, the gender scripts that drive Seneca's use of a female character as an argument against emotion. My *On Agate Hill* example does hint at the gender scripts that underlie Molly's story and my own, but it does not explore gender—or race or class.

While writing this book, my own critique of Nussbaum led to new insights as well. When I first read *Love's Knowledge* and *The Therapy of Desire*, I was less interested in ideological questions than I am now. Her assumption of universal human values did not disturb me; after all, she was powerfully naming my own experience. Returning to Nussbaum, after years of developing my own ideological voice, I found that many of the passages I had once underlined still rang true but that her universalizing discourse disturbed me. How could she talk so confidently about how *all* humans think and feel, how the human heart *always* works? And yet, despite the flaws in these assumptions, why did I still resonate with her words? In reflecting on my reaction, I concluded that I am willing to accept Nussbaum's claims about all humans when they ring true for *me*, when I share her ideology. I noticed, too, that the two chapters of her work that most grabbed me both involve erotic love, as does my reaction to *On Agate Hill*. In the process, I saw more clearly that patriarchal scripts about love are not just "out there" in these books and in my culture, but also "in here" in my own thinking. The critic is not immune to the power of cultural messages: despite my perceptions of myself, I still respond, usually unconsciously, out of a deeply internalized message that love is a universal human condition.

And the Bible . . . ?

Reading our lives alongside the Bible is not a new concept for Christians. In one way, the use of allegory by patristic and medieval interpreters shares this approach: in allegory, biblical characters stand for larger truths, and biblical stories plot the spiritual paths of human lives. Such thinking also runs through interpretations that draw explicit analogies between the biblical text and the believers' own situations, such as when slaves in the American South heard as their own the Exodus narrative of liberation from bondage and when Christian families hear their own struggles in the Genesis narratives detailing the estrangement and reconciliation of Joseph and his brothers.

My appeal to read the Bible as literature, however, goes deeper. It suggests that our interaction with the Bible can be more subtle, more unconscious. Reading the Bible in this way can help readers become aware of that which they are not already aware. Serene Jones struggles for words to explain the way the Bible has pulled her into its narratives and worked on her in often-invisible ways:

> It strikes me that at each step along the way, the stories pulled me into their realm of imagination in radically different ways. . . . Often much to my surprise, I find my thoughts floating onto the landscape of these [biblical] tales I supposedly do not believe in, and I discover that they are forming my experience anyway.[15]

Jones does not describe a simple process of asking, "How is my life like the ones of the Bible?" but a more complex one in which the Bible interacts with the Christian's life at deep, even unconscious, levels.

I affirm that the same value can be found in *ideological critique* of the Bible. Christians can learn not only from looking to the Bible for its wholesome truths but also from looking it straight in the eye and seeing the complexities of human ideologies at play. Insight can come from asking hard questions: How is what is happening ideologically in this text happening in me and in my culture? How do I see the politics of my own situation in the politics of the text? But convincing most Christians of this claim is not an easy task so, again, I offer testimony.

I can still see where I was sitting when I first read a critic refusing to accept Abraham's near sacrifice of Isaac in Gen. 22 as a mark of the patriarch's faithfulness. While I do not remember the author, I vividly recall the way that, in an instant, my world changed. The critic guided me through the multiple ways that this story depends on and reinforces patriarchal ideology—how it assumes that Isaac *belongs* to Abraham to the point that sacrificing Isaac can be portrayed as *self*-sacrifice on Abraham's part; how Sarah and her perspective remain absent; how the story, as I would later read another critic describe it, values sacrifice of children rather than their protection.[16]

The experience of reading this critique did several things. It allowed me to admit that I had never accepted the premise of the story that willingness to kill a child could make someone a hero, even a hero for God. It also helped me understand *why* I resisted this story. At the time, I was just beginning to understand the depths of my own commitment to my daughter; reading the critique helped me understand just how much this text's ideology differed from my own.

But this experience also allowed me to name more clearly the patriarchal ideologies in my culture that seemed to be working against my deepest desires for my daughter, Anna. It caused me to think in a new way about my own childhood, to reinterpret my parents in light of their own socialization. As patriarchy became more obvious in the text, it became more obvious in my church, in my workplace, and in the theology that I had been taught—a theology in which God the father sacrificed his innocent son, Jesus, for a cause, with no female voice to offer another perspective.

My experience has shown me how often this powerful story of Gen. 22, called the Akedah in Jewish tradition, throws thoughtful readers into wrestling with ideology, even when they do not recognize it as such. In the seminary classroom, I have watched the equal fervor with which some students lambaste the story and others defend it at all costs. Engaging this story and ideological critique of it, we have disagreed about what makes good parenting, whether the United States sacrifices its own sons in war, and whether God's call requires Christians to sacrifice their families.

Whenever I think of the Akedah, I think of Lyn, a former student in my Introduction to the Old Testament class. Four years after Lyn completed a thorough study of the Akedah for her final class project and one year after she graduated from seminary, she encountered the text again. Now a pastor in a small church, Lyn faced Gen. 22 in the lectionary readings for the Sixth Sunday after Pentecost. As she explained to me later, she agonized to respond: given how much she had struggled in seminary to find value in this story, what in it could she offer to congregants eager to hear good news? In the sermon, which Lyn emailed to me, I heard the power of honest struggle with a difficult text. She explained to her congregation how all week the problems of the text faced her:

> The questions swirling in my head gave me vertigo. What kind of God would ask this of a parent? What kind of father would agree without arguing or trying to change God's mind? Is blind obedience what faithfulness is all about? Is violence in the name of God sanctioned? What does this all mean for us?

Lyn's sermon explained that, despite all her study in and since seminary, no commentary, interpretation, or sermon had solved the problems of this text for her. She confessed that at some point in her preparation she gave up trying to make this text into something beautiful and uplifting and simply wept. She wept not just for the characters in the story but also for herself and for her culture. In her e-mail to me, Lyn explained that she had done what she thought critical study had pushed her to do: "to take us into the 'death layer' of a text where hidden truths lie waiting to be discovered and brought back to life." In this sermon, Lyn gave her congregation permission that the text had not given Abraham: to weep for the tragic situations of their own lives, for the horrible choices they feel they have no choice but to make. I claim she preached good news.

Four months after sending me the sermon, Lyn e-mailed me a second time. The Akedah had found her again, this time in the context of a spiritual retreat, where meditating on the text led Lyn to new insights about her relationship with her children. She realized that the actions for which she had criticized Abraham were much like her own: in order to heal from early childhood traumas, Lyn had needed to distance herself from her children for a period of time, to "sacrifice" them in order to respond to God's call, in this case a call to wholeness. As she came to understand, even forgive, her own choices, she began to value Abraham's story differently.

Lyn, a faithful and committed Christian, did not come to these insights by submitting to the Akedah's didactic truth. She grew because she was willing to look at the text, and herself, from all angles, especially challenging ones.

Ideology AND Theology?

These stories, I believe, indicate that ideological critique of the Bible can lead to greater understanding of oneself and one's culture. It can help readers to understand more clearly not only the logic of ancient texts but also the current ideologies with which those texts intersect, offering readers deeper insight into the cultural scripts that shape their own thinking and thus inform their responses to the text.

The degree to which those insights should be considered *theological* might be challenged. After all, in the examples I offered, readers did not formulate statements about the nature of God after encountering the biblical text and its critique. But I maintain that ideological critique has a profound role to play in demonstrating the ways that formulations about God's nature and character are shaped by human dynamics of power. By challenging Christians to consider the human politics that shape their thought and speech about God, ideological critique calls for Christians to take responsibility for what they say about God—for the ethics of biblical and contemporary talk about God. By naming invisible allegiances to systems of power, it might function, as Eichrodt, von Rad, and Brueggemann claim the prophets did, to assert sovereignty of God over all forms of idolatry.

Ideological criticism does challenge the easy assumption that the Bible is a transparent window into the divine, and in that way it distances the Bible from the "reality" of God and thus, seemingly, from Christians seeking to know God. But in my discussion of literature, I have argued that distance often opens up space for insight. Perhaps *not* insisting that the Bible teach us who God is will allow us to learn things about ourselves and our culture that have profound implication for our theology. Perhaps, as the Wisdom literature of the Old Testament insists, in learning about life we learn about God. Perhaps we will find God not simply in the words of Scripture but instead in our wrestling with them.

In this way, the Bible might become less a "rule" than a "classic," as described by theologian David Tracy. Tracy defines "classics" as "certain expressions of the human spirit [which] so disclose a compelling truth about our lives"[17] that we return to them again and again. Tracy says,

> When the text is a classic, I am also recognizing that its "excess of meaning" both demands constant interpretation and bears a certain kind of timelessness—namely the timeliness of a classic expression radically rooted in its own historical time and calling to my own historicity.[18]

While my own project does not share all of Tracy's assumptions (he argues for a universal common human experience in ways that I do not), I share his resistance to defining the Christian life as one of obedience to doctrines and dogmas.[19] I share, too, his conviction that the task of theology is not to merely repeat the tradition but to understand it anew. "I can never repeat the classics to understand them," Tracy says. "I must interpret them."[20]

Looking Forward

In the chapters that follow, I apply these reading strategies to a specific set of texts: metaphors for God and nations in the Prophetic Books. Several factors make these difficult texts prime candidates for my consideration of ideology and theology. First, these metaphors are graphic, striking, troubling—thus begging for a response. Second, they obviously operate ideologically: deriving from the realm of human relationships, they depend on the "rules" of relationship for their meaning. And, third, as chapter 2 explained, the critique of these metaphors has polarized (and paralyzed) readers, theologians, and preachers.

The chapters ahead strive, at one level, to explain these metaphors by analyzing the ancient ideologies on which they depend. What "rules" of human relationship drive the metaphor, what understandings of proper authority and control? On another level, they aim to bring into focus contemporary cultural assumptions by investigating the nature of readers' responses to the text. In considering both ancient and modern ideologies, these discussions explore theological implications. How has ideology shaped descriptions of God? What does ideological critique reveal as problematic or "interested" within theological debate?

For reasons I have explained, readers should not expect to find in these chapters metaphysical claims about God or broad, overarching paradigms for understanding reality. They should not search for descriptions about what these metaphors "teach" about the nature of God. Rather, I hope that they will encounter moments of insight into their lives, into the society in which they live, and into the way that they think about—even the way they experience—God.

Chapter 4

God as (Abusing) Husband

*I*n chapter 2, I explained the key role that the marriage metaphor of Hosea has played in the development of feminist critique of the Prophetic Books, and I offered Hosea as an example of the polarization of "love it" versus "hate it" responses. Because interpreters have encountered such difficulty in valuing Hosea while taking feminist critique seriously, I offer it as my first attempt at engaging prophetic metaphor. What value can come from allowing the feminist critique of Hos. 1–2 to inform the theological task? What can readers find life giving in ideological critique of the marriage metaphor?

As suggested in the previous chapter, these questions have ancient, contemporary, and theological dimensions.

Ancient Dimensions

Critique reveals that *patriarchy is not an incidental feature of this metaphor but rather its very core.* My introduction to the feminist critique of Hosea's marriage metaphor in chapter 2 highlighted the pervasiveness of patriarchal ideology within the comparision. The discussion here reviews that exposition and goes beyond it, to show even more patriarchy in Hos. 1–2 than readers usually recognize.

This metaphor shares with the Old Testament as a whole the presumption that a man can and should control "his" women and children. Old Testament texts indicate that in ancient Israel, the oldest male member of a family (usually the father) was presumed to hold authority over the household—a unit tellingly referred to as the *bêt āb*, the "house of the father." This man held the prerogative to decide where the family would live, whom the children would marry, and how problems facing the unit would be resolved. For a daughter, this meant that prior to her marriage she owed full obedience to her father.

After marriage, however, the daughter would reside with her husband's family and come under his authority.

Numerous biblical narratives reveal that women could influence family decisions in indirect ways, as when Rebekah aids Jacob in deceiving his father to order to procure the rights of the firstborn (Gen. 27) and when Tamar deceives Judah into fulfilling his family obligations to her (Gen. 38). These stories demonstrate, however, that women could only influence major decisions by trickery or by otherwise circumventing established rules. In Israel, the default position of power (if not always the realized one) belonged to the oldest male family member.

Interpreters of the Old Testament disagree about whether it treats women as property. On the one hand, women are given status as persons in their own right. As Tikva Frymer-Kensky outlines in her entry on "Deuteronomy" in the *Women's Bible Commentary*, the Ten Commandments include women in the religious requirements to keep Sabbath and to refrain from murder and theft; honor is due mothers as well as fathers.[1] Moreover, women's status may have varied in different periods of Israel's history. Carol Meyers and others have argued that women enjoyed more status in Israel's early period than during the monarchy, when landholding and power shifted from the family to the bureaucratic and militaristic state.[2]

Despite these caveats, however, few deny that in ancient Israel, as in other cultures of the ancient Near East, *rights to sex with a woman* were owned by the man in authority over her. Biblical law recognizes the right and the responsibility of the father to ensure that his daughter remains a virgin until marriage, and if she is raped, payment comes to him (Exod. 22:16–17). After marriage, rights to sex with a woman transfer to her husband; if she has sex with another man, both she and the offending man are to be put to death. Women in the ancient world were not considered free agents when it came to their sexual partners.

Given how the male-female relationship was configured and transacted in ancient Israel, calling the relationship described in Hos. 1–2 a "marriage" is a matter for debate. Not only did these ancient relationships not look like modern ones, but also there is no word in biblical Hebrew for "marriage"; instead, a man is said to "take" (*lqh*) or "rule over" (*b'l*) a woman. Whenever "marriage" or "marry" appears in an English translation of the Old Testament, it has been added by a translator. Similarly, the English translation "wife" reflects the Hebrew word *'išâ*, which technically means "woman," and the word usually translated "husband" is *ba'al* or "master."

Clearly, the relationships between a man and "his" woman in ancient Israel were not egalitarian matters. The woman owed sexual allegiance to her husband, who retained authority over her and their children. Men could have multiple sexual partners, as long as those women were not themselves the sexual property of other men, but women could not.

The difference in ancient Israel's rules for male and female sexuality also can be seen in the Old Testament usage of the word translated in the NRSV as "whore." Literally, the Hebrew root *znh* refers to a professional prostitute: it is the same term used to describe the activities of Tamar (Gen. 38) and Rahab (Josh. 2), and its prohibition is paralleled with that of a male prostitute in Deut. 23:18. By extension, however, *znh* refers to any promiscuous woman. In Deut. 22:21, for example, a young woman found not to be a virgin is called *znh*, and Ezek. 23:3 uses the term to accuse young women of promiscuous behavior. Isaiah 57:3, Jer. 3:8, and Hos. 4:13–14 place *znh* in parallelism with *n'p*, "commit adultery." In most of these cases, it seems, the term *znh* functions as a slur, much like the contemporary American usage of "slut"—a term that demeans women or men being compared to women.

These features are painfully evident in Hos. 1:2. Yahweh tells the prophet, "Go, take [*lqh*] to yourself a woman [*'išâ*] of whoredom [a form of *znh*]" (my trans.). The prophet/God not only takes (*lqh*) the woman/Israel without her consent, but also alone chooses when to dissolve and when to resume their relationship. The man alone names the children and alone determines their fate. The NRSV translation of Hos. 2:19–20 describes Yahweh's relationship with Israel as "betrothal," but the Hebrew word in question (*'rś*) does not refer to the kind of romantic engagement that the English translation implies. The term literally means "to pay the bride-price for." When the word appears in Exod. 22:16, it is more accurately translated in the TNK translation than in the NRSV:

> If a man seduces a virgin for whom the bride-price has not been paid, and lies with her, he must make her his wife by payment of a bride-price. (Exod. 22:15 TNK)

> When a man seduces a virgin who is not engaged to be married, and lies with her, he shall give the bride-price for her and make her his wife. (Exod. 22:16 NRSV)

Literally, the Hebrew of the first phase of Hos. 2:19 reads, "I will pay the bride-price for you for myself forever." The NRSV and other translations add "as a wife" to both verses.

As outlined in chapter 2, the man also assumes his right to punish his wife for infidelity. Even if the acts of violence in Hos. 2 are understood as verbal threats rather than actualized physical violence, the threats only take on power because they appear *credible*. The threats of 2:1–13 make evident the patriarchal assumptions running not only through the establishment of the metaphor in chapter 1, but, more important, through the "honeymoon" phase of the relationship of 2:14–23. While in the new period of tenderness the husband may cease physical violence, he remains in control of their relationship and implicitly retains the right to punish in the future. The husband's actions toward the woman in the "honeymoon" are not a change in his earlier behavior but an extension of it.

The patriarchy of Hos. 1–2 is not a minor blemish on an otherwise pure text nor a minor matter to be delegated to footnotes. Rather, the hierarchy built into the metaphor of (ancient) marriage provides the basis for the author's comparison of the bond between God and Israel as that of a man who has taken a woman. The author seeks to convince readers that Israel owes Yahweh not only affection but also obedience, that Israel deserves punishment for attachments to other deities, and that after the punishment Yahweh might again choose Israel. The vehicle for those claims is a metaphor in which one party holds power and privilege over another, in which one stands as the unquestioned superior. In the world of this text, God and Israel are not equal partners in a mutually chosen relationship; neither are men and women.

The feminist demonstration that patriarchy remains inseparable from Hos. 1–2 has important implications for Christian teaching and preaching about this text. Particularly, it points to numerous dangers that arise from apparently good-hearted attempts to downplay or even "fix" the patriarchal ideology of Hosea. First and most obviously, such readings pass off selective readings of the text as "biblical." Interpretations that point to some of what Hosea says but remain silent about its key features do not faithfully represent the biblical text but rather (even if unintentionally) grant biblical authority to other ideologies. Second, readings of Hosea that do not take its patriarchy seriously allow readers to ignore the very features of the metaphor chosen by the author to make his theological point. When Bowman's sermon, for example, assumes that Hosea's marriage is like his own,[3] he misses the full import of the book's claims about God: through this metaphor, the author underscores that God remains in control over Israel, that Israel owes Yahweh its allegiance and faithfulness, and that God's physical punishment of Israel is justified. Changing the vehicle of the metaphor into that of modern, affectionally based, egalitarian marriage changes its message. Third, mentioning only the "positive" aspects of this text leaves readers insufficiently sensitive to how even the love in Hos. 2 is couched in patriarchal terms. Limiting the reader's exposure to Hosea to God's profession of love in 2:14–23, as does the Revised Common Lectionary for Year C, does not erase the patriarchy of Hos. 1–2 but instead allows it to pass as normal. Keeping invisible the violence of the beginning of the chapter serves to mask the patriarchy of the "honeymoon." Feminist critique of Hosea's marriage metaphor calls Christians to acknowledge the way that this biblical text and others were shaped by the world in which they were produced.

Contemporary Dimensions

Feminist critique of Hosea reveals the *patriarchal ideologies within readers.* Such critique underscores not only the deep-seated patriarchy within the world of the text but also, and perhaps even more important the powerful ways that patriarchal ideology influences readers. The ease with which readers accept the terms of Hosea's metaphor, as well as its continued appeal for those who attempt to resist it, reveal the family resemblance between ancient and modern ideologies of marriage.

As I explained earlier, feminists have argued that a reader must adopt the male perspective of Hos. 1–2 in order to evaluate positively the image of God that it presents. Reading *with* and *for* the male protagonist of the text makes it "work": readers accept his feelings as justified and his desire for revenge (even if not its actualization) as understandable. Readers consider a woman's choice of multiple partners as whoredom and her husband's willingness to forgive her as magnanimous only when they assent to the patriarchal assumptions on which the metaphor depends.

In over twenty years of teaching this text, I have rarely found a Christian who does *not* read Hosea in precisely this way. In the classroom and in churches, the majority of readers cannot see the patriarchy in the text until it is painstakingly pointed out to them. In encountering the feminist critique of Hosea, some are shocked not to have noticed these features before; but even more struggle to comprehend even the basic dynamics of patriarchal ideology in this text.

In my experience, although more women than men come to see the patriarchy in the text, the dividing line between the responses is not neatly drawn by gender. Some women defend the purity of Hosea as fervently as do some men, but with an added zing: "*I'm* a woman, and this text doesn't bother *me!*" Of course, several factors inform such reactions. Most Christian women as well as most Christian men accept the Bible as an authority for their lives and believe that it faithfully reveals God's own intentions for the world; especially for women who turn to the Bible for support against a sexist society, viewing a biblical text as working *against* their liberation is painful if not impossible.

Moreover, women as well as men react in different ways to the adjective with which I introduce the issues: the f-word, *feminism*. Feminism is so caricatured in our culture that few are willing to accept the label or align themselves with what they see as its negative evaluation of contemporary culture.

I do believe, however, that the most significant reason that women as well as men struggle to see Hosea as patriarchal is that all people internalize patriarchal ways of looking at the world. Although our culture often contrasts "men's perspectives" with "women's perspectives," most of us remain well aware that positions on social matters are not so easily identified with a single gender. For this reason, patriarchy is most accurately understood as an ideology; a set of rules; a way of thinking, feeling, and behaving into which both women and men are socialized. Both girls and boys learn early, usually before they can talk, how to sort people, clothes, toys, and jobs by "girl" or "boy," and to apply the appropriate rules to each. Girls also learn early to accept male perspectives as normative. Girls will watch "boy" TV shows and movies, while boys find more difficulty in identifying with female characters. Long before adolescence, girls learn not only to groom themselves to be admired by the male gaze but also to gaze at themselves in the same way, to evaluate their appearance as they believe men would evaluate them.

Socialization happens so early, so consistently, and sometimes so subtly that it usually remains unnoticed as such. In the case of all ideologies, the more that patriarchy remains under the radar, the more we believe that we act as free agents. What is learned best feels to us most normal: "I don't wear makeup to please men. It just makes me feel good about myself." "I know God doesn't have a gender, but it just doesn't feel right to call God a 'she.'"

Some women (I have been calling them feminists) resist patriarchal socialization, with varying levels of intensity; so do some men. Some women find nothing wrong with their socialization, see it as a minor factor in their lives, or disagree with my description of the process altogether; so do some men.

But awareness of socialization does not erase its influence. Most feminists acknowledge that they cannot escape the appeal of patriarchal images and literature. For example, Brenner concludes her discussion of pornoprophetics with this confession:

> As a F[emale] reader, I can resist the fantasy [of pornography] by exposure, by criticism, by reflection. But within the present cultural system, I do so at my own peril. I was raised and educated to comply with that male fantasy and to adopt it as my very own. Like other F[emale] readers, I may deconstruct myself at times; the temptation to reciprocate this M[ale] fantasy, even to appropriate it, may still be there. Awareness helps, but the odds are against me.[4]

The difficulty that some people have in seeing patriarchy in Hosea comes from their difficulty in seeing patriarchy in their own culture, and from their difficulty in acknowledging that their own "gut" responses are shaped by presumptions of male privilege. Most readers never question Hosea's right to punish Gomer and the children or question the character of a man who threatens to kill his wife for infidelity. That "of course" response indicates that patriarchal frames of marriage continue to pass as normal, even for those whose own relationships are more egalitarian.

One positive function that recognizing patriarchy in Hosea can have is to train readers to see patriarchy in the present. For many people, hearing familiar patterns of relationship called "sexist" or "abusive" invites a reconsideration of their own lives. It invites them, too, to reflect on the sheer power of patriarchal ideology—in their culture and in themselves. When the author of Hosea sought to convince ancient readers of the legitimacy of God's punishment of Israel, he found an easily usable cultural analogy: patriarchally framed marriage. Why does that analogy continue to be so effective for many people? Why, in the past and in the present, is gender such a highly effective means to describe hierarchies of power?

Engaging Hosea in light of feminist critique also reveals the degree to which interpreters' responses to Hos. 1–2 are driven by modern ideologies of romantic marriage. Having recognized the vast differences between the relationship described in Hos. 1–2 and that of contemporary marriage, readers are confronted with the question of why interpreters insist on reading Hosea as a modern tale of love, betrayal, and reunion.

I previously named several ways that contemporary interpreters have collapsed the difference between ancient and modern marriage. The trend, I suggested, is evident in the translation of the book. English translators render the Hebrew word *'išâ* as "wife" even though its most basic meaning is "woman"; they add "as a wife" to God's command to Hosea to "take a woman"; and they use vocabulary such as "engage" and "betroth" to describe the ancient practice of sealing an agreement with a bride-price. This tendency to translate in "marriage-friendly" ways runs throughout modern English translators of the Old Testament. In a careful though not exhaustive study of English translations, I found that the more recent a translation is, the more likely it is to add "in marriage" or "as wife" to the Hebrew phrase "to take a woman." For example, the NRSV translation (1989) uses some form of the English word "marry" (including "marrying," "marries," "married," "marriage," "marriages") 92 times in its translation of the Old Testament, while the earlier RSV (1952) only lists 64 occurrences. Some form of "marry" appears in the KJV (1611) 20 times, but in the NIV (1984) 134 times.

A selective reading of the metaphor, as described above, also makes the relationship of Hos. 1–2 appear more like a modern marriage. The priority given to the wooing at the end of chapter 2, such as in the choice of verses in the Revised Common Lectionary and in Brueggemann's focus on the theological importance of these verses, allows the romantic dimensions of the relationship to become the "meaning" of the metaphor, to the exclusion of its other, more central features. Ideological critique challenges readers to consider the contemporary factors that go into making Hos. 1–2 into a romance.

It would be difficult to overstate just how strongly notions of romance factor in contemporary understandings of marriage in the United States. This is a society that insists that people should only marry if they are in love and coaches men on how to make romantic proposals of marriage. Most Americans believe, too, that romance within marriage can and should be lifelong. Should the spark of romance go out, magazine articles, TV shows, the Internet, couples seminars, flower shops, and whole malls sell remedies to rekindle the flame. Partners who do not love one another any more, who are "stuck in a loveless marriage," are seen as prime candidates for divorce or at least pity. Given how romance saturated contemporary pictures of marriage are, it is little wonder that readers are taken by—and actually help create—Hosea's expression of love. Despite all that Hosea's metaphor involves, seeing only love in Hosea becomes easy, given what many of us are taught about marriage from an early age.

Viewing Hos. 1–2 through the lens of romance also allows the modern reader to minimize the threats of violence in chapter 2 as "natural" anger in response to marital infidelity. While feminist critique suggests that the two halves of chapter 2—the threats and the honeymoon—are two dimensions of male control, "hopeless romantics" understand the two divine emotions as two dimensions of romance: because God/the prophet loves Israel/Gomer, he erupts in anger when she betrays him with another. The threats arise from the same passion as the coos of love.

Such a depiction, of course, follows particular gender scripts. The man responds to betrayal with rage, although the woman's feelings about being abandoned by her lovers and stripped by her husband receive no attention. The man does not respond with other "understandable" emotions: sadness, grief, or depression in response to loss. Readers socialized into patriarchal ideologies of marriage and romance do not register surprise at these features of the text because they have learned to expect men to lash out in anger against affronts to their honor and refusals of their affections.

This "gendered sympathy" runs throughout contemporary movies and literature as well. In the 2002 film *Unfaithful*, a woman's affair with another man baffles and then enrages her husband. The husband (played by Richard Gere) tracks down her lover, initially out of curiosity, but in a moment of rage kills his rival. In a powerful scene, the husband confronts his wife (played by Diane Lane) and confesses, "I wanted to kill you." Although she is initially appalled by his confession, she comes to consider his act of violence and his threat against her as acts of love. The couple becomes closer, and the movie closes with them driving away together. The husband's angry violence has been rewarded by greater intimacy with his wife. A key difference between this film and Hosea is instructive. While in *Unfaithful* the husband murders his wife's lover in blind rage, in Hosea the wife alone bears the brunt of her husband's anger. Yet the same contemporary scripts regarding infidelity, anger, and violence allow *Unfaithful* and Hosea to find a ready audience.

It is the "hopeless romantics" who most need the ideological critique of Hosea. By insisting that we read the metaphor as a whole and as wholly patriarchal, feminist criticism forces readers to see how they allow the romance they impute to Hosea to obscure violence and domination—both in this text and in contemporary human relationships. It reminds readers of things they know but tend to forget when the language turns to love: that perpetrators of spousal battering often blame their actions on their wives: "She made me so angry that I hit her"; and that the jealousy which sounds flattering on the surface can quickly turn predatory and terrifying. Many people know, or have at least read about, women who have been threatened or killed by jealous husbands or boyfriends. If domestic violence statistics are accurate, one out of every three women has experienced some form of domestic abuse. Why, then, it is so easy to forget these realities when the language turns romantic?

Unfortunately, the patriarchal assumptions of Hosea's metaphor are so familiar to many of us that they remain invisible. Most readers accept, without recognition, the male privilege on which the comparison of Yahweh's relationship with Israel to that of a husband with his wife depends. Because we know the scripts so well, we feel Yahweh's pain, we sympathize with his plight, we feel the pathos of the situation. Patriarchy is the "fishbowl" in which we swim.[5]

Feminist criticism offers an opportunity to look at the structures of our thinking. Why are modern notions of romantic marriage so powerful that readers will find them in Hosea, despite their absence in the text? Why are readers so insistent on finding stories in which love triumphs over all and relationships weather the storms of betrayal and anger? Why do they like to see men woo women, to be a little jealous, maybe to exert just a little force? Why are these scripts so powerful that they can fuel not only the wedding industry but also the reading of biblical texts?

Feminists have shown that when readers collapse the distance between ancient and modern relationships in order to give biblical sanction to their own constructs, they do so at the price of ignoring the violent, hierarchical, patriarchal parts of the Bible—and of their own culture. Acknowledging both the similarities and the differences between the contemporary world and that of Hosea forces readers to acknowledge that the patriarchy of Hosea is not only in the *text:* it is often deeply embedded within *readers* as well. Feminist critique cautions us to pay the most attention to texts that evoke our sympathies and inflame our passions, for they may teach us the most about the ideological scripts that we follow while thinking we are free to feel and act as we choose.

Theological Dimensions

In my understanding, all of these reflections have theological dimensions. Clearer understanding of the nature of the Bible, as well as of self and culture, directly informs an understanding of the world and the human condition. I do point specifically, however, to two aspects of this discussion that I believe have particular bearing on theological discourse and reflection.

First, reflection on the feminist critique of Hosea reveals the extent to which patriarchy is not an incidental feature of the Bible, of Christian tradition, or of the believer's response to either. As I have demonstrated, the patriarchal ideology of this text runs far deeper than the fact that it talks about men and that it calls God "he." In Hosea, God is not simply grammatically male but also identified with a particular human male and with particular male behaviors, attitudes, and emotions. The starkness of patriarchy in Hosea is valuable in calling the Christian church to acknowledge that the patriarchy of our tradition is not something easily remedied. No simple shift of pronouns for God will alter this consistent picture of God as enjoying male prerogatives of power.

Feminist critique of Hosea also underscores that this pervasive patriarchy is dangerous. Christians who truly believe in the equality of human beings before God, who believe that all are created in God's image, are called to respond to Hosea's metaphor of God as a husband with more than the spoken affirmation that it is "the word of the Lord." They are called to acknowledge that exclusive masculine language for God, intentionally or not, reinforces male privilege in the human realm. Hosea painfully shows us that the masculinity of God is intertwined with human dynamics of power.

As we have seen, however, the matter goes far beyond the substitution of pronouns for God. Simply switching masculine pronouns to feminine ones in Hosea or comparing God to a wife and Israel to an erring husband would not address the problematic nature of this text: how one partner owns another; how children are treated; how anger justifies violence; how happy endings resolve all problems. The patriarchy of Hosea, and of the Bible as a whole, is not a layer of meaning that can be stripped away. Rather, feminist critique calls the church to rethink its understanding and use of the Bible. By forcing Christians to acknowledge the humanness of the Bible, the way in which it is shaped by both ancient and modern culture, such critique offers an opportunity to talk about the power of the Bible to inform human life rather than the Bible as a authoritative set of rules.

This discussion also suggests, however, that only addressing the Bible's patriarchy is insufficient. Because patriarchy also is internalized within readers, it must be addressed in culture as well. Just as recognizing patriarchy within the Bible might make patriarchy in culture more evident, so might greater awareness of the forms that patriarchy takes in their own cultures and psyches allow Christians to see something important, if perhaps painful, about their traditional texts.

Ideological critique challenges Christians to take responsibility for all God language, both the language inherited from tradition (language that feels right and comfortable) and also any new language forged in attempts to respond faithfully to new insights and sensitivities. What does our God-talk imply about others? About the world? What ideologies does it support? As we have seen, metaphors of human relationships come with particular risks, because they carry the most culturally specific ideologies; we find it easy, and dangerous, to equate human and divine prerogatives.

Feminist analysis of Hosea's metaphor also challenges attempts to accept God's love but not God's power. I have argued that God's courtship language at the end of chapter 2 does not imply weakness or even vulnerability on God's part. As in domestic violence situations, the cessation of violence does not mean that the dynamics of power within the relationship have changed; even in his apparent kindness, the man remains in control of the woman and of the relationship. This critique cautions Christians from claiming as "biblical" any attempt to separate divine love from divine power or from pitting the two natures of God against one another. Feminist critique argues instead that Hosea testifies not to a deity whose love and power remain in a paradoxical, tensive relationship but to one whose choice to act in love remains an exercise of full divine sovereignty.

Reading the romantic ending of Hos. 2 in light of its threat-filled beginning also raises the question of how God's power interacts with human will. In Hosea, Gomer is not allowed to say "no" to her husband: if she forsakes him, he punishes her, and even when he speaks tenderly to her she is not free to decline his attentions. Does the same hold true for God? Is it possible to say "no" to God? Is God's power, even when couched in terms of love, ultimately inescapable? In light of ideological critique, Hosea says as much (or more) about divine right and control as it does about divine compassion. Why, then, is love all we can see?

In its ancient context, Hosea's metaphor may have served as a retrospective explanation for the fall of the northern kingdom. Although the dating of the book is much debated, I have suggested elsewhere that the first nine of the twelve Minor Prophets may have been edited in the Persian period in order to provide an introduction to Zechariah.[6] Zechariah 1:2–6 explains the book's outlook in Israel's and Judah's past:

> "The LORD was very angry with your fathers. Therefore say to them, Thus says the LORD of hosts: Return to me, says the LORD of hosts, and I will return to you, says the LORD of hosts. Be not like your fathers, to whom the former prophets cried out, 'Thus says the LORD of hosts, Return from your evil ways and your evil deeds.' But they would not hear or heed me, says the LORD. Your fathers, where are they? And the prophets, do they live for ever? But my words and my statutes, which I commanded my servants the prophets, did they not overtake your fathers? So they repented and said, As the LORD of hosts purposed to deal with us for our ways and deeds, so has he dealt with us." (RSV)

According to Zechariah, earlier prophets had called for the ancestors' repentance, but to no avail. In punishment, Yahweh destroyed Israel and Judah. Zechariah's own audience in the Persian period is warned not to be like their forefathers. If they return to Yahweh, Yahweh will return to them.

When read from a Persian vantage point, the book of Hosea explains the reason for Israel's fall. Despite Hosea's prophecy, the people failed to repent, so that Yahweh declared that "Samaria will bear her guilt" (Hos. 13:16). Yet the close of the book offers promise, using vocabulary that prefigures Zechariah's message: just as the call of Hos. 14:1 for the people to return to Yahweh is met by the report in Hos. 14:4 that Yahweh's anger *did* turn from them, so Yahweh promises in Zech. 1:3: "Return to me and I will return to you."

In such an interpretation, Hosea's marriage metaphor goes beyond a dry explanation that Yahweh's punishment of Israel was deserved to offer a compelling depiction of Israel as Yahweh's bride. Because Yahweh had taken Israel as his own, he had every right to react as any human husband might: to erupt in anger and to exact punishment. The use of the marriage metaphor would make the perception of divine punishment more palatable—and less permanent. If the fall of Israel (and later Judah) had been the reaction of a divine shamed husband, then Hosea's promises of future closeness might soon materialize. If indeed such thinking was at work in the production or editing of Hosea, it suggests that ancient writers (and perhaps modern Christians) need ways of believing that our experiences of suffering have some role in the plan of a good God and that they can end. Hosea allows ancient and modern readers to face suffering in full confidence of God's control and care.

While such theological reasoning might be attractive, feminist critique calls Christians to recognize (in Hosea and in other theological formulations) the potential danger in such thinking. As the analogy with domestic battering reveals, such thinking implicitly portrays God as an abuser to be feared, even in moments of care.

Conclusion

I have tried to model a way of engaging Hosea, and the Bible in general, that does not start—or stop—with the question of what it means to accept the text as authoritative. Rather, I have attempted to show that sustained, honest engagement with both the ancient and modern dimensions of this metaphor can encourage reflection on issues that profoundly matter to human lives, including lives of faith. In the chapters that follow, I suggest how other metaphors in the Prophetic Books can do the same.

Chapter 5

God as (Authoritarian) Father

*O*ne of the most heated controversies within mainstream Protestant denomi-
nations in the late twentieth century erupted in response to feminist challenge
to the image of God as father. In the 1970s and 1980s, feminist theologians
decried the identification of God with a male figure, and the 1980s publication
of the *Inclusive Language Lectionary* offered gender-neutral identifiers for
God. Many Christians raised an outcry in response, pointing to the long
tradition of calling God Father, one that according to the Gospels goes back
to Jesus himself. In the twenty-first century, a minority of Christians have
embraced gender-inclusive language for God, but most have not—and respond
to all challenges with force.

A consideration of how the Prophetic Books use the metaphor of God as
father obviously will not resolve this passion-filled conflict. But, as I hope to
demonstrate, the distinctiveness of the prophetic usage does raise important
issues that inform the debate. This chapter considers the way that the Prophets
characterize God the Father, as well as the implications of this characterization for the way Christians think not only about the gender of God but also
about the nature of good parenting—both human and divine.

Father and Son in the Prophetic Books

Although multiple permutations of the parent-child relationship are possible
(father-son, father-daughter, mother-son, mother-daughter, and combinations
of these relationships), the Prophets rely most on the comparison of God the
father to Israel the son. The Prophets rarely speak of God as mother; in fact,
the only explicit identification appears in Isa. 66:13 ("As one whom his mother
comforts, / so I will comfort you; / you shall be comforted in Jerusalem,"
RSV). "Daughter Zion/Jerusalem" appears in numerous prophetic passages,

77

but given the distinctive nature of the comparison, it will be considered in a later chapter.

Not surprisingly, the prophetic depictions of God as a father often stress Yahweh's affection and care for the people. In Hosea, fatherhood is verbally linked with love: "When Israel was a lad, I loved him, and out of Egypt I called my son" (11:1, my trans.).

Jeremiah makes this connection as well:

> With weeping they shall come,
>   and with consolations I will lead them back,
> I will make them walk by brooks of water,
>   in a straight path in which they shall not stumble;
> for I am a father to Israel,
>   and Ephraim is my first-born. (31:9 RSV)

> Is Ephraim my dear son?
>   Is he my darling child?
> For as often as I speak against him,
>   I do remember him still.
> Therefore my heart yearns for him;
>   I will surely have mercy on him,
> says the LORD.
>
> (31:20 RSV)

Similarly, the poet called Second Isaiah addresses Yahweh as father in order to evoke the Deity's sympathy and compassion for the people:

> Where are your zeal and your might?
>   The yearning of your heart and your compassion?
>   They are withheld from me.
> For you are our father,
>   though Abraham does not know us
>   and Israel does not acknowledge us;
> you, O LORD, are our father;
>   our Redeemer from of old is your name.
>
> (Isa. 63:15–16)

The next chapter, Isa. 64, again calls God a father in the midst of the people's petition for rescue, but this chapter also raises another, extremely important, dimension of the role of fatherhood in ancient Israel:

> Yet, O LORD, thou art our Father;
>   we are the clay, and thou art our potter;
>   we are all the work of thy hand.

Be not exceedingly angry, O LORD,
    and remember not iniquity for ever.
    Behold, consider, we are all thy people.
Thy holy cities have become a wilderness,
    Zion has become a wilderness,
    Jerusalem a desolation.
Our holy and beautiful house,
    where our fathers praised thee,
has been burned by fire,
    and all our pleasant places have become ruins.
Wilt thou restrain thyself at these things, O LORD?
    Wilt thou keep silent, and afflict us sorely?
                                    (64:8–12 RSV)

In this passage, the writer recognizes that fathers not only care for their sons' well-being and act on their behalf but also demand their strict obedience. The image of the father parallels that of the potter, two roles in which the superior retains complete control and ultimate responsibility for the outcome of the "product." (Similarly, Isa. 45:9–11 claims that sons have no right to question their fathers, just as clay has no right to question its potter.) This passage also indicates that fathers punish sons, sometimes in ways that are overly severe.

Such an understanding is not unique to Isaiah 64. As Katheryn Darr stresses in her study of family metaphors in the book of Isaiah, the entire book presupposes the father's right to demand strict obedience of his son and to punish disobedience severely.[1] Isaiah 1:2–6, for example, casts Israel as a son who continues to rebel despite repeated beatings:

Hear, O heavens, and give ear, O earth;
    for the LORD has spoken:
"Sons have I reared and brought up,
    but they have rebelled against me.
The ox knows its owner,
    and the ass its master's crib;
but Israel does not know,
    my people does not understand."

Ah, sinful nation,
    a people laden with iniquity,
offspring of evildoers,
    sons who deal corruptly!
They have forsaken the LORD
    they have despised the Holy One of Israel,
    they are utterly estranged.

Why will you still be smitten,
    that you continue to rebel?
The whole head is sick,
    and the whole heart faint.
From the sole of the foot even to head,
    there is no soundness in it,
but bruises and sores
    and bleeding wounds;
they are not pressed out, or bound up,
    or softened with oil.

(RSV)

Isaiah does not criticize the father's beatings but rather the son's willfulness.

The dual role of father to care and to punish disobedience is reflected, too, in Jeremiah. The metaphor of father-son interweaves, in a telling way, with that of master-son:

Return, O faithless sons, says the LORD, for I am your master. (Jer. 3:14, my trans.)

As in the case of the pairing of father/potter, the pairing of father/master demonstrates the degree to which obedience is demanded.

In subsequent verses in Jeremiah, the refusal of Israel to respond to Yahweh as father transforms Israel from a bad son into a whore—the classical image of the uncontrolled, unfaithful one.

"'I thought
    how I would set you among my sons,
and give you a pleasant land,
    a heritage most beauteous of all nations.
And I thought you would call me, My Father,
    and would not turn from following me.
Surely, as a faithless wife leaves her husband,
    so have you been faithless to me, O house of Israel,
    says the LORD.'"
A voice on the bare heights is heard,
    the weeping and pleading of Israel's sons,
because they have perverted their way,
    they have forgotten the LORD their God.
"Return, O faithless sons,
    I will heal your faithlessness."
"Behold, we come to thee;
    for thou art the LORD our God.

(3:19–22 RSV)

Clearly, when Second Isaiah and Jeremiah speak of God as father, they refer not only to care and affection but also to power and enforced obedience. When Israel fails to be an obedient son, he is dismissed and punished as severely as a slave or a whore would be. For the prophetic writers, obedience to the father is valued, presupposed, and enforced.

Israelite Patriarchal Ideology and Children

As in the case of the (abusing) husband discussed in the previous chapter, the image of the father presented in the Prophets and elsewhere in the Old Testament arises from the social construct of the patriarchal family. In patriarchy, children belong to and remain under the authority of the father. In the Old Testament, fathers not only have the right to choose children's marriage partners but also may sell children into slavery in order to pay debts (Exod. 21:7) and nullify the vows made by their daughters as well as their wives (Num. 30).

Delaney links the sense of ownership of children to ancient Israelite understandings of reproduction.[2] Like other ancient cultures, Israelites understood conception in terms of monogenesis: the belief that children derive biologically only from their fathers. The active male "seed" is planted into the passive "ground" of women's wombs. In ancient perspective, fathers owned their children in ways mothers did not. This belief is reflected in the male orientation of biblical genealogies; the occasional mother mentioned receives honor but not genealogical significance. Delaney traces the belief in monogenesis in early Christianity as well, in which Jesus is the "only begotten son of God," and Mary is merely a receptive and nurturing vessel for God's child.

Not only the gender of the father but also the gender of the son take on significance in this metaphor. In ancient Israel, while fathers owned both sons and daughters, sons (at least oldest sons) alone inherited their fathers' property and authority. After the death of the oldest male member of a family (usually the father), his role would pass to that of the oldest son, who would become the new patriarch. As patriarchs-in-training, sons were to learn obedience, just as they would later demand it of others. In the Bible, then, the relationship of father and son was unique—different from relationships that included female family members.

The right of a father to punish a disobedient son is found throughout Scripture. Although the nature of the punishment is not always spelled out (as in 2 Sam. 13:21), several passages indicate that sons could be struck with a rod, as in the (in)famous passage in Proverbs:

The one who withholds his rod hates his son; and he who loves him eagerly seeks to discipline him. (13:24, my trans.)

The prophetic description of Yahweh as father reflects all these features of the Israelite patriarchal ideology of fatherhood:

1. Like a human son, Israel owes Yahweh the father honor and respect.
2. Like a human son, Israel inherits land from Yahweh his father.
3. Like a human son, Israel can be punished by his father.

The Prophets, then, are not unique in describing God as a controlling, authoritative, punishing father. Yahweh's threat in Mal. 2:3 to throw dung on the priests' faces demonstrates the extent of the punishment allowed: though the threat is often seen as one that would render the priests "unclean" for their duties, the image also resonates strongly with the right of fathers in ancient Israel to punish and shame their children, and especially their sons (Num. 12:14).

The intensity of prophetic rhetoric, however, underscores and intensifies the authoritarian, harsh dimensions of the image of God the Father. The details of the son's beatings in Isaiah 64 and the verbal parallels between sons and slaves and sons and clay in Jeremiah and Malachi arrest a reader with just how patriarchal the model of fatherhood was in ancient Israel.

Ideological Critique of the Metaphor: The Case of Malachi

Interpreters have critiqued other parts of the Bible for their patriarchal ideologies of parenting. Delaney's *Abraham on Trial* challenges the story of Abraham's near sacrifice of Isaac; Danna Nolan Fewell's *The Children of Israel* testifies to the invisible child victims in stories in Genesis and Ezra; and numerous scholars have highlighted how much of what is said about Jesus' death at the hands of his father fits the rhetoric of child abuse.[3]

Fewer scholars, however, have addressed the ideology of parenting in the Prophets. The *maleness* of God the Father has concerned feminist scholars more than what the metaphor entails *for children*, even though the two are closely interrelated. Katheryn Darr's *Isaiah's Vision and the Family of God*, mentioned above, does describe at length how the book of Isaiah uses the image of the rebellious child rhetorically to describe Israel as deserving of punishment. She does not, however, go beyond description of Isaiah to consider how contemporary people might respond to this rhetoric. So rather than survey feminist opinion on the father-son metaphor in the Prophets, I instead explain my own feminist "problem" with this metaphor, specifically as it appears in the book of Malachi.

My Understanding of Parenting

Anyone who knows me even moderately well knows how passionately committed I am to my daughter. I devote a great deal of time, thought, energy, and care into what I believe is good for her—not only in terms of education and experiences but perhaps primarily on an emotional level. I place a high value on parenting her in a way that honors her feelings and nurtures her soul.

Becoming that kind of parent did not come naturally to me. As a child, I showed no particular interest in dolls or playing mother; as a young adult, I never longed for a baby of my own. In fact, the decision to start a family was a difficult one for me; after seven years of marriage, my husband was ready, as were both sets of our parents, but I was just finishing my PhD and was ready to start teaching. The decision was ultimately more rational than emotional: if I were going to have a child, the logical time to do so was before I started a tenure-track job. In those first few days in the hospital after Anna was born, I wondered if we had done the right thing. I secretly worried that I did not feel sufficiently "motherly," that we were not bonding properly. Those feelings continued into her first few months. Having been in some form of school my entire life, engaged with people and thinking new things, I found staying at home with an infant difficult and often boring.

I am not sure when things started to change, but they did. I increasingly began to look at the world as a parent. I began to think about my own childhood and what I did and did not like about it. And I began to fall in love with the child in my care and to become passionate about what kind of world I wanted for her.

What that world looked like took on greater specificity when, the year after she was born, I took on my first full-time teaching position at a Southern women's college. Since I was the only woman on the religion department's faculty, I was encouraged to teach courses in women's studies, not only in the department but also with an interdisciplinary team. My first reaction was to refuse: I had no academic training in women's studies, and I certainly did not consider myself a feminist. I agreed, however, as much from a desire to be a cooperative junior faculty member as anything else.

The interdisciplinary women's studies course that I cotaught with female professors in sociology, art, English, and psychology converted me to feminism. I learned that much of what I and my female friends had wrestled with our whole lives were not just personal issues; they were common experiences for many women. When I confronted for the first time the systemic nature of sexism and the inequities of my own culture, I immediately understood how they would threaten the hopes and dreams I had for my daughter. It would be only a slight exaggeration to say that I became a feminist because of Anna.

When Anna was four, her father and I divorced. He has continued to be an important part of her life, though I consider each of us a single parent, interacting with our daughter on our own terms. Eventually she and I moved out of state, increasing my sense of responsibility and freedom to raise my daughter in ways that matter to me. Even though I have remarried after twelve years of "just us girls," my new husband and I are clear that at this stage of Anna's life, his role is to support my parenting rather than to parent her himself.

Parenting a daughter and feminism have run parallel tracks for me, supporting one another. Critiques of the cultural expectations of motherhood have never threatened my feelings for Anna; in fact, they have given me the freedom to reject the stereotypical role of "mother" and be the kind of parent/mentor/nurturer that would help another (young) woman thrive.

The more I learned about patriarchy academically, the more I saw its dangers for children as well as for women. Reading Donald Capps's *The Child's Song: The Religious Abuse of Children* exposed me to the work of the psychologist Alice Miller and her concern about children's psyches. I came to believe, perhaps because I already did believe, that strongly hierarchical family structures, such as in patriarchy, deny to children a crucial aspect of their well-being: intellectual autonomy, the ability and freedom to think independently of the adults who form their worlds.

All of this was happening, of course, as I was reading, teaching, and writing about the Bible. My graduate work had been traditionally historical, linguistic, and archaeological, but as my thinking changed, my writing changed to incorporate feminist concerns. Biblical descriptions of God as father became as problematic as its depictions of God as husband and male—not because I had a bad experience of my own father (which I did not) but because I had become convinced about a certain style of parenting.

When I approach biblical texts that describe God as father, I want to know how that father treats his children. I do not assume that because the father is male that he must be a bad parent; feminism does not require that of me. But I do come with the firm conviction that a threatening, belittling, obedience-requiring father—or mother—is a bad parent.

When I first read the book of Malachi, I was interested in historical questions, particularly what the book might reveal about the status of the priesthood in the Persian period. But the more I became invested in parenting, the more I noticed what Malachi had to say about fathers and sons.

Fatherhood in Malachi

The patriarchal aspects of fatherhood are strikingly evident in the book of Malachi. The book opens with a description of the nations of Israel and Edom as brothers: though both have a common father, Yahweh has loved one and hated the other.

> Is not Esau Jacob's brother? says the LORD. Yet I have loved Jacob but I have hated Esau. (1:2–3)

As the book continues, Mal. 1:6–2:9 hurls against Israel's priests a diatribe that begins with a description of how things *should* be:

> A son honors his father, and a slave his master. If then I am a father, where is my honor? And if I am a master, where is my fear? says the LORD of hosts to you, O priests, who despise my name. (1:6, my trans.)

In the verses that follow, the writer announces the punishment that the priests, as disobedient sons, deserve. In 2:2–3, the priests are cursed, excrement is spread on their faces, and their offspring are rebuked (a verb commonly used for fathers rebuking their sons).

Clearly, the first sentence of the diatribe (1:6) provides the grounds for the accusation: because (of course) sons should honor their fathers and (of course) Yahweh is a father to Israel, then Israel is wrong not to honor God—and deserves punishment. The persuasiveness of Malachi's string of logic depends on the reader's agreement as to what constitutes proper behavior. Only if the son (Israel) is supposed to act a certain way is the father (Yahweh) justified in his anger and punishment.

The second half of 1:6, which assumes the rightness of slavery, reveals that the submissive posture of sons and slaves is assumed equally by the writer of Malachi. That the posture of the inferiors in both relationships is the same— or at least similar—is underscored by the fact that the second phrase about slaves shares the verb of the first phrase. In both cases, the superior deserves the honor (and obedience) of the inferior. The writer of Malachi does not argue for but trusts that the reader shares the assumption that sons should honor fathers and slaves should honor masters; the very grammar of the sentence suggests that (of course) they do. In the context of chastising Israel for not properly honoring Yahweh, the writer has appealed to two accepted relationships in which a power differential is culturally sanctioned.

Elsewhere in Malachi, the writer again appeals to the fatherhood of Yahweh as the basis for an argument. In 2:10, the fatherhood of God provides the basis for community solidarity:

Have we not all one father? Has not one God created us? Why then are we faithless, a man to his brother, profaning the covenant of our fathers? (my trans.)

More usually, however, references to God as father underscore the same power dynamics of 1:6. The restoration of the proper relationship between Yahweh and Israel is envisioned as a return to the proper hierarchy of the family:

"They shall be mine, says the LORD of hosts, my special possession on the day when I act, and I will spare them as a man spares his son who serves him. Then once more you shall distinguish between the righteous and the wicked, between one who serves God and one who does not serve him." (3:17–18 RSV)

The verb chosen for the father-son relationship is telling: the son serves his father.

The ending of the book appears to suggest that the restored relationship will be affectionate:

And he will turn the heart of the fathers unto the sons and the heart of sons unto their fathers, lest I come and smite the land with a curse. (4:6, my trans.)

And yet, nothing erases the hierarchy between the two. As in Jeremiah, Yahweh might be a loving father, but he is also one who demands respect and obedience.

By describing God as a father who appropriately scolds and shames his son Judah, the book of Malachi both reflects and perpetuates the ultimate control of the male head of the family. In contrast with the commandment to "Honor your father and your mother" and with Deut. 21:18–21, which gives the mother a role in the punishment of her son, Malachi mentions only the power of the father. The father may choose or reject a son as he sees fit, as Mal. 1:2–3 reveals: "I have loved Jacob but I have hated Esau."

Parenting Models

The more I read the book of Malachi in light of my convictions about parenting, the more it angered me. I thus presented a paper and published an article in which I described it as abusive.[4] I learned fairly quickly, however, that not all readers share my disgust with Malachi. When I first shared my views in a classroom setting, I was amazed that many of the students heartily applauded Malachi's views that children should obey their fathers and that physical punishment was good for children. They did not think Malachi's ideology was a problem; they thought *my* ideology was. To them, I was a soft, coddling, ineffective parent.

The differing "takes" on proper parenting extend beyond the classroom to our culture as a whole. Especially in the United States, the debate over "family values" has been angry and polarized. While there are probably as many positions on parenting as there are parents (or even moods of parents), I highlight three major approaches to parenting advocated in mainstream thinking in the United States.

Authoritarian Fatherhood

On a former website and now in publication, Phillip Lancaster has called for a "true and wholesome patriarchy"—the return of male leadership of the family and the culture.[5] A Reformed Presbyterian, Lancaster sees the primary threat to male control of the family as feminism and its various outgrowths.

In his attempt to return a "good name" to patriarchy, Lancaster recognizes that human patriarchs are supported by biblical depictions of God as patriarch:

> God has appointed the husband/father as the leader of his family. . . . He is the original pattern, the perfect example of fatherhood. If men are to rediscover their identity they will need to become reacquainted with the one who made them to be uniquely like himself. . . . Fathers need to spend time with the original Patriarch.[6]

Lancaster not only describes the biblical perspective of fatherhood in patriarchal terms but also argues that such a model of fatherhood is valuable for contemporary families and contemporary society.

Support for authoritarian parenting extends beyond the somewhat extreme example of Lancaster. As sociologists Bartowski and Ellison report, "Conservative Protestant writers and commentators have clearly emerged as the leading spokespersons for 'traditional' hierarchical childrearing practices,"[7] which include male control of the household and the physical punishment of children. James Dobson's Focus on the Family Web site, for example, clearly advocates male leadership of the family and the right of parents to physically discipline their children. Similarly, the Focus on the Family Web site repeatedly stresses that the willingness to administer physical discipline to children is an essential sign of parental care.[8]

Nurturing Parenthood

A polar opposite ideology of parenting can be discerned within other circles, primarily those within the psychological community. Psychologist Alice Miller is an articulate and passionate advocate for raising children in nonviolent ways. In her book *For Your Own Good: Hidden Cruelty in Child-Rearing and the Roots of Violence*,[9] as well as in speeches and Internet articles, Miller forcefully argues that all physical punishment of children is inherently violent: "Physical punishment only produces obedient children but cannot prevent them from becoming violent or sick adults precisely because of this treatment."[10] True care of children, Miller argues, requires of adults a different attitude than authoritarianism: "True authority dismisses humiliation. Its discipline is based on listening and talking, on trust, respect and protection of the weaker."[11] The best that parents can give their children is empathy, respect, and solidarity.

Pastoral theologian Donald Capps, building on the work of Miller, has made a similarly strong and impassioned case that authoritarian parental practices, by both father and mother, are closely aligned with, and provide the necessary precondition for, child abuse. Particularly, the denial to children of intellectual autonomy—the permission to think for themselves—prevents children from recognizing abuse for what it is, from naming the treatment they receive as wrong. Capps, indeed, claims that "a key factor in breaking the vicious cycle of child abuse" is intellectual autonomy for children.[12]

Benevolent Patriarchy

J. Bradford Wilcox, a sociologist at the University of Virginia, takes an apparently middle position, claiming that authoritarian parenting need not be abusive. As reported in *Social Forces*, Wilcox and coresearcher John P. Bartkowski of Mississippi State University claim that even though conservative Protestant parents value obedience from their children more than most parents and that they are more likely to spank their children, this fact does not mean that they are abusive.[13] Because conservative Protestant parents are less likely than other parents to yell at their children and more likely to express affection toward them, critics like Capps unfairly consider them authoritarian.[14]

The Persistence and Significance of These Models

These three approaches to parenting are not unique to the modern context. Philip Greven has argued that three similar approaches competed with one another among Protestant believers in the early years of American history. Evangelicals, as represented by leaders such as Jonathan Edwards and John Wesley, stressed that children were bound to love and fear their parents:

> Within relatively isolated and self-contained households, the focus of authority and the source of love were united in the parents, who dominated

the household and determined the principles and practices that were to shape the temperaments of their offspring. Within the confines of the nuclear family, children found no alternatives, no defenses, no mitigation, no escape from the assertion of power and the rigorous repressiveness of their parents.[15]

In wealthier, more "genteel" families, such as that of Massachusetts governor Thomas Hutchinson and that of Chief Justice William Allen of Pennsylvania, the mode of parenting was different. "Fond affection rather than conscientious discipline shaped the relationships between the generations."[16] Criticized as "indulgent" by others, these Christians were more tolerant of children's willfulness and less likely to engage in physical punishment of children. Greven describes the third parenting model as that of "moderates," such as Rev. Samuel Willard of New England. Willard claimed that while parents have the duty to govern their children, "the authority of parents over their children is limited."[17] Moderates sought to bend children's will through love and guidance, not to break their will through the exercise of authority.

In both past and present contexts, such diverse positions on parenting are not sympathetic to one another. Greven underscores just how critical early American evangelicals were of the way that the genteel spoiled and refused to control their children, as well as how insistent moderates were that authoritarian attitudes to children were dangerous and nonbiblical. Similar arguments can be heard as well in the modern examples discussed here. On the Focus on the Family Web site, James Dobson calls the nurturing model of parenting "little more than repackaged permissive claptrap" and offers parodies of its use.[18] On the other hand, Alice Miller boldly links the obedience expected by the authoritarian model with Nazism.[19] Bartowski and Wilcox claim to have disproved Miller's and Capps's contentions about the abusiveness of authoritarian parenting, even though the two camps define abuse differently; the former claim that the conservative Protestant parenting style cannot be characterized as abusive and authoritarian because this parenting approach is high on parental affection and low on parental yelling, but they do not address the control of a child's psyche that Miller and Capps define as abuse. The debate is, indeed, polarized.

At the core of the disagreement between these positions on parenting is the value that each of them places on obedience and submission to authority. For Lancaster and for early American evangelicals, obedience is clearly valued: children should obey their fathers, wives should obey their husbands, and everyone should obey the Bible. For Miller and Capps and the genteel of the seventeenth century, however, obedience is not a positive trait. Because the teaching of obedience is itself harmful to the psychological and spiritual development of children, authoritarian parenting is by definition abusive, not only when it is combined with yelling and/or physical abuse. Similarly, Capps deems harmful any teaching or practice that denies intellectual autonomy to children, including teaching that Christians should accept the Bible as one's ultimate authority: "Biblical literalism is pernicious because it both encourages a punitive attitude toward children by adults and discourages intellectual autonomy—the capacity to think for oneself."[20] Similarly, in *Creating Love* John Bradshaw claims that one of the most dangerous practices of patriarchal parenting is the insistence on

> blind obedience—the foundation upon which patriarchy stands; the repression of all emotions except fear; the destruction of individual willpower; and the repression of thinking whenever it departs from the authority figure's way of thinking.[21]

Wilcox and early American moderates, while distancing themselves from outright physical abuse of children, also value the obedience of children to their parents and the obedience of their parents to the Bible. In an interview in *Christianity Today*, Wilcox stepped out of his role of researcher to appeal to evangelicals to follow the Bible:

> Married Christians should recall the first commandment God gave to his people: "Be fruitful and multiply."[22]

He argues that marriage is not primarily about an emotional union between spouses but rather an institution that "enlarges the kingdom of God in large part through the bearing and rearing of children."[23]

Bartowski and Ellison concur with my contention that the value placed on obedience separates the parenting styles of conservative Protestants from that advocated by Miller and Capps. Having compared the divergent models of child rearing advocated by conservative Protestants and "mainstream" parenting manuals, they suggest that mainstream commentators focus on "healthy" personality development and social competence; self-esteem, self-confidence, self-discipline, creativity and intellectual curiosity; empathy and communication skills; and common understanding between two interacting individuals. Conservative Protestant writers, on the other hand, believing that humans are born with inherently sinful natures, stress that children must be taught to submit to parental and divine authority.[24]

Obviously, my clash with Malachi (and with some of my students) arises not simply over a little "tough love." It arises from incompatible understandings of who children are and how parents should relate to them.

Political Dimensions of Parenting Models

The implications of these differing parental models, however, go beyond the confines of the family. Greven contends that the competing ideologies of parenting in colonial America carried over into the disagreements over British rule of the colonies. The genteel, who had learned through their family models to view parental authority as loving and benign, found no reason to doubt that "Mother England" and "Father (King) George" were equally benign. Evangelicals, who had experienced firsthand the tyranny of their parents and especially of their fathers, adamantly insisted that British control was tyrannical. And moderates, whose childhoods had in theory balanced affection and control but in practice had underscored the ultimate control of parents, could in theory accept limited monarchical control but in practice remained fearful of political authority. According to Greven,

> The choice between being a monarchist or becoming a republican thus involved the entire way of life of every person throughout the colonies. But the choice also, above all else, involved the entire self, and thus became a matter of temperament. The political choices and the ideological commitments that accompanied them rested, in the last analysis, upon intensely personal inclinations.[25]

My own modification of Greven's statement substitutes "ideological" for "personal."

In *Moral Politics: How Liberals and Conservatives Think*, George Lakoff has argued that ideologies of parenting also undergird political debates in the United States today.[26] Tracing two parental models rather than three, he claims that both progressives and conservatives transfer their definitions of a good parent to their definitions of good government. According to Lakoff, progressives work out of the "nurturing parent" model, both in their homes and in their politics: because they believe parents should encourage children to develop their own personalities and to care for others, they define the role of government as providing protection, education, and equal treatment of all persons. In contrast, conservatives think along the lines of a "strict father" model: because they believe in the inherent danger of the world and the natural sinfulness of human beings, they define good government as that which serves to maintain order, administer punishment, and instill discipline. Progressives and conservatives disagree, Lakoff insists, not simply in their politics but also in the frames within which they perceive the world.

Disagreements about Malachi, it seems, are not simply disagreements about what the book actually says. They also are reflections of deeply held values and highly formative experiences. The battle over "family values" within and beyond Malachi has wide-ranging ramifications. If Lakoff is right, Malachi and I would not just be unable to parent together; we also would clash in the workplace and vote against each other.

Reading the Father-Son Metaphor in Light of Ideological Critique

What then do I *do* with Malachi? Is it possible to appreciate, even learn from, a biblical book that so thoroughly contradicts what matters most to me?

As in the case of Yahweh the Husband, approaching this text while asking the question, "Can I accept this text as authoritative?" is likely to reach a dead end quickly. If after engaging in ideological critique of Malachi's metaphor of God the Father, the only responses I am allowed to make are to (1) accept it or (2) reject it, given my violent reactions to the ideologies of the text and their implications, I will simply reject it and quickly move on.

But, as I have argued, asking different questions about the Bible invites a different kind of theological engagement. When I approach the prophetic image of God the Father with the question "How does ideological critique of this text invite me into theological reflection?" I enter a more fruitful conversation about my society and about the nature of God.

Cultural Assumptions about Parenting

Power

Ideological critique of the Prophetic Books calls to clear, even painful, attention just how essential the dimension of authoritarian control is to the biblical image of God the Father. The prophets repeatedly interweave the metaphor of father with that of other metaphors of domination: God the Father is also master and potter. Carefully working through one biblical example of the father metaphor, such as Malachi, makes that power dynamic harder to miss. As in the case of God the Husband, love and power remain intertwined.

Also as in the case of God the Husband, ideological critique challenges any attempt by readers to "fix" the harshness of the metaphor. I have watched numerous students, pastors, and laypeople attempt to salvage the prophetic language of God as father by reading the metaphor selectively, accepting what the prophets say about the love of God the Father but rejecting what the prophets say about the punishment that the father metes out. Our study has shown several problems with that approach. The first is that the prophets, as a rule, place far greater emphasis on Yahweh's intent to punish than on Yahweh's intent to show mercy. While almost all the prophets talk about both mercy and punishment, they (especially the preexilic prophets) focus on the latter. To preserve only the tender aspects of fatherhood and dismiss the authoritarian aspects would be to avoid what the prophets are claiming: that, just as a father appropriately punishes his son, so too God's pending punishment of the nation is justified and expected. The second problem with accepting the prophetic language of fatherly love while rejecting the prophetic language of fatherly punishment is that, as we have seen, the Prophetic Books do not cast the love of the father as a *counterbalance to* his discipline but rather as a *justification for* it. The father does not love, on the one hand, and punish, on the other. The father's punishment is itself a sign of love.

What ideological critique of this metaphor also shows, however, is how deeply engrained the ideology of the patriarchal father remains in contemporary thinking. The description by the womanist writer bell hooks of her own patriarchal upbringing echoes that of biblical portrayals of God the Father. After explaining the rigid gender roles both of her parents taught her and her brother, hooks reports a traumatic moment when she tried to break gender scripts by playing with her brother's marbles. Her father told her to stop, and when she would not, he punished her:

> His voice grew louder and louder. Then suddenly he snatched me up, broke a board from our screen door, and began to beat me with it, telling me, "You're just a little girl. When I tell you to do something, I mean for you to do it." He beat me and he beat me, wanting me to acknowledge that I understood what I had done. His rage, his violence captured everyone's attention. Our family sat spellbound, rapt before the pornography of patriarchal violence. After this beating I was banished—forced to stay alone in the dark. Mama came into the bedroom to soothe the pain, telling me in her soft southern voice, "I tried to warn you. You need to accept that you are just a little girl and girls can't do what boys do." In service to patriarchy her task was to reinforce that Dad had done the right thing by putting me in my place, by restoring the natural social order.[27]

This story by hooks underscores that the logic of patriarchal parenting is not merely a thing of the past, nor one confined in the modern world to her own family: "Listen to the voices of wounded grown children raised in patriarchal homes and you will hear different versions with the same underlying theme, the use of violence to reinforce our indoctrination and acceptance of patriarchy."[28]

Even those who consciously promote the nurturing parent model continue at some level to assume that children should comply with their dictates. Parents expect—and are expected—to be in control. In the contemporary setting, while many parents prefer the term "discipline" over "punish," they too justify their own exercise of power with the rhetoric of care. In *Don't*

Think of an Elephant, Lakoff argues that even those who predominantly operate out of a "nurturing parent" frame often switch to a "strict father" frame when they are afraid—a dynamic that most "nurturing" parents have experienced themselves.[29]

Greven argues that in colonial America, becoming authoritarian parents was a way for evangelicals to reconcile themselves to the strictures of their own childhood.

> Evangelicals rarely acknowledged any feelings of resistance or hostility toward the sovereign powers that had shaped their personal lives from earliest childhood through adulthood.[30]

Rather, evangelicals praised their parents' success in controlling the sinful natures of their childhood selves and applied the same model to their own children.

Recognizing the authoritarian nature of ancient Israelite ideology of fatherhood calls readers of the Old Testament not only to read the Bible carefully but also to confront the dynamics of their own views of parenthood and their own experience of their parents. I often wonder how much deep-seated fear of parental punishment stifles people's ability to move away from the image of God the Father.

Gender

Ideological critique also underscores the degree to which parental power in ancient Israel was gendered. The father took on roles and prerogatives that the mother did not; to "gender-switch" Malachi's metaphor to that of a mother would not communicate the authority implied in the metaphor.

I believe that the same observation holds true for the modern context. Despite the fact that many people have experienced authoritarian mothers and nurturing fathers and the fact that TV sitcoms frequently show fathers as inept, a dominant cultural paradigm continues to identify the father as the authority, or strong one, within the family. Whatever mothers actually are, to be "motherly" still means to be "nurturing." Even modern Christian attempts to balance father and mother imagery of God are constrained by these cultural assumptions. For example, while Brian Wren's hymn "Bring Many Names" speaks of a "strong Mother God" and "warm Father God," it reshuffles gender stereotypes rather than moving beyond them. The only female image chosen is that of the mother, even though the biblical text from which the verse draws (Prov. 8) uses no maternal language.

While of course many more issues are at stake, I believe this analysis hints at why attempts to cast God as mother rather than father provoke such reaction.

The images are not interchangeable. Given current cultural understandings, to call God Mother is to say something different than to call God Father, even when adjectives like "strong" are attached to the female. Greven argues that one of the greatest fears of evangelical men in the 1700s was of becoming effeminate, of being subordinate in the way that women and children were.[31] That denigration of the feminine is still alive and well, as is easily seen in the different social responses to men in stereotypical female professions and to women in stereotypical male professions. For many people, to make God female is to make God effeminate and thereby detract from "his" status and power.

Taking Sides

Ideological critique of the prophetic metaphor of God the Father, however, has shown that gender is not the only issue at stake in Christian response to these texts. It has also called to our attention the way that God-language reinforces—and is reinforced by—particular ideologies of parenting. According to the Prophets, Yahweh the Father loves his son Israel and also has the right to demand that son's obedience and submission, as well as to administer physical punishment when the son fails to obey. The prophetic use of the father image not only depends on the patriarchal model of family life to make sense, but it also serves to normalize this ideology, to make it seem right and natural.

These writings, then, take a side in the family values debate. Conservative readers accurately recognize that biblical writers not only permit but also expect the physical discipline of children. Physical punishment of sons in the Prophets is not restrained and rare, stopping at preadolescence, as recommended on the Focus on the Family Web site. Rather, in the Prophets God the Father shames, even destroys, his son, while the texts remain silent on maternal discipline. God in the Prophets is not a loving father, who in partnership with his wife administers occasional restrained physical punishment. Phillip Lancaster—with his call for male headship and severe discipline of children—may be more representative of the prophetic view of fatherhood than is Focus on the Family. Those who ascribe to the nurturing parent model need to know that the biblical depiction of God the Father stands in tension with their own understandings of parenthood, and they need to come to terms with that reality.

Some might be tempted to suggest that this problem lies only with the Prophetic Books or Old Testament and that the New Testament offers a different model. Although it is beyond my task here to analyze New Testament portraits of God as a father, I suggest that the similarities are more striking than most people recognize. The Prophets only make more evident an ideology than runs throughout most, if not all, of the Bible.

Continuing to read and proclaim the prophetic language about the father without engaging in critique of its patriarchy serves, intentionally or not, to reinforce the frame of the strict father model of parenting. Why, then, do even those who adopt the nurturing model find it difficult to abandon God-the-Father language? Are there ways in which we are not as far from a strict father model, individually and as a society, as we like to think we are? Does calling God something other than Father challenge our ability to justify both how we were parented and how we parent our own children?

Politics

Greven and Lakoff have argued that promoting a particular parenting frame also supports the political system associated with that frame. If being a strict father is the best way to parent, it is also the best way to govern a nation; if punishing a disobedient child is appropriate, then so too is taking military action against states or international leaders that do not follow real or perceived rules.

In *Don't Think of an Elephant*, Lakoff claims that the worst thing the advocate of one position in a political debate can do is to invoke the other position's frame. Just as being told *not* to think of an elephant guarantees that the hearer immediately *will* do just that, so too adopting an opponent's frame, even in challenge, supports the validity of the frame. When a social progressive continues to repeat language that invokes the strict-father frame, she reinforces the very political thinking that she wishes to challenge.

Ideological critique helps us understand that even those with whom we disagree are "logical"; their parenting and their politics make sense within a particular frame. In turn, it helps us to see that what is obvious to us, even indisputable, itself only makes sense within a particular frame. Listening for metaphors can help us understand what is at stake in our discussions and how we might communicate better with one another. I have a better understanding than I did several years ago about why some students cheer on Malachi's tirade while I find it appalling, and I recognize that in order to explain my reaction I not only have to point to particular features of the text but also explain my own assumptions about parenting.

Christian Understandings of God?

Stuck with an Abusing God?

The enduring nature of the metaphor of God as father invites reflection not only on why the dynamics of childhood retain their strong influence on adult thinking but also on what this metaphor reveals about human thinking about the divine. If on a human level the frame of the authoritarian father portrays the father's control of the child as benevolent and necessary, then perhaps it functions in a similar way on a divine level. Just as readers desperately want, even need, to believe that the parents who once controlled their lives acted out of concern for their best interests, they also need to believe the same of the God whom many of them have been taught controls not only humans but also the universe itself. When we suffer, calling God a father allows us to trust that there is a plan, a purpose beyond our pain. Either God is punishing us "for our own good," or our suffering is somehow necessary or at least unavoidable in the grand plan of the good world the father has created.

Perhaps, too, the preference for father metaphors rather than mother images indicates that while we want our parent deity to be loving, we also need that deity to be powerful and strong. In the Prophets and in the imaginations of many people, seeing God as a father allows the Deity to be affectionate but not soft; "he" is in charge, tough, tenacious—strict not only to his children but to anyone who breaks the rules. God the Father insures order and discipline, at home and in the world. The world is not chaotic or undisciplined. All is in the strong, capable, loving hands of a divine father.[32]

Although these theological projections are understandable, they can lead to disturbing theological conclusions. For example, in *Facing the Abusing God*, David Blumenthal crafts a Jewish post-Holocaust theology that accepts the biblical and rabbinic portrayal of a God who "acts like an abusing male: husband, father and lord."[33] He does not challenge the texts that portray God as an abusing father but instead accepts them as accurately describing humans' utter dependency on a God who is not always good. Israel remains bound to the God who causes it harm in the same way that children victims remain bonded to the parents who abuse them. Just as children cannot "unchoose" abusive parents, so too Israel is stuck with an abusing God. For Blumenthal, the good news, if there is any, is that God is not *always* abusive. *Sometimes* God is incredibly beneficent.

Blumenthal's theology reveals the logical outcome of accepting biblical images of God the Father without critique or resistance. Indeed, while he calls his project a "theology of protest," his protest is against God's abuse of Israel rather than against traditions that paint God in this image. His theology also underscores just how engrained the image of the parent is in the human psyche. Faced with the theological crisis of the Holocaust—how can Israel be elected and God not save?—Blumenthal finds an understandable, ready analogy in the all-to-common experience of abuse at the hands of parents.

In her critique of Blumenthal in *The Female Face of God at Auschwitz*, Jewish feminist Melissa Raphael claims that he, along with other male post-Holocaust theologians, are pushed into such theological corners by their assumption that the question posed by the Holocaust is one of divine power: was God impotent to stop the horror, did God turn his face from his people's suffering, or, as Blumenthal suggests, did the sometimes-abusive God harm his own people? Raphael claims that such theological questions result from patriarchal ways of thinking:

> It was a patriarchal model of God, not God-in-God's self, that failed Israel during the Holocaust. . . . [It was a patriarchal] model of God which was reliant upon an idea of masculine power that simply could not withstand the actual masculine patriarchal power that confronted it.[34]

Raphael offers an alternative, feminist, post-Holocaust theology, one that does not look for signs of God's power at Auschwitz but for signs of divine presence. Through her reading of the memoirs of women in the camps, she finds glimpses of the divine in the small acts of human dignity that the women were able to assert for themselves and for others.

Raphael's critique highlights just how deep-seated the image of God the patriarchal father is. The human desire to believe that someone is looking out for us, that we are not alone, that there is always someone who is obligated to love us—even if we have to be punished—keeps many people holding fast to the image of God the Father, even though that image leads them to condone dangerous dynamics in human families as well as disturbing theological formulations. They hold on to the image of God the Father even though it requires them to justify suffering, to think of themselves as trapped in a relationship in which abuse is always a possibility, or even to lose their ability to see God in the times of their most profound trauma.

Clinging to the image of God the Father has other troublesome consequences. As Rosemary Radford Ruether has argued, in this metaphor believers remain dependent minors, forever striving to avoid the displeasure and abuse of the divine father:

> God becomes a neurotic parent who does not want us to grow up. To become autonomous and responsible for our own lives is the gravest sin against God. Patriarchal theology uses the parent image for God to prolong spiritual infantilism as virtue and to make autonomy and assertion of free will a sin.[35]

Missing from the frame of the God-as-Father metaphor are any dimensions of human maturation, of the self-differentiation required for humans to achieve healthy adolescence and adulthood, and of the pain and pride that a parent experiences as she watches her child need her less and less. In terms of human action, remaining a perpetual child can prevent individuals and societies from taking seriously their own responsibility for the state of the world.

In demonstrating that the image of God the Father reinforces not only scripts about gender but also scripts about parenting, ideological critique challenges "simple fixes" to the metaphor. Simply substituting "she" or "mother" for "he" and "father," or even speaking of the divine as gender-balanced Father/Mother, might indeed challenge certain gender stereotypes, but it does not address the inherent dangers of the parental metaphor.

Moreover, this particular metaphor remains colored by the individual's experience of parents. Different schools of modern psychology find different dynamics at work in the child's early interaction with her parents, but few deny the crucial role that early caregivers play in the development of the adult. Comedy skits parody Freud's insight about the early importance of the mother by making into a stock scene the image of a client reclining on a couch complaining to his psychiatrist about his mother, but few people would deny how important as well as how emotionally charged their relationships with their parents are or were. Imagining God as father and/or mother cannot help but carry with it the "baggage" of these intensely felt relationships.

This observation holds true even when believers attempt to envision God as a different kind of parent from their own. I have witnessed numerous Christians cast God as the parent they never had: an ideal father or mother as a substitute for the flawed or absent father or mother in their lives. Ideological criticism helps explain the appeal of such thinking, how it allows the scripts of proper parenting to continue despite painful experience, how it allows believers to continue to believe that someone cares about them in ways that their parents *should* have. But ideological critique also shows the way in which holding on to parental models infantilizes the believer before God and before the world. Rather than trying to heal by making God into a new parent, the wounded might find value in understanding God as the "enlightened witness,"[36] the one who stands apart from dysfunctional family systems and names them for what they are.

The Bible as the Father's Book?

A similar dynamic can be discerned in models by which readers understand the nature of the Bible. Usually, a strict father model of God carries over into a view of the Bible as an authoritative, unquestionable rule book. In this thinking, the Bible outlines what the Father requires of us; it provides instructions for how to please God and, more important, how to avoid his displeasure. Believers obey biblical injunctions because they are the father's rules for life, and they seek to internalize those rules in order to remain good children of God.

The premise of this volume is that such a model of reading the Bible limits our interaction with these rich, complex texts. My treatment of metaphors in Hosea and Malachi suggests what can happen when, rather than simply asking whether we can or cannot obey these images, we engage them in conversation, even debate, all the while recognizing the power that these texts and the images they employ exercise in our lives. Reflecting on ideological engagement with the Bible can allow readers to explore not only their own cultural assumptions but also the contours of how they understand God. Seeing themselves less as dependent infants and more as adult children interacting with adult parents, perhaps they can come to respect what the Bible has to offer while still being honest about how their own thinking might differ and why.

Chapter 6

God as (Angry) Warrior

*R*ecently, I was leading a church workshop on "Reading the Bible as an Adult." The premise of the workshop was that many Christians have never gotten beyond their childhood understandings of biblical stories and Christian faith in general. We were experimenting with reading the stories of David and Goliath and Jonah and the Big Fish in ways that relate to the concerns of adult lives.

During a break, a retired pastor kindly but firmly grasped my arm and implored, "What can I do with the image of God as a warrior in the Old Testament?" Even though the violence of the Old Testament was not the topic for the day, he desperately hoped that an Old Testament scholar could answer the question that continued to trouble him. This man was a seminary graduate and a gifted minister who had preached and taught the Bible for more than thirty-five years, but he still had no idea about how to think or talk about the image of God as a violent warrior.

That pastor is not alone. While some Christians find no problem with envisioning God as violent, most of the people I encounter recoil from such images. In fact, in my experience the one thing that most troubles people about the Old Testament is its violence. People regularly plead with me to say something positive about the violence of the conquest of the land in the book of Joshua, the violence of God's smiting of the people with a plague in the book of Numbers, and of course, the violence of God's angry tirades in the Prophetic Books.

There are a whole host of reasons that Christians and non-Christians alike resist such images. Most Christians, for instance, have been taught that God is love and that Jesus taught followers to denounce violence; they are sure that God cannot really be like the enraged, vengeful warrior that the prophets describe. For some, reading these texts brings back bad memories of fire-and-brimstone preachers who try to scare people into submission by threatening them with God's pending wrath. These folks want nothing of punitive preachers and nothing of a punitive God, and they often leave traditional Christianity in order to get away from both. While humans have always feared war and bloodshed, many people today believe that global violence is on the rise and that strongly held religious beliefs fuel division and hatred. Many people are afraid of war and violence and are afraid of any aspect of religious language that has the potential to enflame religious zeal against the enemy. Finally, many people see anger itself as a negative emotion, something that rational and controlled people can and should eradicate from their lives. If anger is not a good thing for humans, then certainly it has no place in Christian understanding of God.

For those who read the Prophetic Books and pay special attention to the fate of women, the problems of the image of God as warrior run deeper still. In the prophetic depictions of the punishment that God the Warrior will exact, the one who receives punishment is usually described in feminine terms: when Judah, Israel, or the nations are slated for destruction, they become women, and the language used for their devastation is that of graphic sexual assault. God's vengeance on those who oppose the divine will is portrayed as a warrior's sexual humiliation of a woman.

If a reader does not condone violence, war, and/or violence against women, what value can come from reading texts that describe a deity as angry and vengeful? How can feminists value the image of a Rambo-like, testosterone-crazed God who threatens to destroy all who challenge his honor and his absolute control? In a world such as ours, the stakes for reading these texts seem very high.

Precisely because the stakes are so high and because our own issues are so pressing, it seems appropriate to pay careful attention to the contours of these particular texts before we consider our response to them. How do the Prophetic Books depict the Divine Warrior? How do these texts work? What ideologies inform them?

The Divine Warrior in the Prophets

There is no escaping the image of God the Avenging Warrior in the Prophets. It surfaces in Isaiah, in Jeremiah, in Ezekiel, Hosea, Joel, Amos—to one degree or another in every Prophetic Book. To be fair, the Prophetic Books do provide captivating images of hope, salvation, and peace—of swords beaten into plowshares, of every man sitting under his own vine and fig tree, of lions lying down with lambs, of a future of peace and justice. But most of all the Prophetic Books launch scathing rebukes of humans and their actions and announce God's punishment on their unfaithfulness. God is angry not just a little bit, but a lot, in the Prophets.

Elsewhere in the Canon

Other parts of the biblical canon also describe Yahweh as a warrior. In order to see the distinct way that the Prophets use this image, a look at the Warrior in the Hebrew Bible as a whole is instructive.

A line of scholars trained at Harvard under Frank Moore Cross and his successors has argued that the Divine Warrior motif evolved over time. This "Harvard school" maintains that the first stage of the motif is reflected in texts dated to the earliest periods of Israel's history. Here, the Warrior is portrayed as battling other gods and personified cosmic forces. These texts adopt the vocabulary of the mythologies of other ancient near Eastern cultures and challenge their claims by positing Yahweh's ultimate power over all other powers.[1]

In both Canaanite and Babylonian mythologies, the world was formed as the result of combat between gods. In the Canaanite account, the god Baal fought and defeated Yam (Sea) to create order in the world; in the Babylonian myth, the god Marduk slew the chaos monster Tiamat and created the heaven and the earth from her body. Biblical texts adapt this language in praise of Yahweh. Exodus 15 and Deut. 33, for example, seem to draw from common ancient Near Eastern mythological motifs to portray a deity who triumphs against cosmic forces; in Ps. 74, Yahweh breaks the heads of dragons and of the beast Leviathan; and in Ps. 89 Yahweh rules the sea and crushes the mythical Rahab.

The second stage in the development of the warrior motif appears in biblical texts written during the monarchy. Here, the Divine Warrior supports the power of the Davidic king. For example, Ps. 18 recounts the ways that Yahweh strengthens the king for battle. When the king was overwhelmed with woes, Yahweh descended from on high to grant deliverance: "He delivered me from my strong enemy, / and from those who hated me; / for they were too mighty for me" (Ps. 18:17).

The Harvard school explains that the Prophetic Books mark a new, third stage in the development of the Divine-Warrior motif. While mythological motifs linger, the distinctive contribution of the prophetic materials was to portray the Divine Warrior as willing to fight evil inside the community as well as outside it. In keeping with the prophetic task of judgment, the prophets portray Yahweh as the champion of justice—against all foes.

The Divine-Warrior motif reaches its final stage in apocalyptic literature. In Dan. 7–12, certain passages in Isa. 56–66, and ultimately in the New

Testament book of Revelation, the cosmic scope of the Warrior's powers again take center stage. This literature affirms that when the world is overtaken by unrelenting evil, Yahweh the Warrior will disrupt human history to defend his people against their enemies.

The Warrior in the Prophets

While I am not fully persuaded that the Divine-Warrior motif underwent an unbroken linear evolution, the presentation of the Harvard school does underscore (1) that the image can function in different ways in different situations and (2) that the Prophetic Books focus on the role of the Warrior in (re-)establishing justice against *all* foes.

This last point is crucial for understanding the distinctive way that the Divine-Warrior image functions in the Prophetic Books. In these books, the march of the Divine Warrior follows a consistent pattern: (1) there is injustice, either inside the community or outside it; (2) that injustice enrages Yahweh; and (3) Yahweh's rage leads him to orchestrate the destructions of nations, usually through the means of military defeat by others.

Step 1: Injustice

While cosmological motifs appear in the prophetic descriptions of the Warrior, they are always set in the context of the administration of justice. Cosmological elements appear most often in theophanies, in which Yahweh's appearance shakes the earth. In Habakkuk 3, Yahweh fights River and Sea, which are also the names of Canaanite deities. Throughout the Prophets, God appears in a storm as mountains and hills shake and the earth heaves (Nah. 1:2–8; Hab. 3; Amos 1; Isa. 29; 59:15a–18; 63:1–6; Zeph. 3:17). But, in all of these cases, Yahweh appears to right the wrongs of the world.

This day in which Yahweh acts for the sake of justice is called "the day of Yahweh"; in English translations, "the day of the LORD." The military language in Isa. 13:4–13 powerfully shows that this fateful day is the day of reckoning by the Divine Warrior:

> Listen, a tumult on the mountains
>   as of a great multitude!
> Listen, an uproar of kingdoms,
>   of nations gathering together!
> The LORD of hosts is mustering
>   an army for battle.
> They come from a distant land,
>   from the end of the heavens,

the LORD and the weapons of his indignation,
> to destroy the whole earth.
Wail, for the day of the LORD is near;
> it will come like destruction from the Almighty!
Therefore all hands will be feeble,
> and every human heart will melt,
> and they will be dismayed.
Pangs and agony will seize them;
> they will be in anguish like a woman in labor.
They will look aghast at one another;
> their faces will be aflame.
See, the day of the LORD comes,
> cruel, with wrath and fierce anger,
to make the earth a desolation,
> and to destroy its sinners from it.

As stressed by the Harvard school, the Warrior can march either against the nations or the community itself. The classic example of the former is the prophetic Oracles against the Nations, in which Yahweh announces pending judgment on countries such as Egypt, Babylon, Moab, and Edom. For example, Amos 1–2, Isa. 13–23, and Ezek. 25–32 announce Yahweh's judgment on a series of nations. Jeremiah 46 begins with the explanation that these are the words that Yahweh speaks concerning the nations:

That day is the day of the Lord GOD of hosts,
> a day of retribution,
> to gain vindication from his foes.
The sword shall devour and be sated,
> and drink its fill of their blood.
For the Lord GOD of hosts holds a sacrifice
> in the land of the north by the river Euphrates.
> > (46:10)

The book of Obadiah claims not only that Yahweh is angry at the neighboring country of Edom, but also that soon all nations will receive their just deserts:

For the day of the LORD is near against all the nations.
As you have done, it shall be done to you;
> your deeds shall return on your own head.
> > (15)

The Prophetic Books launch equally harsh words against the community, insisting that the Warrior soon will march against Israel and/or Judah themselves. The classic example of this usage of the Warrior against Israel is found in Amos 5:18–20:

> Alas for you who desire the day of the LORD!
>> Why do you want the day of the LORD?
> It is darkness, not light;
>> as if someone fled from a lion,
>> and was met by a bear;
> or went into the house and rested a hand against the wall,
>> and was bitten by a snake.
> Is not the day of the LORD darkness, not light,
>> and gloom with no brightness in it?

Sometimes these texts spell out the injustices the offending party has committed. In Obadiah, Edom is to be punished for its treatment of Judah; in Amos and Micah, Israel will be conquered because of its mistreatment of the poor; in Hosea, Israel will fall because of its failure to worship Yahweh alone. Sometimes, however, the injustices that spark Yahweh's anger are only implied via the use of generic language such as "sin," "transgression," or "sinners" (as in Isa. 13:4–13, quoted above).

In her study of the language used in the Hebrew Bible to describe emotions, Ellen van Wolde explains that both people and Yahweh become angry when someone thwarts their intentions: "the emotion of anger must always have an object; an individual cannot be angry without being angry *at* something."[2] In the Prophets, the object of Yahweh's anger is injustice.

Step 2: Injustice Provokes Anger

Throughout the Prophetic Books, Yahweh reacts to injustice with anger. Vocabulary related to anger abounds in this material, as seen in the frequency with which the words "anger," "angry," "fury," and "wrath" appear in English translations. In the Hebrew of the texts, even more anger-related vocabulary surfaces, including language referring to "heat" and "the nose" (which in Hebrew seems to be the part of the body most related to anger). In the book of Isaiah alone, the ASV translation (a somewhat literal translation of the Hebrew), associates the words "anger," "angry," "wrath," and "indignation" with the Deity forty-nine times, all in the context of Yahweh's response to nations' sins.

This connection can be seen in Isa. 5:24–25:

> . . . they have rejected the instruction of the LORD of hosts,
>> and have despised the word of the Holy One of Israel.
> Therefore the anger of the LORD was kindled against his people,
>> and he stretched out his hand against them and struck them;

the mountains quaked,
and their corpses were like refuse in the streets.
For all this his anger has not turned away,
   and his hand is stretched out still.

A similar example is found in Isa. 42:24–25: because the people sinned against Yahweh, would not walk in his ways, and would not obey his laws,

. . . he poured upon him the heat of his anger
   and the fury of war;
it set him on fire all around, but he did not understand;
   it burned him, but he did not take it to heart.

Not only in Isaiah but throughout the Prophetic Books, Yahweh's passion for justice is expressed in terms of the Deity's fury.

Step 3: Anger Leads To Vengeance

Yahweh's anger is not simply a felt emotion; it almost inevitably propels the Deity to take vengeance on wrongdoers. This feature of the Divine Warrior texts can be seen in the example of Isaiah 5 given above: when Yahweh is angry, he stretches out his hand against his enemies.

Sometimes Yahweh's retribution takes place on a cosmic level, as in the theophanies discussed earlier—those accounts of Yahweh's anger shattering trees and mountains, shaking the very foundations of the earth. But, mostly retribution is a very this-worldly matter. Divine retribution comes in the form of military defeat and destruction, as Yahweh guides international affairs in order to punish wrongdoers. According to Isaiah, Yahweh will use the Assyrians to punish unjust Judah:

Ah, Assyria, the rod of my anger—
   the club in their hands is my fury!
                              (10:5)

According to Jeremiah, the Babylonian destruction of Judah is Yahweh's doing:

It is I who by my great power and my outstretched arm have made the earth, with the people and animals that are on the earth, and I give it to whomever I please. Now I have given all these lands into the hand of King Nebuchadnezzar of Babylon, my servant, and I have given him even the wild animals of the field to serve him. (27:5–6)

I am going to send for all the tribes of the north, says the LORD, even for King Nebuchadrezzar of Babylon, my servant, and I will bring them against this land and its inhabitants, and against all these nations around; I will utterly destroy them, and make them an object of horror and of hissing, and an everlasting disgrace. (25:9)

The prophetic tendency to trace Yahweh's hand in the successes and defeats of human armies is often seen as the primary difference between the Prophetic Books and apocalyptic sections of the canon. According to such an argument, apocalyptic books like Daniel, Revelation, and isolated passages later added to the Prophetic Books (such as Isa. 63) show Yahweh working outside of human history, disrupting international affairs rather than orchestrating their outcomes. While it is difficult to draw a clear dividing line between "prophetic" and "apocalyptic," the Prophetic Books do consistently make the bold claim, problematic for many, that God determines the winners and the losers of wars.

Van Wolde argues that, unlike the Japanese language in which anger is understood as a powerful emotion that must be controlled, biblical Hebrew envisions anger as uncontrollable. She notes that in the Hebrew Bible even Yahweh is not in control of his anger: "He is more than five hundred times represented as subjected to the explosive force of fury and aggression leading to violence."[3] This aspect of the Divine Warrior is evident in the Prophetic Books, even when they discuss divine mercy. The famous credo of the Old Testament, repeated in Joel 2:14, that Yahweh is "gracious and merciful, slow to anger, and abounding in steadfast love, and relents from punishing," stresses the fact that Yahweh does not get angry easily. Yet once his anger is activated, it usually does not abate until punishment is meted out:

> The anger of the LORD will not turn back
> until he has executed and accomplished
> the intents of his mind.
>
> (Jer. 23:20)

The hope of repentant people is not that an angry God will decide not to punish but rather that God will cease being angry, since anger "automatically" entails dire consequences:

> "Who knows? God may relent and change his mind; he may turn from his fierce anger, so that we do not perish." (Jonah 3:9)

> Who is a God like you, pardoning iniquity
> and passing over the transgression
> of the remnant of your possession?
> He does not retain his anger forever,
> because he delights in showing clemency.
>
> (Mic. 7:18)

> For my name's sake I defer my anger,
>> for the sake of my praise I restrain it for you,
>> so that I may not cut you off.

(Isa. 48:9)

Like the husband and father explored in earlier chapters, the image of Yahweh the Warrior communicates the pathos of God. In this case, however, the pathos of Yahweh is expressed as anger. Because God cares, God is enraged, which in turn motivates God to right the wrongs of the world.

The Warrior and Women

As suggested above, however, there is another feature of the prophetic Divine-Warrior texts, one more nearly inevitable step in the process of the Warrior's response to injustice, a step that complicates theses texts even further. In the Prophetic Books, the physical retaliation that the Warrior exacts is usually depicted as taken out on women or those personified as women.

Feminists have given most attention to the way in which the Warrior's vengeance on women or communities personified as women is described as sexual violation. Examples of the sexualized nature of the punishment envisioned by the prophets abound. The threat to "lift up your skirts" is clearly applied to countries imagined as women: in Nah. 3:5 the threat is made against woman Nineveh, and in Jer. 13:26–27 it is lodged against Judah, who is also accused of "whoring" and neighing like a mare.

Violence against a woman's genitals is also threatened. English translations often obscure this aspect of the texts, but Rachel Magdalene has well argued that in texts such as Isa. 3:26 the word translated "gate" in the NRSV is a wordplay on the word for "opening" or "vagina":[4] "And her gates shall lament and mourn; / ravaged, she shall sit upon the ground." In fact, this word is closely related to the word translated in the NRSV of Isa. 3:17 as "secret parts":

> The Lord will afflict with scabs
>> the heads of the daughters of Zion,
>> and the LORD will lay bare their secret parts.

The language of sexualized violence against women is so striking in prophetic texts that feminist scholars such as Drorah Setel, Athalya Brenner, and Cheryl Exum have compared them to pornography: in both cases, violence against women is sexual in nature and is intended to titillate male viewers/readers.[5]

While often in the Prophets violence against women is set within a domestic context (as in Ezek. 16 and 23 and Hos. 2, discussed previously in chapter

4), of particular interest here is the connection between sexual assault and the activities of the Divine Warrior. The Divine-Warrior texts of the Prophets compare God's vengeance to that of a soldier assaulting civilian women in the context of war. One example is found in Jer. 13:25–27, as Yahweh joins Babylon in military action against female Judah, and himself exacts her punishment:

> This is your lot,
>   the portion I have measured out to you, says the LORD,
> because you have forgotten me
>   and trusted in lies.
> I myself will lift up your skirts over your face,
>   and your shame will be seen.
> I have seen your abominations,
>   your adulteries and neighings, your shameless prostitutions
>   on the hills of the countryside.
> Woe to you, O Jerusalem!
>   How long will it be
>   before you are made clean?

Thus, to the progression of anger that van Wolde describes, the Prophetic Books add an additional step: injustice leads to anger, anger leads to vengeance, and vengeance is taken out on actual or personified women.

Nahum as a Case Study

The book of Nahum provides a good case study of Divine-Warrior imagery, as well as of the difficulty that Christian interpreters have in responding to biblical violence. This short book devotes single-minded attention to announcing Yahweh's punishment against Nineveh, the capital of the Assyrian Empire in the 8th century BCE. In so doing, it allows us greater insight into how a Divine-Warrior text works and also how it evokes very different responses.

Nahum as a Divine-Warrior Text

Nahum exhibits all the features of prophetic Divine-Warrior texts. Steps 2–4, as described above, are especially evident. This prophet announces God's anger and readiness to march in vengeance:

> A jealous and avenging God is the LORD,
>   the LORD is avenging and wrathful;

the LORD takes vengeance on his adversaries
and rages against his enemies.

(Nah. 1:2)

The verses that follow describe the Warrior's march in cosmological terms:

His way is in whirlwind and storm,
and the clouds are the dust of his feet.
He rebukes the sea and makes it dry,
and he dries up all the rivers;
Bashan and Carmel wither,
and the bloom of Lebanon fades.
The mountains quake before him,
and the hills melt;
the earth heaves before him,
the world and all who live in it.

(1:3b–5)

Attention to Yahweh's anger returns:

Who can stand before his indignation?
Who can endure the heat of his anger?
His wrath is poured out like fire,
and by him the rocks are broken in pieces.

(1:6)

The cosmological dimensions of the Warrior in chapter 1 give way in chapters 2 and 3 to the depictions of Yahweh engaged in warfare on the streets of Nineveh. Yahweh's power is unstoppable: he is a shatterer (a "scatterer" in the Hebrew behind the English translations of 2:1)[6] whose army overwhelms those who attempt in vain to defend Nineveh. The city falls, amid cries of woe (2:10). Chapter 3 reveals the devastating consequences of Yahweh's rage:

Horsemen charging,
flashing sword and glittering spear,
piles of dead,
heaps of corpses,
dead bodies without end—
they stumble over the bodies!

(3:3)

In typical fashion, the image of Nineveh's humiliation becomes that of sexual assault in Nah. 3:4–11. Nineveh is described with a form of the Hebrew *znh* (in NRSV, a "prostitute," the same term used in Hosea to describe the infidelities of Gomer). Yahweh's lifting her skirts so that others can gaze on her shame makes her into a spectacle. The language of sexual assault may continue into verse 3:13, where "gates" may refer both to the city and, as argued above, to female genitals:

> Look at your troops:
> they are women in your midst.
> The gates of your land
> are wide open to your foes;
> fire has devoured the bars of your gates.
> (3:13)

Step 1, the recognition of injustice, is not explicit in the book of Nahum. The book does not state clearly what Nineveh's crimes are. However, several clues in the book may suggest that justice is its underlying theme. The book's opening superscription, depicting what follows as an oracle against Nineveh, signals to readers that the foe in the book is the Assyrian Empire, not a petty state but the dominant empire of the eighth century BCE. The Assyrian Empire (more properly called the Neo-Assyrian) is best known to Bible readers as the nation that destroyed the northern kingdom Israel in 721 BCE, but it was notorious throughout the ancient Near East for its prowess and brutality in battle as well as its hunger for territory and the resources that came with it. Over time, Nineveh and Assyria became symbols for evil, such as in the books of Jonah and Judith (found in the Apocrypha for Protestants), two pieces likely written long after the eighth century.

Other clues within the book suggest that its vision of the defeat of Nineveh was understood as the exacting of justice. Nineveh is called "the wicked" (1:15) and "a city of bloodshed, utterly deceitful" (3:1). The closing taunt of the book rhetorically asks of Nineveh, "Who has ever escaped your endless cruelty?" (3:19), and Nineveh's defeat is seen as good news for those who trust in Yahweh:

> The LORD is good,
> a stronghold in a day of trouble;
> he protects those who take refuge in him,
> even in a rushing flood.
> He will make a full end of his adversaries
> and will pursue his enemies into darkness.
> (Nah. 1:7–8)

In Nahum, Nineveh's cruelty provokes Yahweh's anger; that anger leads Yahweh to take vengeance on enemies; and the destruction of those enemies is described as the sexual assault of a woman.

Responses to Nahum

Christians and Jews have reacted in very different ways to the book of Nahum. As in the case of Hosea's marriage metaphor, responses have fallen on two opposite poles. Few have attempted, and even fewer have succeeded, in finding any value in Nahum while taking ideological critique of the book seriously. The "love it or hate it" dilemma faced by interpreters of Hosea confronts readers of Nahum as well.

Hate It

Nahum most often is lambasted for its violence. For example, professional commentator Mary Ellen Chase refused in 1952 to call Nahum a prophet because of his violent, though beautiful, rhetoric:

> [Nahum deserves praise] as a poet and not as a prophet. . . . A complete and confirmed nationalist, he hated the bloody city of Nineveh. . . . It is a poem of bloodshed and horror, of vengeance and destruction, with little to relieve its savagery and violence; but it must be admired for the sheer power and force of its expression and for its awful, but brilliant imagery.[7]

Lay interpreters also tend to dislike Nahum. When in the classroom and in churches I have people read Nahum for the first time, they rarely see the beauty of the book; instead, almost always they react negatively to its violence. In fact, most readers struggle to get past the description of God as vengeful in 1:2 and angry in 1:6.

Not surprisingly, feminist commentators have protested the way that Nahum depicts Yahweh assaulting Nineveh as though the city were a woman. In the *Women's Bible Commentary*, Judith Sanderson calls readers to see the danger of Nahum's use of feminine language for Nineveh and claims that it has no positive value for the present:

> No aspect of God's relationship with humankind can be represented in the modern world by an image that depends on a destructive view of women's bodied selves. . . . What would it mean to worship a God who is portrayed as raping women when angry? . . . To involve God in an image of sexual violence is, in a profound way, somehow to justify it and thereby to sanction it for human males who are for any reason angry with a woman.[8]

Sanderson acknowledges that Assyrian brutality gave rise to the intense anger expressed in the book of Nahum but maintains that modern readers must resist the continued use of the misogynistic metaphor in which it is couched.

My own study of Nahum argues that gender issues are even more preva-
lent in the book than Sanderson's commentary indicates.[9] The punishment of
Nineveh is not the only aspect of the book that reflects gender ideologies.
Throughout, the feminine is vulnerable: Judah, who is also portrayed as feminine in 1:15 due to the Hebrew form of the word "you," is dependent on Yahweh to save her. And true masculinity is defined as power and control. The
king of Assyria is taunted in 1:14, 2:13, and 3:18–19 as impotent to defend
his people:

> Your people are scattered on the mountains
> with no one to gather them.
> (Nah 3:18)

Similarly, the ineffectiveness of Assyrian warriors is described as a lack of
manliness:

> Look at your troops:
> they are women in your midst.
> The gates of your land
> are wide open to your foes;
> fire has devoured the bars of your gates.
> (3:13)

In contrast, Yahweh is a powerful, fierce, and victorious warrior who defends
(feminine) Judah against the foe. Even his anger defines Yahweh as masculine
in the thought world of the Hebrew Bible. As van Wolde points out, not a single woman in the Hebrew Bible is described with the vocabulary for anger.
Women express grief, fear, and sorrow in the Bible, but not anger.[10] The thoroughgoing gender ideology of Nahum is hard to ignore and, for those who care
about challenging such stereotypes of men and women, hard to forgive.

Love It

On the other extreme, some interpreters argue for the positive value of the
book of Nahum. Peter Craigie is one example. His interpretation insists that
readers take seriously the brutal nature of the Assyrian Empire, which he compares to the Nazi regime of the early twentieth century. He scolds those who
consider themselves ethically superior to Nahum for failing to acknowledge
the evil that Nineveh represents:

> If, from the comfort of study or pew, we complain that the sentiments of this
> book are neither noble nor uplifting, we need to remind ourselves that we
> have not suffered at Assyrian hands.[11]

Another example of one who appreciates Nahum is Wilhelm Wessels. A South African, Wessels has suggested that Nahum is best understood as resistance literature, much like the kind produced in South Africa during the apartheid years. It is poetry meant to liberate the imagination, to give oppressed people the confidence that justice will one day come. Nahum, he argues, "is not so much a call to violence or a legitimation of violence, but a call on the imagination of the people to picture the defeat of their enemy at the hands of a sovereign power."[12] Nahum allowed ancient readers to experience something that they could not witness in the flesh: they could imaginatively witness the spectacle of Assyria's defeat, which in turn gave them hope for the future.

While the prophets' insistence on the anger of God is often seen as their failing, some interpreters have argued to the contrary that divine anger is good news. A generation ago, the Jewish theologian Abraham Heschel insisted that God's anger against injustice is a sign of God's goodness, that a God who cares about humanity must be angered at its suffering. According to Heschel, the prophets perceived God's wrath not as a fundamental characteristic of God but as a temporary response to human sin:

> The ultimate meaning of history lies in the continuity of God's concern. His wrath is not regarded as an emotional outburst, as an irrational fit, but rather as a part of His continual care. Because the prophets could not remain calm in the face of crimes committed by men and disaster falling upon men, they had to remember and to remind others: God's heart is not made of stone.[13]

For interpreters such as Heschel, the book of Nahum reveals God's care for humanity. For Nah. 1:7 to claim that God is good *after* claiming that God is working vengeance is not an oxymoron. Similarly, according to Elizabeth Achtemeier, God's vengeance does not promote human violence but rather substitutes for it:

> Nahum is not primarily a book about human beings, however, not about human vengeance and hatred and military conquest, but a book about God. And it has been our failure to let Nahum be a book about God that has distorted the value of this prophecy in our eyes.[14]

And, likewise, Duane Christensen maintains,

> Nahum is primarily a book about God's justice, not about human vengeance, hatred, and military conquest.[15]

According to these commentators, to denigrate the book of Nahum is to denigrate the cause of justice.

Reflecting on the Responses

As was the case in our discussion of other images of God in the Prophets, interpreters' responses to the Divine Warrior in Nahum take two opposite extremes. Either Nahum is a *bad* book—violent and misogynistic—*or* it is a *good* book, one that champions justice for the oppressed.

Several elements of the discussion so far offer explanations for why the responses to Nahum differ so greatly. (1) As suggested above, the two camps focus on different steps in the process of Yahweh's anger. Chase, Sanderson, and those who generally dislike the book direct their attention to *the final outcome* of Yahweh's anger, while Craigie, Wessels, Achtemeier, and Christensen stress the *originating cause* of Yahweh's concern: injustice. (2) In the previous chapters, I argued that some responses prioritize a metaphor's vehicle while other interpretations focus on its tenor. In the case of Nahum, Sanderson's critique obviously focuses on the metaphor's vehicle, the all-too-familiar depiction of women's bodies as the battlefields for men's wars, so well outlined by Susan Brownmiller in *Against Our Will: Men, Women and Rape*.[16] On the contrary, Wessels, Achtemeier, and Christensen focus on Nahum's tenor, its concern with justice; they ignore the frame invoked by gendered language. While in our study of other metaphors we saw some commentators attempt both appreciation and critique, I have not found commentators on Nahum who acknowledge that it is *both* concerned with justice *and also* violent and sexist. Apparently, there is no middle ground to hating or loving Nahum.

But, as in the case of other metaphors for God in the Prophets, neither of these polarized positions helps readers decide "what to do" with Divine-Warrior texts like Nahum. Focusing on how evil the Assyrians were may appropriately challenge modern readers who think of themselves as superior to Nahum, but any interpretation that fails to take seriously the violence and misogyny of Nahum clearly fails to consider the whole of the book or the problems that most readers have in appreciating it. At the same time, simply rejecting Nahum as a bad book, offensive to modern sensibilities, provides little for readers to engage. The "hate it" strategy gives readers a false confidence that the problems they find with Nahum remain in the world of the text and can be solved by a simple refusal to read, or at least to approve of, the book. For readers who find walking away from a biblical text difficult, this strategy also leaves unresolved the dilemma that gives rise to my project: readers are allowed *either* to appreciate *or* to critique biblical texts, but not to do both.

Perhaps even worse, when these two approaches are pitted against each other as mutually exclusive options, readers are left to decide whose oppression matters most. Will they read, like Wessels, for the sake of those who

groan under the weight of empire? *Or* will they read for women who are physically and metaphorically raped in war? Having to pick the greater victim not
only poses a moral problem for readers; it also keeps them from recognizing
the complex relationship between various forms of oppression.

I see that tendency in the way in which "liberation" readings of the Prophets
often exclude women from such liberation. For example, in discussing the con-
demnation of the "daughters of Zion" in Isa. 3:16–24, D. N. Premnath explains
that wealthy women deserve their punishment because they oppress the poor:

> Why should Isaiah go to such lengths to condemn the women of the elite
> group? One can see from the list of the personal items that only the rich
> could afford these. This relates to their penchant for luxury items. . . . It is
> this lack of justice and denial of a basic decent living to the peasants that
> led the prophets to speak out against the situation and those who were
> responsible for it.[17]

What Premnath does not consider, however, is that women did not enjoy independent wealth in ancient Israel; the seizure of land that would have made
ancient Israelite elites rich remained the prerogative of men.

For these reasons and a host of others, neither of these responses to Nahum
or to the metaphor of the Divine Warrior rises to the challenges posed by this
text and its critique. As in the case of other chapters, I suggest a different
approach to reading Nahum.

Another Way of Engaging Nahum

Rather than asking whether we like Nahum or whether we are willing to live
the way it prescribes, what happens when we consider what pressing human
questions this book and its critique invite us to consider? What good can come
from reading Nahum, problems and all? How, for example, does ideological
critique illumine ancient and modern understandings of anger and justice?
And what do the metaphor of the Divine Warrior and its ideological critique
suggest for Christian theological formulations?

Ancient and Modern Understandings of Anger

Nahum's claim that Yahweh is angry (1:2) *and* good (1:6), implying that Yahweh is good *because* he is angry, encourages readers to reflect on what they,
as individuals and as members of a society, believe about anger. As explained
above, van Wolde's study suggests that in the Hebrew Bible anger is understood to be motivated by an offense and uncontrollable once enflamed. What
do modern people believe about anger and its expression?

Current thinking about anger can be seen in the semantic range of the word in American English. Our vocabulary for anger compares it to fire: anger is a fire within; it burns; it is a flame; people see red when angry. Similarly, anger is often likened to combustible fuel: anger fuels aggression and is highly volatile. Anger also is compared to hot water: anger boils; it builds in pressure; it can be vented when people blow off steam.

"Proper" human response to anger, however, is variously described:

1. *Anger as manageable*: A quick, unscientific Internet search suggests that the dominant perspective on anger in our culture views anger as dangerous but also unavoidable, so that the appropriate response to one's own anger is to dissipate its energy. Although we can be provoked to anger, our anger can be controlled, handled, dealt with, coped with, resolved, channeled, and, most of all, managed. The commercial success of books, seminars, and miscellaneous programs for "anger management" demonstrate that we differ from the Old Testament in believing that anger does not necessarily lead to acts of violence. Acting out on anger is unacceptable, but so is keeping it bottled up inside; we thus learn techniques to "take out our anger" by punching a pillow, going for a walk, or engaging in talk or scream therapy rather than by physically harming others.

2. *Anger as loss of control*: A competing view of anger, however, runs deep in some communities, families, and churches. This view considers anger a moral failing, a sin, or at the very least a sign of a person's inability to remain in control. Because anger is an irrational impulse, humans should train themselves to quit getting angry and instead respond to the world with love and understanding. This actually was what I was taught growing up in the Christian church in the American South: good Christians (or at least good Christian girls) do not get angry. It just is not nice. Rather than feeling anger at those who wronged me, I was to follow Jesus' teaching in the Sermon on the Mount by loving my enemies and by not even allowing myself to despise someone in my heart.

This perspective runs beyond my own upbringing. As Robert A. F. Thurman describes in *Anger: The Seven Deadly Sins*, both a dominant strain of Eastern thought as well as of ancient Greco-Roman Stoicism teaches that to be truly whole, humans must eradicate their anger.[18] As in Seneca's version of the Medea myth, discussed in chapter 3, Stoics maintained that anger cannot be managed or controlled but instead drives people to act in ways they do not intend; "blind rage" leads them to commit "crimes of passion." The only solution for a violent world is for people to eradicate their anger.

3. *Anger as a motivator for justice*: Another view of anger holds that it can be a positive force when it energizes people to address wrongs. This perspec-

tive talks about "just anger," or "righteous anger," or even more often "righteous indignation." For example, in her poem "A Just Anger" Marge Piercy claims that

> A good anger acted upon
> Is beautiful as lightning
> and swift with power.
> A good anger swallowed,
> a good anger swallowed
> clots the blood to slime.[19]

Anger invests energy in causes that matter. It motivates and impels action, a counterbalance to passivity and depression. Anger's force can fuel individual action: "I'm mad as hell, and I'm not going to take it any more." It can also energize social protest against injustice.

4. *Anger as diagnostic of values*: Although many people consider anger a fickle emotion, one that overrides reason and logic, numerous thinkers within philosophy, psychology, and pastoral counseling have argued that anger is instead a form of intellectual response. In *Love's Knowledge*, philosopher Martha Nussbaum insists that anger only arises when that which we most fundamentally believe is threatened.[20] For example, I might have a physical, visceral response of anger when a twenty-five-year-old in a red sports car cuts in front of me. But if I get new information—that he has changed lanes quickly to avoid hitting a child who has run into the street—my anger will evaporate, because my belief in the value of a human life is stronger than my belief in orderliness. Nussbaum suggests that rather than denying anger, we listen for what it is telling us about our true mind, which may differ from our idealized versions of ourselves.

In *The Angry Christian*, pastoral counselor Andrew Lester takes Nussbaum's case a step further. He agrees with Nussbaum that "an anger event always begins with an interpretation of a life situation"[21] and that paying attention to what angers us might reveal what we really believe, even if that differs from what we would like to think we believe. Lester, however, extends his discussion to insist that Christians can and should bear responsibility for *what* angers them. Writing from a Christian perspective, he claims that true growth in faith entails growing into getting angry only at the right things: one who professes Christianity bears some culpability if, over time, she continues to get more angry about someone scratching her Lexus than she does about poverty in the world.

An experiment reported in a 2007 issue in *Personality and Social Psychology Bulletin* suggests that anger even helps people make better decisions. As summarized on www.livescience.com, the experiment proved that anger helps people focus on the cues that matter most to making a rational decision and ignore cues that are irrelevant to the task of decision-making. This could be because anger is designed to motivate people to take action— and that it actually helps people to take the right action.[22]

Understanding that contemporary readers hold different, even competing, views of anger offers one explanation for why responses to the anger of God in the Prophets differ. If readers cannot agree on the value of human anger, how will they agree on the value of divine anger? In fact, I would suggest that how people value divine anger is directly related to the way in which they value anger in themselves and others.

On the one hand, those who understand human anger as a failing, both those who consider it to be "natural" and those who consider anger to be "treatable," find little value in the prophetic insistence that Yahweh gets angry. They see such texts as reflecting ancient, limited understandings of God, understandings that evolved to higher planes in the New Testament and continuing into the present. The skeptically minded suspect that ancient writers attempted to manipulate their readers by making them afraid of God.

On the other hand, those who understand human anger as an appropriate response to injustice in turn highly value God's anger against mistreatment of the weak, as do those who understand human anger as diagnostic of deeply held values. Heschel provides a striking example of the connection between viewing divine anger positively and committing oneself to causes of justice. He reported that his study of the Prophetic Books convinced him not only of God's suffering and anger in the face of human injustice but also of his own need to take up the cause of social action. At the encouragement of Martin Luther King Jr., Heschel became active in the civil rights movement and was photographed with other civil rights leaders in a famous photo of the 1965 Selma march. Heschel also encouraged King to speak out against the Vietnam War, and this scholar of the Prophets helped found the anti–Vietnam War organization, Clergy and Laity Concerned about Vietnam. His daughter Prof. Susanna Heschel explains that her father's understanding of the prophets carried over into his own social action:

> The prophets presented God as profoundly emotional and resonant to humanity, whether in anger, love, or forgiveness; the prophetic God is characterized above all as compassionate. . . . Acting on his conviction that the prophets form models for Jewish behavior today, Heschel became deeply engaged in social and political issues.[23]

While I have likely not addressed all perspectives that humans have toward anger, the ones discussed here help demonstrate that readers' responses to the anger of God in the Prophets are not only theological; those responses are closely related to their own understandings of (and personal histories with) anger. Engaging these texts fully invites us to explore how cultural assumptions inform readers' responses to biblical texts, and it allows individuals to name more accurately what features of the Prophets lead them to love or hate what they find there.

For me, an exploration of the different functions of anger led me to clarify exactly what offends me about Nahum. In reading Heschel and Wessels, I realized that my problem with Nahum is not the fact that God gets angry, since I do believe that the emotion of anger arises from an attitude of care rather than the lack of concern. Rather, my problem with Nahum is the way that Yahweh is described as acting on his anger and the way that women become the symbol of all that is evil.

Ancient and Modern Understandings of Justice

When I first encountered the writing of Wessels, who compares Nahum to the antiapartheid poetry of South Africa, I felt convicted: like other commentators, I had too easily read the book from a position of privilege, not paying enough attention to the way that this book sets the anger of God in the context of speaking against the Assyrian Empire. By focusing only on the violence against women in Nah. 3, I had ignored the significance of Assyrian violence in the world of the writer.

My first reaction was to feel torn: Is Nahum the voice of the Judean oppressed by Assyria *or* the voice of the male oppressor of women? How could I insist on feminist critique of a book that offered liberation to others? The more I reflected on this tension, however, the more I realized that reading Nahum from different ideological perspectives had confronted me with a very real, very contemporary issue: how to sort through competing claims of justice. Why did commentators only focus on one aspect of Nahum? And why, when confronted with competing perspectives of Wessels and Sanderson, did I feel the need to choose between the two?

My initial impulse to choose sides may reveal something about me, but I suspect it also reveals something about the way our culture pits one cause of justice against another. Dozens of examples come to mind. I am especially aware of how women's issues so often take a backseat or are simply overlooked in the fight for "bigger issues." Throughout American history, when the rights of women were raised in the context of other social movements, other goals were understood to be more important: women who pressed their own cause during the fight for independence for the United States, the abolition of slavery, Prohibition, and civil rights were told to wait until other injustices were addressed. At the same time, the feminist movement has been roundly challenged for addressing the concerns of some women at the expense of others. White women in the feminist movements of the 1960s and 1970s assumed that their issues—the right to work, the struggle against male power—were the issues of *all* women. African American women have argued that their concerns are not with all men but with white male power and not with the right to work but with the ability to be treated fairly in the work that they have never had the privilege of not doing; their concerns are not "feminist" but "womanist." Asian and Latina women have argued, too, that their lives are not just determined by gender but also by other dimensions of power, including race and class.

On a global scale, many in the United States are quick to criticize political struggles beyond our borders as stymied by the "who's the real victim?" competition. The Palestinian-Israeli conflict is often portrayed in this way. Yet these critics often fail to see how they do the same, as individuals and as communities—arguing whether girls or boys are more disadvantaged in the classroom, whether the discrimination against same-sex couples or African Americans is more egregious, whether conservatives or liberals are more silenced in the media.

These and other examples reveal that a simple appeal to "justice" does not resolve debates. As a colleague reminded me once, everyone claims to support justice; what people differ on is how they *define* justice. In fact, any appeal to justice can be trumped with the qualifier "whose," as in "whose justice?" If "justice" means "what is fair and right," then humans are not likely to reach consensus on when justice has been achieved because they do not share a common definition of the "right."

In terms of Nahum, this observation compels me to look beyond the claims that the book supports generic "justice" to consider *what justice looks like* in Nahum and *who benefits* from its particular definition of justice. Indeed, it is precisely those "gaps" in justice, the "blind spots," that reveal ideologies—assumptions about what is right and natural. When my attention to gender in Nahum does not extend to noticing political oppression, I reveal that, despite my own self-perception, I am less aware of political oppression than of gender oppression. When the attention of other interpreters to different forms of oppression does not extend to noticing the book's violence against women, they reveal their own lack of sensitivity to patriarchy. In both cases, readers reveal how much their own biases and self-interests inform their definitions of justice.

Engaging Nahum through the lens of ideological critique makes me more aware of my own potential for defining justice in ways that benefit some at the expense of others; at the same time it reminds me that my own concerns need not be brushed off for the sake of "bigger issues." Nahum itself might not be a manifesto for equal justice for all, but my engagement with it in light of ideological critique helps me take up that cause yet again. The dialogue with ideological critique leads me to critique not simply Nahum and my world but also to critique myself and the institutions in which I hold power when any of us fall short of truly inclusive justice.

Christian Theology and Divine Anger

Engagement with both the implied historical setting of Nahum's metaphor and its ideological critique challenges Christians to recognize divine anger not as an Old Testament problem that required a New Testament solution but rather as a powerful claim of divine concern for human suffering. As Heschel forcefully argued, the portrait of an impassive, impartial God is not biblical; the prophets in particular insist on a God passionately invested in human affairs and emotionally affected by their outcomes. When Christians distance themselves from "an angry God," they fail to grasp that this image of God has positive potential for causes of justice.

Yet critique of the metaphor underscores that human definitions of God's justice are shaped by cultural ideologies. Just as Nahum's (and Premnath's) visions of justice do not encompass justice for women, so must all human visions of justice be understood as contingent on human understandings. This insight is easily extended to those with whom we disagree. Christian liberals, for example, readily lambaste those who label Hurricane Katrina's devastation of New Orleans or the terrorist attacks of 9/11/01 as outpourings of God's justice against a morally bankrupt country. Yet the same liberals confidently identify divine justice with the abolition of slavery, the granting of women's voting rights, or desegregation. Personally, I do see God's justice working through all of the "liberal" examples, but my encounter with Nahum reminds me that I must continue to listen to those whom my own definitions of justice render invisible. Christians must at the same time insist on justice and remain open to learning more about what full and true justice entails.

This call for boldness with humility also bears implications for the way that Christians undertake theodicy: both philosophical and pragmatic attempts to defend the goodness of God in the face of evil and suffering. I believe Christians must never blindly accept the inevitability of suffering: they must name, protest, and bring to the divine ear the realities of human pain. At the same time, these discussions suggest that our very theological wrestling with the "problem of evil" is shaped by our own implicit understandings of how the world "should" work and how God "should" relate to humanity. Behind phrases such as "when bad things happen to good people" and "What did I do to deserve this?" lie assumptions about moral cause and effect and definitions of "bad" and "good."

Again, I do not suggest that Christians cease struggling for all they are worth to understand what they can about themselves, their world, and God. But I do believe ideological critique calls all people to build into that task as much self-awareness as possible about why they expect the world to operate in a particular way and why the failure of those scripts challenges belief in God or in God's goodness and/or power.

Engaging the Divine Warrior metaphor, as engaging the Prophetic Books as a whole, leads me to a paradoxical conclusion. To be faithful, I must act passionately for the establishment of justice, yet I must also be open to the possibility that what I believe to be most true and holy may remain only a partial truth. I believe that Eichrodt, von Rad, and Brueggemann are right in defining as most "prophetic" the insistence that all institutions, beliefs, and even ethical formulations remain subordinate to the freedom of God. Ideological criticism makes that case even more strongly, in its willingness to critique even the theological formulations that the prophets and their interpreters hold most dear.

Chapter 7

Jerusalem as (Defenseless) Daughter

*I*n the previous three studies of prophetic images of God, I considered issues that arise when the texts are engaged ideologically. In exploring how the Prophets describe Yahweh as husband, father, and warrior, we saw (among other things) the interplay of divine pathos and power, the role of gender in depictions of and justifications for power, and the masculine nature of divine anger.

These dynamics carry over into the two additional prophetic metaphors treated in this volume: the comparison of Jerusalem to a daughter and the comparison of the nation of Edom to a brother. While metaphors for communities might not seem to be as theologically significant as metaphors for the divine, I will argue that language used for nations—one's own and others— not only reveals cultural assumptions about the human roles to which those nations are compared but also has profound implications for international relations. The metaphors also have indirect but important bearings on understandings of God.

The Daughter Metaphor

The designation of Jerusalem as a daughter appears widely in the Prophets, in the books of Isaiah, Jeremiah, Micah, Zephaniah, and Zechariah. It appears only infrequently in non-Prophetic Books: in 2 Kgs. 19:21, which is actually a parallel to Isa. 37:22; and in Ps. 9:14. For this reason, most scholars understand the metaphor as distinctive to the Prophetic Books.

At first glance, the metaphor seems a simple variation of the father-son metaphor explored in an earlier chapter. As we will see, however, the metaphor of Jerusalem the daughter not only employs different gender scripts than does that of Israel/Judah the son; it also raises different interpretative issues and invites different reflections on the human and divine dimensions of metaphor

Cities and Countries as Women

The comparison of Jerusalem to a daughter belongs to a much broader prophetic tendency to characterize cities and countries as women. Already in this volume, we have seen the prophets portray Israel as Yahweh's wife (chap. 4) and call both Israel and Nineveh whores (chaps. 4 and 6). These two metaphors run throughout the Prophets and are joined by other female images. As Katheryn Darr shows, Isaiah alone casts Jerusalem and/or foreign cities in multiple female roles—mothers, wives, whores, widows, virgins/maidens, queens, and daughters.[1]

These female personifications are more obvious in Hebrew than in English translations. In Hebrew (as in French or Spanish), nouns, verbs, third-person pronouns, and the second-person pronoun "you" take either masculine or feminine form. Because most of these parts of speech are not marked by gender in English, English translations often fail to reflect the gender assignments of the original language. For example the NRSV translation of Jer. 49:17 seems devoid of gender:

> Edom shall become an object of horror; everyone who passes by it will be horrified and will hiss because of all its disasters.

In the Hebrew of the verse, however, "shall become," "object of horror," "it," and "its" are all feminine forms. This use of the feminine for Edom reflects the choice of the author and not a mere fluke of the Hebrew grammar, as seen by the fact that several verses earlier the same author employs numerous masculine forms for Edom:

> But as for me, I have stripped Esau bare,
> I have uncovered *his* hiding places,
> and *he* is not able to conceal himself.
> *His* offspring are destroyed, *his* kinsfolk
> and *his* neighbors; and *he* is no more.
> (Jer. 49:10, my italics)

Israel was not unique in the ancient world in associating cities with female images. Mesopotamian texts describe cities as having patron goddesses who fight on their behalf and weep over their destruction. F. W. Dobbs-Allsopp has argued that Hebrew writers transferred much of this goddess imagery to the city of Jerusalem itself; the book of Lamentations, he suggests, draws from the genre of Mesopotamian city laments to show Jerusalem, rather than a patron goddess, as lamenting the city's fall.[2]

The logic and ideology underlying this female personification have been well studied and described by various scholars. Some focus on historical dimensions, others on literary ones, but most agree that prophets use feminine language to communicate particular features of cities and/or countries. Darr lists these features as subordination and dependence, weakness and vulnerability, haughtiness, submissiveness, limited knowledge and competence, objects of familial and conjugal love, fertility, bereavement and mourning, and sexuality as a source of danger.[3] A few examples demonstrate the way in which these features appear. In the oracle against Tyre in Isa. 23, Tyre is to wail (feminine form), for although she once was prideful, she now is an object of shame: she is infertile, oppressed, ruined, and destined to be a forgotten prostitute. The oracle against Damascus in Jer. 49:23–27 also portrays the ruined city as a woman: like a woman, Damascus is feeble, in anguish as if in labor. The extended female imagery for Zion in the book of Isaiah is described this way by Christl Maier:

> In relation to its ruler Jerusalem would be possessed like a woman; in relation to its inhabitants she would provide shelter and food like a mother for her children; and in relation to God, the title "daughter" would imply her need for protection.[4]

Prophetic rhetoric relies heavily on female imagery.

Cities/Countries as Daughter

Within this larger realm of female personification, the role of daughter performs a special role. Prophetic texts use the term "daughter" frequently, not only for Jerusalem/Zion but also for other nations/cities. This application of the metaphor to foreign entities is distinctive to the Prophets, the only other example being Ps. 137:8, which addresses "daughter Babylon."

The following offers a representative, though not exhaustive, list of foreign (from the perspective of Judah and Israel) countries or cities that are designated as "daughter" in prophetic texts:

Sidon (Isa. 23:12)
Egypt (Jer. 46:11, 24)
Babylon = Chaldea (Isa. 47:5; Jer. 50:42; 51:33; Zech. 2:7)
Dibon (Jer. 48:18)
The Ammonites (Jer. 49:4)
Tarshish (Isa. 23:10)

In this last case of Tarshish, the designation "daughter" is missing from the NRSV, which reads:

> Cross over to your own land,
> O *ships of Tarshish*;
> this is a harbor no more.
>   (Isa. 23:10, my italics)

It appears, however, in the RSV translation, which is more faithful to the Hebrew:

> Overflow your land like the Nile,
> O daughter of Tarshish;
> there is no restraint any more.
>   (Isa. 23:10)

I highlight two aspects of prophetic daughter language for nations other than Israel and Judah. First, every example appears in the context of judgment. Throughout, when the foreign one is called daughter, she is also told to mourn, to prepare for exile, to accept devastation:

> Come down and sit in the dust,
>   virgin daughter Babylon!
> Sit on the ground without a throne,
>   daughter Chaldea!
> For you shall no more be called
>   tender and delicate.
>   (Isa. 47:1)

> Pack your bags for exile,
>   sheltered daughter Egypt!
> For Memphis shall become a waste,
>   a ruin, without inhabitant.
>   (Jer. 46:19)

Second, these texts do not imply to whom Egypt, Babylon, Dibon, and so forth belong: they do not criticize the nation or city for insubordination to a father (or mother) figure. Rather, the language invokes the more generic image of "any daughter." The literary context of these passages hints at precisely what being a daughter entails. Like daughters, the nations remain defenseless, weak, and unable to protect themselves—traits, as we shall see, linked in the Old Testament with the role of daughter.

Jerusalem as Daughter

Having considered the general way in which the Prophetic Books apply "daughter" language, we now turn to the specific metaphor of Jerusalem as a daughter. In so doing, we face two immediate issues of interpretation.

Issues of Translation

While the NRSV translates the Hebrew phrase in question as "daughter Zion," readers of the KJV, NIV, and RSV encounter the phrase "daughter *of* Zion." Do prophetic texts actually compare Jerusalem to a daughter?

The Hebrew phrase, *bat ṣîyôn*, is a grammatical form called a construct chain, in which two nouns are directly joined. Most often, the construct chain signifies possession, so that English translations connect the two nouns with the preposition "of" in order to convey this sense (for example, the English phrase "sons of Israel" translates a Hebrew construct chain). The construct form, however, can convey other meanings. It can function to attribute to the noun a characteristic (as in "a man of honor"), or it can serve as an apposition, further identifying the noun in question (as in "the city of Atlanta"). In the case of *bat ṣîyôn*, interpreters debate whether to translate the phrase as possessive or as appositional: does it refer to someone else as Zion's daughter, or does it identify Zion itself as the daughter? The NRSV accepts this latter interpretation, as does the TNK translation, which renders the phrase as "Fair Zion."

In some prophetic passages the daughter does seem to represent something or someone related to, though separate from, the city. In Mic. 4:10, daughter Zion is told to groan

> like a woman in labor;
> for now you shall go forth from the city
> and camp in the open country;
> you shall go to Babylon.

A daughter who *is* the city can scarcely *leave* the city. A similar passage is Jer. 31:21, in which "maiden" (not "daughter") Israel is promised that she will *return to* her cities.

On the basis of such passages, Antje Labahn claims that "daughter of Zion" refers not to the city itself but to its people.[5] Several examples support his contention. A frequent phrase in the Hebrew of Jeremiah is "daughter [of] my people," appearing in Jer. 4:11; 6:26; 8:11, 19, 21, 22; 9:1, 9. This phrase is recognizable in the RSV translation of Jer. 8:19:

> Hark, the cry of the daughter of my people
>   from the length and breadth of the land:
> "Is the LORD not in Zion?
>   Is her King not in her?"

The NRSV, however, translates the phrase as "my poor people":

> Hark, the cry of my poor people
>   from far and wide in the land:
> "Is the LORD not in Zion?
>   Is her King not in her?"

The same phrase in Jer. 9:7 is translated by the NRSV as "my sinful people":

> Therefore thus says the LORD of hosts:
> I will now refine and test them,
>   for what else can I do with my sinful people?

These examples underscore not only that "daughter" sometimes refers to the people and not to the city, but also that English translations often obscure Hebrew usage.

Jeremiah 14:17 offers yet another example of a passage in which "daughter" appears to refer to the inhabitants of the city:

> You shall say to them this word:
> Let my eyes run down with tears night and day,
>   and let them not cease,
> for the *virgin daughter—my people*—is struck down
>   with a crushing blow,
>   with a very grievous wound.
>
> (my italics)

Tikva Frymer-Kensky has offered an alternative explanation of these passages, suggesting that "daughter" represents the essence or the spirit of the city. In discussing the phrase *Yoshevet Zion* in Isa. 12:6, a feminine singular form that literally means "she who dwells in Zion" even though it is translated in the NRSV as "Royal Zion," Frymer-Kensky claims:

> Zion is very much the physical city of houses and walls, but Zion is also a person who dwells within this physical city. . . . *Yoshevet Zion* is the essence of the city seen as a female, the immanent presence that lives within the walls. . . . [Zion is] the inner spirit of the city.[6]

A logical conclusion drawn from this discussion is that while in some cases "daughter of Zion" might not mean "the daughter who is Zion," in most prophetic examples "daughter" *does* refer to the city itself. The literary context of the phrase supports this claim, since the words for "daughter" and "city" regularly appear in close proximity, often as synonyms:

The LORD has proclaimed
  to the end of the earth:
Say to *daughter Zion*,
  "See, your salvation comes;
his reward is with him,
  and his recompense before him."
They shall be called, "The Holy People,
  The Redeemed of the LORD";
and *you* [feminine form] shall be called, "Sought Out,
  A *City* Not Forsaken."
                            (Isa. 62:11–12, my italics)

In the RSV translation of Jer. 6:2–6, the "comely and delicately bred" daughter Zion is described as "the *city* which must be punished; / there is nothing but oppression within her" (my italics), and in Isa. 1:8,

Daughter Zion is left
  like a booth in a vineyard,
like a shelter in a cucumber field,
  like a besieged *city*.
                        (my italics)

Zechariah 2 and 9 also seem to describe Jerusalem/Zion as daughter. In summary, while the appellation "daughter" may function in different ways in prophetic literature, many prophetic passages *do* employ the label as a metaphor for the city of Jerusalem itself.

The Nature of the Daughter-Parent Relationship

To whom does daughter Jerusalem/Zion *belong*, if anyone? Does the metaphor have an implied parent, such that she is the daughter of Yahweh or perhaps of the inhabitants of the city? Or is the label "daughter" used more broadly, making her a generic daughter rather than the daughter of a particular parent?

Jeremiah 3 presents one case in which Jerusalem seems to be the daughter of *Yahweh*. Verses prior to this chapter introduce the female personification of the people: the people are like a virgin or a bride (Jer. 2:32). Jeremiah 3:1 builds on this female personification and complains that female Judah has played the whore. Therefore, the Judah who calls Yahweh "My Father" in 3:4 has already been characterized as female. The same language returns in 3:19, in a striking way. Yahweh reports that he had been willing to set female Judah among his sons, perhaps signifying that he would allow her to inherit along with the males, and had hoped that she would call him "My Father." But, rather than behave as a grateful daughter, Judah instead acted as a faithless wife (3:20).

This passage does imply that the Prophets could imagine Jerusalem as Yahweh's daughter, but it also shows how difficult it is to distinguish between the various female roles used metaphorically in the Prophets. Within twenty-five verses, Judah assumes various female roles: the text compares the country to a virgin, a bride, a daughter, and a wife. Indeed, most interpreters treat the complex of female metaphors as a whole rather than considering each of them separately. For example, in her description of the gendered language of the Prophets, Cynthia Chapman does not draw a line between the image of Jerusalem as daughter and the image of Jerusalem as a wife:

> Cast as both father and husband of Jerusalem, Yahweh had as his central concern in this metaphor to protect his honor by controlling the sexual access to his daughter and/or wife.[7]

She claims both that "the term 'daughter' communicates a kinship relationship between Jerusalem and Yahweh wherein Yahweh is responsible for paternal protection" and also that the city is a "woman whose children and divine husband dwell in her midst."[8] Similarly, Kathleen O'Connor claims that

> wife and daughter are the same literary character. Wife describes her relationship with YHWH and daughter identifies her with the city of Jerusalem.[9]

According to Chapman, Isa. 37:22 (// in 2 Kgs. 19:21) also envisions Jerusalem as Yahweh's daughter.[10] In response to the Assyrian envoy who calls for the city's surrender, the prophet announces,

> This is the word that the LORD has spoken concerning him:
>   She despises you, she scorns you—
>   virgin daughter Zion;
>   she tosses her head—behind your back,
>   daughter Jerusalem.
>
> (Isa. 37:22)

Because Yahweh defends his daughter, Jerusalem can toss her head behind the back of her Assyrian conquerors. While I find Chapman's interpretation of the passage plausible, I am not convinced that Isa. 37:22 requires Jerusalem to be *Yahweh's* daughter. The passage focuses more on the stereotype of a young woman as headstrong, flip, and haughty than on the kinship between Jerusalem and Yahweh. Indeed, as we will see, "daughter" can evoke the image of a self-confident young woman, independently of any particular familial tie.

In numerous prophetic texts, "daughter" evokes the image of a defenseless girl or young woman. As seen earlier in the chapter, "daughter" functions in this general way when texts apply it to foreign cities/nations: when Yahweh calls Sidon "virgin daughter" in Isa. 23:12, Yahweh does not imply that she is *his* daughter. The close parallels between the oracles against the foreign nations and the oracles against daughter Zion suggest that in the latter cases as well as in the former the language of "daughter" functions in a general rather than in a specific way. For example, Jeremiah's announcement of war against daughter Zion corresponds with the book's announcement of war against Daughter Egypt:

> They grasp the bow and the javelin,
>> they are cruel and have no mercy,
>> their sound is like the roaring sea;
> they ride on horses,
>> equipped like a warrior for battle,
>> against you, O daughter Zion!
>> (Jer. 6:23)

> Pack your bags for exile,
>> sheltered daughter Egypt!
> For Memphis shall become a waste,
>> a ruin, without inhabitant.
>> (Jer. 46:19)

Various passages also demonstrate that Jerusalem's protector does not always function in the role of father. Rather, Yahweh takes the title of king and warrior in his salvific role. This is especially clear in Zech. 9:9:

> Rejoice greatly, O daughter Zion!
>> Shout aloud, O daughter Jerusalem!
> Lo, your king comes to you;
>> triumphant and victorious is he,
> humble and riding on a donkey,
>> on a colt, the foal of a donkey.

Jerusalem's savior acts a warrior in Isa. 62:10–11 and Zech. 2:10–13 and as both a king and a warrior in Zeph. 3:14–17.

These observations suggest that the daughter metaphor in the prophetic texts works in a more general way than do the son or wife metaphors treated in earlier chapters. The earlier examples appeal to conventional social rules for the interaction between two parties: Israel owes Yahweh fidelity because the sexuality of wives belongs exclusively to their husbands, and Israel should obey Yahweh because a son honors his father. No such rules of relationship govern the prophetic application of "daughter." Rather, it attributes to the city the distinctive characteristics associated with daughters in the Old Testament, characteristics that we now consider.

The Social Status of Daughters in the Hebrew Bible

The Hebrew Bible consistently depicts daughters as under the total authority and control of their fathers. Fathers exercise control over their daughters' marriages, as seen in the cases of Laban deciding to give his daughter Leah to Jacob even though he had worked for Rachel (Gen. 29) and of Saul giving his daughter Michal first to David and then to Palti (1 Sam. 18, 25). Fathers retain the right to annul vows made by their daughters (Num. 30), to sell their daughters into slavery (Exod. 21:7), and to hand them over to violence (Gen. 19:8; Judg. 11; 19:24).

Biblical texts also devote much attention to the father's right to control sexual access to his daughter. According to Deut. 22:13–21, if a husband falsely disputes his new wife's virginity, he must compensate the woman's father and cannot dissolve the marriage. If the charge proves true, then the woman shall be stoned because she has shamed her father's house. In the ruling regarding sex with a virgin for whom no bride-price has been paid (Exod. 22:16–17), the rights of the father also take priority: the father receives compensation from the offender in the form of a dowry and retains the right to determine if the couple is to marry. Exodus does not treat the crime as one against the woman; it reflects no consideration of her consent, and her feelings remain irrelevant to her father's right to restitution.

In the Old Testament, sex acts with a daughter still under the authority of her father require not only financial compensation but also the restitution of family honor. In Gen. 34, Dinah's brothers treat her rape as an offense against the family, one that they must avenge. Dinah plays a minor role in the narrative: the text reveals none of her feelings or wishes and expresses no concern for her welfare. When in Gen. 34:17 the brothers speak to Shechem's father, they call Dinah "*our* daughter" (my italics), underscoring that the sexual purity of the daughter concerns not only the father but also the family unit as a whole.

At the same time, biblical language makes clear that ancient people cared about daughters—and about the young in general:

> May our sons in their youth
> be like plants full grown,
> our daughters like corner pillars,
> cut for the building of a palace.
> (Ps. 144:12)

Indeed, "daughter" in the Hebrew Bible often serves to express affection and tenderness. The term appears often in the book of Ruth. Naomi calls Ruth "daughter" four times (2:2, 22; 3:1, 16), as does Boaz (2:8; 3:10, 11, 18). In all of these cases, the speaker calls Ruth "daughter" while expressing concern for her; the term never refers to biological relatedness. Similarly, the narrator of the story of Jephthah's daughter in Judg. 11 portrays the daughter as a beloved child whose life is tragically cut short by her father's unfaithful vow. The narrator informs readers that "she was his only child" (11:35) and delays the account of the actual repayment of the vow so that readers linger over the horror of what Jephthah's words have wrought. In 2 Sam. 12, the prophet Nathan engages David's sympathies, ultimately provoking him to recognize his own guilt, by telling a parable about a poor man who has a beloved lamb: she was to him as precious as a daughter. These examples show the "daughter" to be one who must be cared for, protected, even avenged. A similar dynamic can be seen in the New Testament, especially in Mark 5, which intertwines the fates of a father distraught over the death of his daughter and that of a bleeding woman whom Jesus calls "daughter."

All women in ancient Israel were dependent on the men who owned the land on which they lived, made the decisions about their welfare, and controlled the property of the households in which they spent their lives. Cultural rules, however, kept daughters even more vulnerable—they were not only females but also dependent children. As argued in chapter 3, the Hebrew Bible insists that *sons* must obey and submit to their fathers' authority; as patriarchs-in-training, they must learn the rules of obedience so that one day they will be able to demand obedience of others. As this discussion has shown, ancient Israel also expected *daughters* to submit to their fathers but, unlike sons, daughters could anticipate no time in the future when they would assume roles of authority. To be forever a daughter is to remain ever dependent on and vulnerable to others, defenseless when those in control fail to offer protection and care.

Understanding the Daughter Zion Metaphor

In keeping with this broader biblical understanding of the daughter, prophetic depictions of Jerusalem/Zion as daughter almost always underscore the vulnerability of the city. The one exception, as seen above, is Isa. 37:22, which portrays daughter Zion as a proud young woman, wagging her head behind the back of the king of Assyria. Weakness may not be far removed from this passage, however: the Assyrian king is especially humiliated if even a weak young woman can taunt him.

Daughter Zion imagery appears often during announcements of Jerusalem's punishment. The language may evoke pity for the desolate land, but it primarily underscores just how helpless the land is when Yahweh withholds protection. Several interpreters highlight the poignancy of Isa. 1:8, in which multiple metaphors describe daughter Zion's vulnerability:

> And daughter Zion is left
> > like a booth in a vineyard,
> like a shelter in a cucumber field,
> > like a besieged city.

As Katheryn Darr and Christl Maier suggest, all of the images describe a tenuous existence. The booth and the shelter are tiny and ephemeral places designed to offer a short-time shelter but not protection for military assault. They underline what the title "daughter" refers to in a sociological sense, namely, that Zion needs protection and cannot shelter her inhabitants.[11] In Jer. 6, "the comely and delicate one, the daughter of Zion" (ASV) so offends Yahweh that he pours out his wrath on children in the street and invites foreign armies to conquer her:

> They grasp the bow and the javelin,
> > they are cruel and have no mercy,
> > their sound is like the roaring sea;
> they ride on horses,
> > equipped like a warrior for battle,
> > against you, O daughter Zion!
> > > (6:23)

These cases underscore that without Yahweh's protection Jerusalem faces doom.

The daughter metaphor also appears in oracles of salvation. In announcing that Jerusalem will be rescued, the prophetic writers compare the city to a daughter once rejected but now saved from destruction:

Shake yourself from the dust, rise up, O captive Jerusalem; loose the bonds from your neck, O captive daughter Zion! (Isa. 52:2)

As noted earlier, the daughter's salvation comes not at the hand of a father but at that of a warrior and/king. As Chapman has argued, the daughter metaphor always appears in a military context, in which Jerusalem is the pawn in a contest of male power.[12] Zephaniah 3:14–20 supports this understanding, for it encourages daughter Jerusalem/daughter Zion to sing and rejoice at the prospect of imminent rescue by Yahweh, her champion:

The Lord, your God, is in your midst,
   a warrior who gives victory;
he will rejoice over you with gladness,
   he will renew you in his love;
he will exult over you with loud singing.
                                    (3:17)

Similarly, Zech. 2:10–11 instructs daughter Jerusalem to rejoice over her impending salvation: Yahweh, who has "roused himself from his holy dwelling" (Zech. 2:13), will dwell in her midst, and she will again be chosen. The same dynamic emerges in Zech. 9:9–10: daughter Zion/Jerusalem should rejoice and shout because a king comes to save her. The passage does not identify this king, but the verses clearly reveal Yahweh to be the Warrior who rescues Jerusalem by bow and sword (Zech. 9:13, 15).

Even when saved, however, daughter Jerusalem remains dependent on the protection of her male patron, Yahweh. Indeed, in numerous passages female personification disappears when Jerusalem grows strong. Zechariah 12:2–3 describes Jerusalem as female: "on that day of vindication Jerusalem will become not only a cup of reeling but also a heavy stone, hurting all those who attempt to lift *her*" (my trans.). Yet in the following verses Yahweh promises to provide strength not to her but to her *people*:

"The inhabitants of Jerusalem have strength through the Lord of hosts, their God." (12:5)

In other places as well, Zion ceases to be female when strengthened by Yahweh's intervention. While, as noted above, Zech. 9:9–10 describes the weakness of daughter Jerusalem/Zion with feminine forms, in the following chapter *the flocks of Judah* become "warriors" (*gbr*, 10:5); Yahweh will "strengthen" (*gbr*, 10:6) Ephraim and Joseph (male pronouns used for both), such that Ephraim becomes a "strong man" himself (*gbr,* 10:7). Prophetic texts rarely apply feminine pronouns or descriptors to the nation being strengthened for battle. Maier outlines this defeminizing process in the book of Isaiah. While the oracle of judgment in Isa. 3:16–4:1 describes the humiliation of daughter Zion and her women, the oracle of salvation that follows in Isa. 4:2–6 turns to the imagery of Zion as an ungendered mountain: "The result of that process is a space of glory but void of female embodiment."[13]

When feminine language *does* appear in visions of the restored land, daughter language remains conspicuously absent. In the "oracle of consolation" in Jer. 31, for example, father-son language underscores Yahweh's renewed commitment to the people: "I have become a father to Israel" (31:9); "Is Ephraim my dear son?" (31:20). Feminine imagery appears when Yahweh proclaims his love for "virgin Israel" (31:4) and calls her to dance with joy over her restoration; and mother Rachel weeps over her children (31:15). And yet, amid all of these metaphors—male and female, kinship and nonkinship—Jeremiah only mentions the daughter in 31:22, where she is called a "faithless daughter." This term clearly offers no praise to the daughter. Jeremiah lambastes the Ammonites with the same phrase in 49:4, and Jer. 3:14 and 3:22 sling the same "faithless" accusation at sons.

Daughter language also is largely missing in Isa. 40–66, where Maier sees the development of positive female imagery. In these chapters, Jerusalem is a nurturing mother and a rehabilitated wife, but in these visions of restoration the only two daughter refrences remind the reader of Jerusalem's former devastated state:

> Shake yourself from the dust, arise,
> O captive Jerusalem;
> loose the bonds from your neck,
> O captive daughter of Zion.
> (52:2 RSV)

> The LORD has proclaimed
> to the end of the earth:
> Say to daughter Zion,
> "See, your salvation comes;
> his reward is with him,
> and his recompense before him."
> (62:11)

The health of the city, like that of human daughters in ancient Israel, depends solely on the strong arm of a man.

The direct connection between the social status of daughters and the status of the city can be further seen in prophetic texts that blur the distinction between literal and metaphorical daughters. In its denunciation of Jerusalem (portrayed as female due to a feminine verb in 3:8), Isa. 3 excoriates the daughters (plural) of Jerusalem for their haughtiness. Because of their pride and finery, Yahweh will afflict them with scabs and expose their genitals. In 3:25–26, however, the feminine plural forms give way to the feminine singular, likely referring to Jerusalem itself: *your* (feminine) men will fall, and *her* gates (or genitals, as discussed regarding Nineveh in chap. 6) will be ravaged. An oracle that began addressing female Jerusalem turns to human daughters and ends with judgment for daughter Zion.

Prophetic texts describe the vulnerability of all young people. Joel 3:3 and 8 lament that boys and girls become spoils of war, and Amos 8:13 paints the horror of the disaster ahead as one in which young men and women will die of thirst. But, by calling cities or countries "daughter," prophetic texts compare their state to one doubly vulnerable—one who is both young and female. The occasional use of the compound phrase "virgin daughter" (as in Isa. 37:22 and Jer. 14:17) further underscores the weakness of young females. While English Bibles often translate *bĕtulâ* as "virgin," as in the NRSV of Jer. 31:4, 21 ("virgin Israel"), the Hebrew term highlights the youth of the woman, not her biological state. All of these combinations of designation for a city or country—"daughter," "virgin daughter," or simply "virgin"—stress this vulnerability. In Isa. 47:1, "virgin daughter" Babylon is called tender and delicate.

The strong correlation between "daughter" texts and the theme of lament suggests that these texts seek to evoke pathos: the daughter's punishment, although deserved, is tragic. Barbara Kaiser argues that the author of the book of Jeremiah occasionally speaks in female persona for precisely this purpose.[14] She interprets the speaking voice of Jer. 4 as shifting from male to female between verses 18 and 19. While in 4:1–18 the male prophet speaks, in 4:19 the speaker becomes daughter Zion: *she* is the one who writhes (4:19) and whose tents are destroyed (4:20). According to Kaiser, the narrative shift to a female speaker allows the author to convey greater emotion: "The Israelite poets 'become women' when expressing the full intensity of the community's suffering."[15]

Dobbs-Allsopp claims the same for the book of Lamentations, which though not technically a Prophetic Book provides a strong parallel to prophetic language. Because "daughter" has "undertones of affection, sympathy, vulnerability,"[16] the complaints of Lamentations take on greater power because they are voiced by daughter Jerusalem. The female imputes pathos.

As in the metaphors of Yahweh the husband and Yahweh the father, both pathos and power permeate the metaphor of Jerusalem as daughter. In telling contrast to the previous two, however, the pathos evoked by the daughter metaphor does not serve to soften or obscure dynamics of power. Rather, this metaphor makes explicit the daughter's total dependence on the power of others: her powerlessness itself provokes sympathy. The subordinate status of the daughter and her helpless state do not lurk in the background of the prophetic description of Jerusalem as a daughter: they take center stage.

The Daughter of Micah 4–5

The characteristics of the daughter discussed here can be seen clearly in Mic. 4:1–5:4. The first subunit of the chapter, verses 1–5, uses masculine pronouns: for Yahweh, for the mountain on which Zion sits, and for the individual (as seen in the RSV translation of vv. 4 and 5, which describe a man under his fig tree and a man walking in the name of his god). Zion is mentioned in 4:2 but without any feminine forms.

In the next subunit, 4:6–7, the words for the "lame," "those driven away," and "those whom I have afflicted" are feminine forms in Hebrew. While H. W. Wolff suggests that the imagery here is of the flock, relying on the language of Ezek. 34,[17] the reference seems more abstract. Feminine participles appear also in Zeph. 3:19, in a similar description of those weak ones whom Yahweh the Warrior is about to save, suggesting that both Micah and Zephaniah describe the current weakness of the people by referring to them with feminine forms. In these verses of Micah, Yahweh will transform the currently weak into a powerful nation and serve as king over them.

In 4:8, Zion becomes "daughter Zion," a personification that continues into subsequent subunits. In verse 8, however, Yahweh exalts not daughter Zion herself but rather, as in 4:1–5, the hill on which she sits. It is to Migdal-eder ("tower of the flock"), the fortified hill of daughter Zion, to which the "former dominion shall come." In keeping with the observation made earlier that female personification ends when power comes, the masculine for "you" is used when the empowered hill is addressed.

The NRSV rendering of the phrase in 4:8 as "the sovereignty of daughter Jerusalem" suggests the empowerment of the female figure herself, her rule. This translation interprets the Hebrew preposition prefixed to Jerusalem as one of possession, as do many interpreters. The preposition *lāmed*, however, can also indicate location, indicating that kingship will return *to* Jerusalem. Such an understanding is reflected in the NIV: "The former dominion will be restored to you; kingship will come to the Daughter of Jerusalem."

In this understanding, Jerusalem does not herself rule but is promised that she soon will be ruled again by a Davidic king. Read in this way, Mic. 4:6–8 is consistent in using feminine forms to describe the weakness and vulnerability of the people and city while rescue comes in the form of the male: Yahweh will rule (4:7) and kingship will return (4:8).

Micah 4:9–13 continues the female personification for Zion. In 4:9, the narrator criticizes her for crying like a woman in labor, since she has a king (Yahweh or a human king?), implied to be a source of confidence. In 4:10, however, daughter Zion is *commanded to* cry out like a woman in labor and told that after she has gone (into exile) to Babylon, Yahweh will become her redeemer. As in previous verses, female Jerusalem finds rescue and security in a powerful male figure. The female imagery of Zion extends further into 4:11–13: she is like a woman threatened with rape. Nations have assembled against her, gazing at her and calling for her pollution—language connected elsewhere with sexual violation (Jer. 3:1–2, 9; Nah. 3:5–6).

Zion's salvation, however, has already been orchestrated by Yahweh. He has prepared the nations for threshing, so that when she is told (in feminine imperatives) to "arise and thresh," she does so not to show her own power but that of her savior. While feminine pronouns continue in 4:13, the imagery is no longer of a human female but of an animal. Zion has horns and hooves and pulverizes the nations, an image of strength also found in Hos. 10:11. In Micah, as Hillers explains, "God the harvester will use Zion as the beast."[18]

While James Luther Mays is correct that this verse constitutes a call to battle, which "looks for the transformation of the daughter of Zion into the irresistible power by which the peoples are overwhelmed,"[19] Zion's empowerment comes *at the hand of* and *for the sake of* Yahweh. She can thresh only because Yahweh has prepared the threshing floor, and all gain is devoted to Yahweh, who enjoys the wealth of the nations.

Micah 4:14–5:4 also opens with an address to a "daughter," though the translation of 5:1 is debated. The NRSV's rendering, "you are walled around with a wall," requires a change to the Hebrew text, as indicated in the footnote. The Hebrew as it stands more literally says "daughter of a troop." Those interpreters who attempt to read the Hebrew as it stands argue that the "daughter" in this verse is a continued reference to daughter Zion, whose vulnerability to attacking armies is here underscored. According to Mays, "The feminine personification, 'daughter of marauders,' characterizes the population as a people whose identity is given them by their life under attack."[20] Such an understanding fits well with the pattern established in Mic. 4: daughter Zion stands defenseless on her own and needs the protection of Yahweh.

In the verses that follow, Yahweh's protection comes in the form of a Davidic king. From Bethlehem, Zion's savior will come. He will rule and feed the flock. He will be great, and because of him Israel will live in peace (5:4–5). While in the transition from present to future, Zion becomes Yahweh's agent of threshing (4:13); in the ideal future Davidic kingship will return and mark an era of perfect peace. Vulnerable Jerusalem will be protected by her (male) king and her (male) God.

Critique of the Metaphor

In comparing cities to daughters, the prophets employ a powerful metaphor. They communicate, clearly and effectively, that the safety of a city, like that of a daughter, is precarious, tenuous; Jerusalem, like a daughter, faces sure destruction when, either by choice or through divine punishment, it loses the protection of its patron. But as in the case of other prophetic comparisons, the same features that make the metaphor compelling also cause the most difficulties for readers.

Two Responses

According to feminist interpreters, when the Prophetic Books call the most vulnerable "daughter," they not only reflect the patriarchal culture in which they were written but also perpetuate such thinking in contemporary readers. I have already mentioned such interpreters—Darr, Chapman, O'Connor, and Maier. O'Connor's entry on Jeremiah in the *Women's Bible Commentary* summarizes well their perspective:

> No matter how daughter language is used, however, it reflects a patriarchal world where a daughter's value is ambiguous at best (6:26). It arises from the bride-price she will bring or from alliances families might make through marriage arrangements. Even when this language expresses tender regard for the daughter, it conveys a structure of relationship in which males represent God and females again symbolize erring nations and cities.[21]

Interpreters such as these agree that in depicting cities and countries as defenseless females, prophetic texts support an ideology that keeps women subordinate and always dependent on others to protect them.

Other commentators, however, find more positive potential in the metaphor of daughter Jerusalem. Archie Smith claims the value of the metaphor in contexts of pastoral care and counseling. Daughter Zion, he insists, is "an important yet complex metaphor for pastoral theology and care" because it provides individuals and groups with a model for speaking out against the suffering of the world, even to the point of protesting God's actions.[22]

Kaiser also sees the metaphor as positive for women. Despite the metaphor's limitations, it nonetheless places value on female experience:

The distinctively female experience was regarded highly enough to function as the chief metaphor through which the poet expressed his own agony over Jerusalem's fate and encouraged community catharsis. . . . Certainly women today are not satisfied to be represented as a persona in a worship context. But recognition of the vitality of the female persona within the Hebrew Bible might be a useful step toward the full and free acknowledgment of women as persons.[23]

According to Kaiser, by empathizing with a female character, readers might learn to empathize with real-life contemporary women.

Analyzing the Responses

The difference between feminist commentators on the one hand and Smith and Kaiser on the other does not rise from the distinction between a metaphor's vehicle and its tenor drawn by interpreters of other metaphors. While in the case of Yahweh as husband some interpreters focused on the danger of the vehicle Hosea uses to convey its message and others focused on the theological tenor of the book, in the case of daughter Jerusalem both sets of interpreters focus on the metaphor's vehicle. They differ in the value they grant the vehicle itself. Does the metaphor of Jerusalem as a daughter give women, however indirectly, a voice in the Bible, allowing their suffering to be heard? *Or* is the metaphor demeaning to women, supporting mentalities that lock women into the roles of dependent daughters?

I believe that neither question fully engages the metaphor of Jerusalem as daughter. The feminist interpretations that I have discussed do not adequately consider the distinctiveness of the "daughter" label within the larger realm of female personifications. Why is Jerusalem called "daughter" rather than "woman," and why do the female roles shift within a single prophetic text?

Likewise, the more positive evaluations do not consider deeply enough the ideology of the metaphor. Smith pays more attention to the content of daughter Zion's speeches than the ways that the prophetic texts describe her—weak, vulnerable, dependent—and he minimizes the cultural realities that make a woman's voice in the Bible seem so extraordinary. Kaiser assumes that when a female voice speaks in Jeremiah that it necessarily witnesses to female experience. If the male writer of Jeremiah adopted a female speaking voice, however, he remains a ventriloquist: he speaks *as if* he were female rather than necessarily granting insight into a female worldview. In the past as in the present, the female characters in narratives written by men often reflect more about men's perceptions of women than women's own view of the world.

Both approaches join, however, in assuming a fairly direct correlation between the fate of a female character and the status of women in society. The feminist interpreters mentioned here posit that the characterization of a female character necessarily reflects and replicates in readers an equivalent understanding of all women. Smith and Kaiser, for example, assume that the positive portrayal of a female character has positive potential for women in general. Do images of women correlate so directly to societal roles for women?

A Consideration of Film Theory

Academic as well as armchair critics of literature and other media have long debated how images relate to the societies that produce and consume them. Does watching violence always make children more violent? Do some kinds of violence work differently on viewers than others?

Debates within feminist film criticism provide a good example of different stances on how depictions of women function in society. One of the first feminist film critics, Laura Mulvey, argues that classic films reflect and reinforce patriarchy at a deep, psychological level.[24] Films from the early-to-mid-twentieth century, she asserts, mirror male psychological processes described by Freud. Filming techniques as well as actual story lines lead male viewers to identify with the ideal male on the screen (narcissism) and to take pleasure in viewing violence against the female (scopophilia), a process that makes men feel safe from the threat of women (castration anxiety). Female viewers unwittingly watch as if they were men, even though they do so at their own peril.

Mulvey offers as her example Alfred Hitchcock's *Rear Window*. In the 1954 film, the male protagonist (played by Jimmy Stewart) watches from his wheelchair the life of his neighbors. His obsession to view others through the zoom lens of his camera deepens when he suspects his neighbor of murdering his own wife. The photographer's love interest (played by Grace Kelly) soon joins his fascination with watching the suspect and at his encouragement breaks into the neighbor's apartment to seek for evidence. Stewart watches in horror and fascination as the neighbor returns, placing his woman in danger.

According to Mulvey, the patriarchal conventions of the film force viewers to identify with Stewart, to see his neighbor and his woman from his vantage point. Like Stewart, the audience finds the woman most interesting when threatened with violence. Because such films necessarily reinscribe a patriarchal view of women, they must be resisted. Analysis, Mulvey suggests, will disturb the pleasure of consuming such negative portrayals of women.

In her study of horror films, Carol Clover also claims that films work through the psychological anxieties of male viewers through their depiction of female characters.[25] She argues that in such movies as *Friday the 13th* and

Halloween the single girl who survives, whom she calls the Final Girl, is a psychological stand-in for the adolescent male. As the Final Girl fends off the threat of penetration by taking on stereotypically masculine traits, often using weapons shaped like a phallus to kill the monster, she helps adolescent males work through their own fear of male-on-male sex. Like Mulvey, Clover understands film conventions as normalizing male psychology and male perspectives on women.

bell hooks and Jaine Gaines criticize theories such as these for assuming that all viewers respond in the same way to female characters on the screen. hooks insists on the differences that race makes to the viewing process.[26] Historically, when African American males have gazed at white women on the screen, they have done so not in the exercise of universal male privilege but in direct defiance of the rules that would punish them for such "looking" outside the theater. In addition, African American female spectators have not automatically identified with white female characters on screen; they have not seen themselves as the Scarlett O'Hara who depends on Mammy or scolds Prissy in *Gone with the Wind*, or as the Mae West who in her moment of triumph orders her black maid, "Beulah, peel me a grape" in *I'm No Angel*. Gaines argues that sexual orientation "queers" the viewing process as well.[27] When a lesbian views a film, she does not automatically identify with the female object of the male gaze but rather gazes in desire at the woman on screen. The pleasure derived from looking at a woman can be called the "male gaze" only when heterosexuality is assumed to be the norm.

These discussions remind readers that multiple ideologies shape the way that viewers—and readers—respond to images. They also bring into focus the unspoken ideologies at work when an interpreter insists on a particular definition of "the way things are." They question a clear cause-and-effect relationship between images and reality, such as that posited by Smith and Kaiser.

Reflection on the Metaphor and its Critique

As in other chapters, I suggest an approach to the daughter Zion metaphor that attempts to hold multiple dimensions of the metaphor together in creative tension. What issues does engagement with this metaphor raise? Can an interpreter both take feminist criticism of daughter Zion seriously and also acknowledge the complexity of the image and the different ways that it functions for readers? How can reflection on daughter Zion challenge readers to think more deeply about their own culture and assumptions, as well as about the Bible and the divine?

The Changing Roles of Daughters

Seeing what ancient Israel expected of daughters should lead us to ask what our own culture expects from daughters. In *The Essential Daughter*, Mary Collins outlines the changes in expectations for daughters over the past two hundred years in the United States.[28] Daughters were once essential to the functioning of a household; they were expected to care for children, cook, sew, and do laundry. Today, in the wake of major changes in mores and technology, the daughter's role in most families is largely an economically unproductive one. Rather than clean or cook, daughters shop. While many Americans consider the leisure of children as a boon, a liberation from a hard life, Collins argues that in losing their work in the household, children have lost any sense of their worth to the family. They are not contributors to family well-being but dependents.

For several years, a colleague and I have led Girls and God retreats as part of our institution's youth leadership development program. Several times a year, thirteen-to-eighteen-year-old girls gather to talk about their lives, and especially about what they believe their families, churches, and society expect of them. At every retreat, we are struck by the complexity of girls' experience, particularly how much they struggle to feel that they are an important part of their families and their world while at the same time they are bombarded with the message that their worth is dependent on consuming the right goods—clothes, makeup, music, stuff in all its forms. We also are amazed by just how tired girls are, how overscheduled their lives are, how much they need playtime away from electronics.

Ancient Israel saw daughters as perpetually dependent, forever obedient to the men who control their lives. In some ways, modern U.S. society also traps daughters into dependency. Ironically, by attempting to free children from expectations in the home, we have surrendered them to the expectations of the marketplace. In the case of young women, the expectations that they be beautiful—thin, acne free, and clothed in the latest fashions—have made daughters' bodies their work. Joan Brumberg's *The Body Project* traces the changing definitions of the perfect female body and how girls spend their time and their parents' money to achieve worth through their beauty.[29]

The studies that I have cited, however, do not acknowledge that these descriptions of "the state of the daughter" fit only those of a particular socioeconomic class. Not all daughters around the world remain out of the workforce; not all daughters shop; not all daughters have parents who can fund their "body projects." In the past and in the present, daughters restrained by poverty and/or racial discrimination have faced other challenges and have been forced to prioritize other "projects." To speak of "our culture," as I have, is to portray white, middle-class families as the only, or only important, ones.

The Dynamics of Protection and Paternalism

Both ancient Israel and some strands within the contemporary United States consider young women as sexually vulnerable, able to be penetrated against their will. As we have seen, the legal rulings of the Pentateuch suggest that in Israel the concern was for family honor and the rights of the father. Today, the concern seems to be for young women themselves, and yet, as in ancient Israel, repeatedly calling attention to the vulnerability of women and young girls can lock them in those very positions. An example of this tension between protectionism and paternalism can be found in the way that many parents and organizations teach women and girls how to "avoid" being raped. In rape-prevention classes, as well as in homes, young women learn strategies to insure safety, such as never walking alone, never starting their cars without looking underneath and in the backseat, watching over their drinks at parties, and so on—strategies that might protect them but that also curtail their freedom and place on them the responsibility for their own safety. Young women are caught in a double bind: their freedoms are restricted (for their own protection) because they are weak, but because they are responsible for their own safety, they are at fault when they fail to take all necessary precautions against being victims of violence. Some of the ways that daughters are "protected" threatens not only their freedom but also their own sense of agency.

Parallels also can be drawn between ancient and modern uses of kinship terms to advance these ideologies. In the same way that African American men resist being called "boy" by those who are not their parents and that many women in the workplace chafe when males in power call them "girl," those who are called "daughter" should recognize that a term that might appear tender and caring can at the same time be an assertion of a hierarchy of power and status. Such language for those not bound by biological relationship implies familiarity with the subject and also the position of a parent, neither of which may be welcomed. When, for example, a church in which I spent several years of my young adulthood recently referred to me as a "daughter of the church," I had mixed feelings. On the one hand, I appreciated that the congregation claims me as "one of ours" and recognizes seminary teaching as ministry. On the other hand, I felt that by calling me daughter, the congregation presumed a level of involvement in my development that I do not myself recognize. The congregation was taking credit for my choice of vocation, without having asked me how I evaluate its role in my life. I felt "claimed" in a negative as well as a positive sense.

Daughters as "Affective Magnets"

In many ways, children in general and daughters in particular continue to function as "affective magnets" for a society's anxieties. This is the language Ann Burlein uses to describe the way that adults project onto children their own deepest fears and desires. Burlein traces how white supremacist movements couch their own values as the fight for what is best for children. She reports hearing a speech by Virgil Griffin of the KKK in which Griffin explains,

> I'm not in this organization for Virgil Griffin. . . . I want to win rights for that little boy right there.[30]

Griffin not only casts racial division as "for that little boy," but he also stresses that racial mixing fails to protect girls. He laments that people will keep an expensive dog behind a fence but will put "their little six-year-old daughter" on a bus with those who will "mongrelize" her.[31]

In reflecting on Griffin's speech, Burlein notes that talking about children is not "just" rhetoric. Rather, for-the-children thinking activates the emotions that attend our own deepest values. What we want for our children is what we most want. And what we fear for children is what we most fear. "Do it for the children" is not just the language of extreme movements: it animates many causes and many parents' reactions to the choices and the treatment of their own children. In all of these cases, "it" is not simply for the children. "It" is for us, our issues, and our ideologies.

What, then, do the specific concerns with daughters reveal about the anxieties of ancient Israel and of modern culture? In the case of ancient Israel, the sexual vulnerability of the daughter left the family open to shame, especially when the assault was perpetrated by one outside the community, as the case of the rape of Dinah shows. Such concerns may reflect the community's own sense of vulnerability to foreign invasion, the shame of being humiliated in the eyes of the world. In underscoring the sexual nature of concern for daughters, the Bible reminds readers of the power dynamics understood to govern sexual relations in the ancient world: to be penetrated was demeaning because it entailed taking the role of the woman.

In the case of contemporary culture, rhetoric about protecting daughters from violence and especially rape may reveal an underlying fear of domination and victimization. The message to daughters that they must protect themselves from assault may arise from the perception that in this violent world we rely only on ourselves for protection.

International Dimensions

Understanding attitudes toward human daughters as projections of societal anxieties invites reflection as well on the metaphors applied to contemporary states. In the present as in the past, the choice of a particular metaphor to describe national and international bodies serves an ideological function.

On the one hand, calling one's own city or country "daughter" might seem appropriately to assume a stance of ownership and care. It recognizes vulnerability and suggests an attitude of tenderness. On the other hand, we have seen that such language can foster an attitude of protectionism. On a political level, the nation's weakness and the constant threat of its unlawful penetration justifies any policy defined as "protection," even if that very policy limits the freedom of the one being protected.

Similarly, depicting another country as "daughter" justifies military action against threats to its safety. In his analysis of the metaphors used for Kuwait during the 1993 U.S. invasion of that country, the linguist George Lakoff underscores the political ramifications of how a state is imagined.[32] As I will explore further in the chapter on Edom as brother, Lakoff argues that while Arab nations considered Kuwait a "brother" who should share his wealth with other Arab brothers, U.S. leaders described Kuwait as a female in need of protection. Because Kuwait was "the defenseless maiden to be rescued in the fairy tale," the United States was justified in acting as "her" protector. Such thinking was clearly at work when General Schwarzkopf called the Iraqi invasion of Kuwait a "rape."

According to Lakoff, the "defenseless-maiden" metaphor shares with all metaphorical frames the ability to constrain thinking—to make only certain interpretations of events and certain responses to those events appear rational and just. When the conflict in Kuwait is cast as a "rape," then only the most callous and immoral would fail to come to "her" defense. Metaphors also necessarily call attention away from aspects of the situation that do not fit the frame. Lakoff argues that viewing Kuwait as a defenseless maiden "hides the monarchical character of Kuwait and the way the Kuwaiti government treats its own dissenters and foreign workers." Civilians might hesitate to rally the troops to defend the ruling family of an authoritarian monarchy, but they might rush in to save a victim. The choice of metaphors, then, is an ethical one. In Lakoff's works, "metaphors can kill."

Writing as I am during the war in Iraq, as the country fervently debates whether to "continue the surge" or to "bring the troops home," I hear the way that metaphors for this war compete for my sympathies and my votes. As a

USA Today article notes, members of the U.S. House of Representatives throw out a host of analogies: one representative arguing for troop withdrawal compares Iraq to a neighbor who shoots at you after you are kind enough to step in and mow his overgrown lawn; another insists that questioning the administration's policies are "second-guessing the coach"; yet another portrays the U. S. decision to enter Iraq as a medical misdiagnosis.[33] In all of these cases and more, metaphors seek to persuade a particular course of action. My own study of metaphors, especially ones for international conflict, teaches me to be wary and always to ask, "What aspects of this situation does the metaphor obscure or ignore?" Voices like those of hooks, Gaines—even Wessels and Craigie[34]—remind me to ask *whose* perspective the metaphor reflects and *to whom* it grants power. What metaphors might Iraq use for U.S. military intervention?

Reflections on Theology(ies)

I hope to have made the case that attention to the ideological import of metaphors is an essential task of ethics. Because metaphors seek to constrain thinking and to mandate a particular course of action, they claim moral power and thus must be evaluated in that light.

Reflection on the metaphor of Jerusalem as daughter also bears on Christian theology by highlighting the diverse political ramifications of the affirmation of divine sovereignty. On the one hand, the prophetic use of the metaphor challenges any nation's claim to moral and tactical supremacy. Prophetic texts insist that no political process or human army can save daughter Jerusalem: she depends on Yahweh alone for protection. When prophetic texts call other nations "daughter," they do not encourage Judah to defend the helpless foreign maiden; rather, this language underscores the desperate straits of nations about to be judged by Yahweh. In the introduction, I outlined how the emphasis on divine sovereignty in the theologies of Barth, Eichrodt, and von Rad functioned in precisely this way: it supported their conviction that God's power was greater than that of German nationalism. I have heard this thinking in my classroom as well: early in my seminary teaching career, a Mennonite woman explained to me that belief in divine sovereignty allowed her to remain a pacificist: "Because God is sovereign," she said, "I and my country do not have to be."

On the other hand, more militaristic ideologies also invoke divine sovereignty to their benefit. In 1839 in the United States, the politician John L. Sullivan claimed that the country's "Manifest Destiny" to expand its territory was granted by divine providence. In the contemporary Israeli-Palestinian conflict, Gen. 12 is often cited as proof that God intends the Jewish people to control a particular plot of land. The theological insistence on divine sovereignty does not solve disputes about the appropriateness of military action; in fact, it can become a powerful argument for both of two competing claims. Significantly, the daughter Jerusalem metaphor consistently casts divine sovereignty in military terms: Jerusalem's protection depends on a Divine Warrior and king. While the metaphor vaunts Yahweh's might over that of human armies, it nonetheless acknowledges that true power resides in military and political control: while Yahweh may be the ultimate warrior and the ultimate king, his power only comes from assuming those roles.

As discussed above, critics like Lakoff call readers to consider what metaphors hide, what they try to render invisible, and critics like hooks call readers to notice whose perspectives too often go unconsidered. The military dimensions of Yahweh's power point to something missing in the metaphor: the power of the father. While, as seen in chapter 5, the Prophetic Books often portray the father as an unquestioned authority, the daughter metaphor suggests something different: the limitations of the father's power. This observation reveals the tension between the patriarchal metaphors in prophetic texts and invites those who enshrine the God-as-father metaphor to consider its limitations.

Also missing from the daughter Jerusalem metaphor are other possible reasons for Jerusalem's fall. Prophetic texts blame the city's destruction on its own failure to remain safely under the protective care of Yahweh. Just as teaching girls to protect themselves from assault leads to a "blame-the-victim" mentality, such an interpretation blames Jerusalem for its own destruction. Other possible causes for the Neo-Babylonian invasion receive no consideration—including the possibility that the real failure was that of those responsible for Jerusalem's safety (its political leaders, its army, or even Yahweh himself). The metaphor also presupposes that Jerusalem is a single entity, an individual with a single mind and will. It obscures the diversity of Jerusalem's inhabitants—the poor, the powerless, and those who disagreed with national policy.

These observations caution readers of the Prophetic Books against accepting too readily their metaphorical descriptions as direct windows into the realities of the ancient world. They also caution Christians against overconfident claims to know exactly how God works in the world and exactly how punishment follows sin. Mostly, however, they remind us to ask what questions and concerns are obscured by our own theological formulations. What do we deny and ignore—about others, about the world, about God—by the theological language we use?

Chapter 8

Edom as (Selfish) Brother

*I*n numerous contexts, contemporary people use language drawn from the family to describe relationships with those to whom they are not biologically related. In churches, members speak of each other as "brother" or "sister" and refer to their "church family." In labor unions, members call one another "brother." I often refer to one of my woman friends as "sister."

Calling someone else "brother" would seem to imply a close bond as well as equality between the two parties. While the metaphors discussed in previous chapters—husband, father, warrior, and daughter—all express differentials of power within a relationship and the authority of one party over another, "brother" instead suggests mutuality. But "brother" language also can function in less noble ways, masking self-interest behind the rhetoric of commonality. Especially when the powerful seek to control the weak by invoking the language of brotherhood, the ties that bind are less blessed than manipulative.

I will explore this dynamic by focusing on the book of Obadiah, a small book among the twelve Minor Prophets. Obadiah complains that Edom, a small nation south of Judah in what is now Jordan, failed to act as a proper brother to Judah. According to the book, Edom participated in and exploited Judah's defeat by the Babylonian armies in 587 BCE, rather than protecting "family."

Few Christians know much about Obadiah. One factor may be its small size. The book is only one chapter in length and has only verse numbers; it rarely fills more than two pages in printed Bibles. Readers easily miss Obadiah when thumbing between the more-famous (and longer) books of Amos and Micah. In my experience, those who *do* find and read Obadiah usually react negatively to its call for revenge against Edom, its claim that "as you have done, it shall be done to you" (v. 15). I focus in this chapter, however, less on Obadiah's "this-for-that" mentality and more on its rhetorical use of brother language to convince readers of Edom's evil. As I will argue, while most readers (and commentators) treat Obadiah's charges against Edom as a straightforward account of what "really" happened, the claims that Obadiah makes are not so simple and objective.

I bring the same concern to Obadiah's "brother" language that I have brought to other prophetic metaphors: how readers might see the ideologies at work in the metaphor and reflect on how similar ideologies inform their own thinking. But in the case of Obadiah I first must establish that "brother" functions *metaphorically* rather than historically, and to do so requires an analysis of the biblical and archaeological evidence usually cited as proof of Obadiah's claims. I seek to establish a critical distance between Obadiah's "narrative" and the "reality" of the sixth century BCE so as to provide a space to discuss the ethics of calling another nation "brother," making the same case with Obadiah that Richard Kearney makes with memories of personal trauma:

> If it is true that on an aesthetic level it matters little whether there is an accurate correspondence between narrative and reality, it matters hugely on an ethical level.[1]

An Overview of Obadiah

The book opens with a terse label: "The vision of Obadiah." A report of Yahweh's word immediately follows and announces the Deity's pending punishment of Edom for its crimes against Judah. After outlining the devastation that the nation will suffer, the book explains Edom's transgressions:

> For the slaughter and violence done to your brother Jacob,
>   shame shall cover you [Edom],
>   and you shall be cut off forever.
> On the day that you stood aside,
>   on the day that strangers carried off his wealth,
> and foreigners entered his gates
>   and cast lots for Jerusalem,
>   you too were like one of them.
> But you should not have gloated over your brother
>   on the day of his misfortune;
> you should not have rejoiced over the people of Judah
>   on the day of their ruin;
> you should not have boasted
>   on the day of distress.
> You should not have entered the gate of my people
>   on the day of their calamity;

you should not have joined in the gloating over Judah's disaster
　　on the day of his calamity;
you should not have looted his goods
　　on the day of his calamity.
You should not have stood at the crossings
　　to cut off his fugitives;
you should not have handed over his survivors
　　on the day of distress.

(vv. 10–14)

In these verses, the author of Obadiah interweaves two important claims: (1) Edom shares guilt for the devastation of Jerusalem, usually understood to be the Babylonian destruction of the temple in Jerusalem in 587 BCE; and (2) Edom's actions are reprehensible because of the brotherhood between Edom and Judah. A brother should not do the things that Edom did to Judah.

Most readers take both components of Obadiah's charges against Edom at face value. They treat Obadiah as historical evidence that Edom acted against Judah in the sixth century BCE and that Edom and Judah shared a special relationship that would have made such activity a clear betrayal of trust. Typical of this position is Paul Raabe, who claims, "Only if the Edomites actually engaged in such activities does the prophet's expression of shock and disbelief make sense."[2] Hans Walter Wolff charges Edom with "fratricide" and asserts,

> What Obadiah says is so independent and so specific that we can only conclude that it was directly based on happenings during those catastrophic days; he cannot have fabricated this material. It would therefore seem most plausible to assign these sayings to a date not later than a few years after 587.[3]

Other commentators defend Obadiah's claims by offering additional literary and archaeological evidence. Using passages from elsewhere in the Prophets and from the Psalms, they attempt to re-create the scenario that Obadiah describes. In what follows, I first explain the evidence used to support this "consensus" on Edom's activities in the sixth century. Then, I will sort through that evidence in order to suggest that the case against Edom is not quite so airtight as it is usually presented. The discussion will involve more detail than many of the previous chapters, but my goal is single-minded. I seek to establish that Obadiah's charges are not simply fact but ideological in nature. Obadiah's use of the rhetoric of brotherhood was driven by ideological interests.

The "Consensus" about Obadiah's Claims

Edom was Brother

Interpreters who defend the factual nature of Obadiah's description of Edom as Israel/Judah's brother have done so in several different ways. Some see the language as biological; some, as ancient tradition; and others, as treaty language. All, however, understand the language of Obadiah to reflect some reality beyond itself.

The first variation of this interpretation is the most straightforward: a literal reading of the Genesis narratives regarding the brothers Jacob and Esau proves that Edom and Israel/Judah were brothers. In a cycle of stories that extends from Gen. 25–36, readers learn that these twins competed with one another while still in the womb and that in adulthood the younger twin, Jacob, tricked the older Esau out of the rights of the firstborn. In a climatic scene in Gen. 33, the brothers reunite peacefully but go their separate ways. If accepted at face value, these narratives indicate that Obadiah's reference to Edom as Judah's brother simply reports genealogical information.

A second variation of the dominant interpretation recognizes the symbolic nature of the Genesis story. While scholars today actively debate the true origins of ancient Israel, most interpret the Genesis accounts of the patriarchs as explaining the writers' understandings of national and group relations rather than as historical accounts of one single family. In this understanding of Genesis, the story of Jacob and Esau explains a complex relationship between the countries of Judah and Edom. By casting the brothers as twins, the story underscores the closeness of the two nations; by casting Esau as unsophisticated, dim-witted, and easily tricked, it underscores that country's inferior status. The story also answers the question of why Esau, a legitimate heir of the line of Abraham, does not remain in the line of the covenant: Esau himself forfeited his birthright for a bowl of food, while Jacob and his mother, Rebekah, are to blame for Esau's loss of his father's blessing. Edom's inferiority to Judah is due both to Edom's failures and Judah's superior cunning.

In this understanding, prophetic references to Edom as brother do not provide independent evidence for the brotherhood of these nations but instead simply allude to the Genesis narratives. This explanation has also been offered for Hos. 12:3, which seems to know the story of the twins, and for Amos 1:11, which charges that Edom "pursued his brother with the sword and cast off all pity."

"Tradition" also serves to explain the opening oracle of the book of Malachi. In response to Israel's question of God, "How have you loved us?" Yahweh replies,

Is not Esau Jacob's brother? says the LORD. Yet I have loved Jacob but I have hated Esau; I have made his hill country a desolation and his heritage a desert for jackals. If Edom says, "We are shattered but we will rebuild the ruins," the LORD of hosts says: They may build, but I will tear down, until they are called the wicked country, the people with whom the LORD is angry forever. Your own eyes shall see this, and you shall say, "Great is the LORD beyond the borders of Israel!" (1:2–5)

The author of Malachi sees in the fall of Edom evidence of Yahweh's preferential care for Judah, a long-standing rivalry expressed in the received tradition of brotherhood.

Yet another variation of the "factual" interpretation of the brotherhood of Edom links this "brother" to treaty making in the ancient world. In the ancient Near East, equal partners entering a mutual treaty called one another "brother." For example, Amos 1:9 describes a "covenant of brotherhood" (RSV) between Judah and Tyre, which may refer to the treaty between Solomon and king Hiram of Tyre described in 1 Kgs. 5:12. If Edom and Israel/Judah had entered a similar treaty arrangement, then the biblical language describing Edom as "brother" would be reflective of a political reality, one that may be echoed in Amos 1:11, which asserts that Edom "pursued his brother with a sword."

While they vary in details, all these variations on the "consensus" find little that is distinctive in Obadiah's use of brother language for Edom. Whether the author appealed to actual genealogical information, to earlier Israelite tradition, or to a widely recognized, perhaps even formal, relationship between the two countries, his description of Edom's brotherly ties to Judah was derivative rather than innovative.

Edom Committed Crimes against Judah in the Sixth Century

The second contention of the consensus position is that other sources—biblical and archaeological—confirm Obadiah's description of Edom's crimes against Judah in the sixth century BCE.

Biblical Evidence

A number of biblical passages are often cited as corroborating Obadiah's charges. For example, Psa. 137:7 charges that the Edomites encouraged the Babylonians to destroy Jerusalem:

> Remember, O LORD, against the Edomites
> the day of Jerusalem's fall,

> how they said, "Tear it down!
> Tear it down! Down to its foundations!"

Ezekiel 35:15 claims that Edom gloated over the destruction:

> As you rejoiced over the inheritance of the house of Israel, because it was desolate, so I will deal with you; you shall be desolate, Mount Seir, and all Edom, all of it. Then they shall know that I am the LORD.

Ezekiel 35:5–6 and Joel 3:19 also charge the Edomites with bloodshed during the ordeal:

> Because you [Edom] cherished an ancient enmity, and gave over the people of Israel to the power of the sword at the time of their calamity, at the time of their final punishment; therefore, as I live, says the Lord GOD, I will prepare you for blood, and blood shall pursue you; since you did not hate bloodshed, bloodshed shall pursue you. (Ezek. 35:5–6)

> Egypt shall become a desolation
> and Edom a desolate wilderness,
> because of the violence done to the people of Judah,
> in whose land they have shed innocent blood.
> (Joel 3:19)

Ezekiel 36:5 further claims that Edom took advantage of the Babylonian destruction to capture Judahite land:

> Therefore thus says the Lord GOD: I am speaking in my hot jealousy against the rest of the nations, and against all Edom, who, with wholehearted joy and utter contempt, took my land as their possession, because of its pasture, to plunder it.

Several passages also use *generic* language to accuse Edom of wrongdoing. For instance, Ezek. 25:12–13 charges Edom for "acting vengefully":

> Thus says the Lord GOD: Because Edom acted revengefully against the house of Judah and has grievously offended in taking vengeance upon them, therefore thus says the Lord GOD, I will stretch out my hand against Edom, and cut off from it humans and animals, and I will make it desolate; from Teman even to Dedan they shall fall by the sword.

Both Isa. 34 and 63 announce that Yahweh will take revenge against Edom for an unspecified crime against Jerusalem:

> When my sword has drunk its fill in the heavens,
> lo, it will descend upon Edom,
> upon the people I have doomed to judgment.

The LORD has a sword; it is sated with blood,
  it is gorged with fat,
  with the blood of lambs and goats,
  with the fat of the kidneys of rams.
For the LORD has a sacrifice in Bozrah,
  a great slaughter in the land of Edom.
Wild oxen shall fall with them,
  and young steers with the mighty bulls.
Their land shall be soaked with blood,
  and their soil made rich with fat.
For the LORD has a day of vengeance,
  a year of vindication by Zion's cause.

(34:5–8)

"Who is this that comes from Edom,
  from Bozrah in garments stained crimson?
Who is this so splendidly robed,
  marching in his great might?"
"It is I, announcing vindication,
  mighty to save."
"Why are your robes red,
  and your garments like theirs who tread the wine press?"
"I have trodden the wine press alone,
  and from the peoples no one was with me;
I trod them in my anger and trampled them in my wrath;
  their juice spattered on my garments,
  and stained all my robes.
For the day of vengeance was in my heart,
  and the year for my redeeming work had come.

(63:1–4)

Finally, parts of the oracle against Edom in Jer. 49:7–22 parallel almost ver-batim numerous verses of Obadiah. Especially strong is the overlap between verses 1–4 and Jer. 49:14–16; verse 5 and Jer. 49:9; and verse 8 and Jer. 49:7. Scholars debate the origin of these similarities: Did Jeremiah use Obadiah? Did Obadiah use Jeremiah? Did both use a common source? Did a third party add the passage to both places? Despite the different conclusions reached on these questions, the consensus view holds that the double inclusion of this anti-Edomite oracle indicates widespread Judean enmity against Edom. Edom must have been an important enemy for this oracle to find its way into the Bible twice.

In the consensus, these passages all add up to the same conclusion: Edom acted vilely against Judah. And all agree with Obadiah. Indeed, notes to Obadiah in annotated Bibles often cite the passages listed above, just as the notes to those passages cite Obadiah. Since "Obadiah's words of judgment bear striking similarities to this larger corpus of prophetic oracles against Edom,"[4] the case for Obadiah's claims seems strong.

Archaeological Evidence

Numerous interpreters also assert that archaeological evidence supports Obadiah's claims. One such example is Itzhaq Beit-Arieh of Tel Aviv University. Based on his excavations in the Negev (the southern area of Judah bordering on Edom), Beit-Arieh argues that Edomites took Judean land in the seventh and sixth centuries.[5] He links his findings with the Judean construction of fortresses in the Negev during this period, as well as with inscriptions found in southern Judah, some that express fear of Edomites and others that indicate the presence of Edomites in the area. When combined, he claims, all this evidence indicates that Edom seized land from Judah during or soon after the Babylonian conquest:

> This new evidence of Edomite expansion into Judah also helps explain the presence of a series of Israelite defense fortresses . . . [built] during the seventh century BCE. Although archeologists have long known that a line of fortified Israelite outposts was erected in the eastern Negev at about this time, the reason for the protective barrier remained a mystery. It is now possible to affirm that these fortresses were built to protect against Edomite invasions, backing up the Biblical references to the conflict between the two peoples with concrete archeological evidence.[6]

Beit-Arieh offers the "plausible explanation" that at the end of the first temple period Edom attempted to

> exploit the weakness of the Judaean kingdom at the very time that the latter was engaged in a life or death struggle against the Babylonian army. By seizing certain Judahite-controlled areas in the eastern Negev, Edom at last was able to satisfy its generations-old ambition to expand its territory westwards.[7]

In his commentary on Obadiah, Raabe also draws on the evidence from the Negev to support the truthfulness of Obadiah's claims:

> This evidence [from the Negev] shows that Edomites resided in the southern parts of Judah during the upheavals of the early sixth century. Thus they could very well have engaged in the activities that Obadiah and the other texts mention.[8]

The same appeal to archaeological finds in the Negev also appears in the third edition of the *New Oxford Annotated Bible*, in the notes accompanying the anti-Edom oracle in Isa. 63:

> Edom, lying to the south and east of Judah, profited by the Babylonian conquest to encroach on Judean territory, a situation confirmed by the archaeological record.[9]

When the biblical and archaeological evidence is presented in the way that I have reviewed here, Obadiah's language is easily seen as reflective of the realities of the sixth century. If indeed Edom took advantage of the Babylonian invasions to seize Judean land, and if indeed the two nations had strong ties, then Obadiah's language against Edom, while perhaps more nasty than other biblical materials, nonetheless reflects accurately the relations between Edom and Judah in the sixth century BCE.

Challenging the Consensus

Closer attention to this "evidence" and the conclusions drawn from it, however, not only raises questions about the consensus but also highlights what is unique—and ideologically driven—about Obadiah.

Brother Edom

In assessing the biblical material referring to Edom as Israel/Judah's brother, several dimensions of this literature deserve attention. First and most important, the biblical testimony provides only an Israelite/Judean perspective on the relationship between the countries. To date, no Edomite literature is available for comparison purposes. Even if Israel/Judah considered the nations to be closely related, did Edom share that perspective? If Israel/Judah claimed to have a treaty with Edom, was it a treaty Edom recognized?

A second factor that complicates the consensus is the difficulty with dating biblical books. For example, although the narratives of Genesis talk about the early stages of Israel's life and faith, for centuries scholars have suggested that some or all of the Pentateuch reflects the social and political realities of much later periods. John Bartlett, for example, has argued repeatedly that the tradition of Edom as Judah's brother cannot date any earlier than David's conquest of Edom in the tenth century BCE: the stories of Jacob and Esau attempt to justify David's taking of Edomite land and to deny Edom's right to reclaim it.[10]

Within the past twenty years, scholars increasingly have dated the Pentateuch even later, to the Persian period—the fifth and fourth centuries BCE. Theodore Mullen argues that Genesis through Numbers was composed after the exile as an alternative to the depiction in Deuteronomy through Kings of Judah as a nation ruled by a king.[11] To create an alternative vision, the writers composed ancestor stories such as that of Jacob and Esau: this "ethno-mythography"[12] reveals the thinking of Persian period authors, not the situation of earliest Israel. Mullen's claims question how "traditional" the tradition of Edom as brother could be at the time Obadiah was written. Obadiah could precede rather than echo Genesis.

The consensus on the traditional nature of this brotherhood also is challenged by the recognition that not all biblical materials describe Edom as brother. In the Prophetic Books, for example, of the thirty-two times Edom is mentioned and of the eleven times Esau is named, only a few explicitly name Edom as Judah's brother. The passages previously listed from Ezekiel and Isaiah, for example, do not make this connection. Even in passages that do link some form of the word *brother* with Edom, multiple interpretations present themselves. Amos 1:11 claims that Edom "pursued his brother with a sword," but it does not identify that brother as Israel/Judah. Several verses earlier in the same chapter, Amos describes the tie between Tyre and Israel as a "brotherly covenant" (1:9 ASV): if the author of Amos saw Edom as Israel's brother, then he did not consider Edom to be Israel's *only* or even closest brother. Malachi 1:2–5 does stress the brotherly bond between the nations, although, as I will argue below, for a different purpose than Obadiah.

Edom's Crimes

The consensus view that Obadiah records Edom's "actual" actions against Judah in the sixth century also faces challenges from biblical and archaeological materials.

Biblical Evidence

Biblical evidence supports Obadiah's claims less clearly than the consensus suggests. Importantly, the major narrative accounts of the fall of Jerusalem in 2 Kgs. 24 and Jer. 39 make no mention of Edom's participation. Especially striking in this regard is 2 Kgs. 24:2, which claims that in addition to the Chaldeans (Babylonians), bands of Arameans, Moabites, and Ammonites came up against Jerusalem: Edomites are conspicuously absent. Jeremiah 40 indicates that Judeans fleeing the Babylonians escaped to Moab, Ammon,

Edom, and elsewhere, making Edom sound more like a haven for refugees than a land-grabbing opportunist.

When those passages that *do* blame Edom for sixth-century crimes are read in their larger literary contexts, they do not single out Edom for special censure. In Ezek. 25, the charges against other nations are equally, if not more, direct than those against Edom. In a litany of blame, Ezekiel charges the *sons of Ammon* with gloating over the fall of Jerusalem, *Moab* with saying that Judah is not just one nation among many, *Edom* with "acting vengefully," and the *Philistines* with "acting in vengeance." This chapter directs the longest and most specific criticism to Ammon: only in the words against Ammon are the sanctuary of Jerusalem and the exile of Judeans mentioned. In other passages, such as Jer. 9:26; 25:17–27; and Ezek. 32, Edom appears within a list of enemy nations: it is one enemy among many.

Indeed, the generic nature of the language in numerous passages makes identifying Edom's crimes difficult. Ezekiel 25 uses the same nonspecific language to describe the actions both of Edom and of the Philistines: some form of the Hebrew root *nqm*, translated in the NRSV with words related to "vengeance," appears ten times in Ezek. 25:12–17. By its very nature, generic language can fit multiple historical scenarios. For example, the oracle against Edom in Amos 1:11–12 is usually seen to reflect events in the eighth century, but its language sounds very much like the language Obadiah and others use against Edom in the sixth century:

> Thus says the LORD:
> For three transgressions of Edom,
>   and for four, I will not revoke the punishment;
> because he pursued his brother with the sword
>   and cast off all pity;
> he maintained his anger perpetually,
>   and kept his wrath forever.
>
> (1:11)

A careful comparison of Obadiah with Jer. 49:7–22, its "parallel" passage, reveals what differs between the two. Missing from Jeremiah are the specific crimes that Obadiah levels against Edom: the list in Obadiah of the actual actions of the Edomites (vv. 10–14) find no counterpart in Jeremiah, which instead uses the same general terms found in the surrounding oracles against Ammon, Moab, and Damascus. Moreover, in Jeremiah the oracle against Edom appears within a longer collection of oracles against foreign nations that run from chapters 46 to 51. While in Obadiah Edom is deserving of special criticism, in Jeremiah Edom is one guilty nation among other even more guilty nations.

Perhaps the most noteworthy observation of all, however, is that these passages differ in specifying Edom's wrongdoing. Some assert that Edom encouraged the Babylonians; others, that it gloated; others, that it committed bloodshed; and yet others give no specific reason for the writers' hatred of Edom. None of the passages gives the full list of crimes that Obadiah offers, and none explicitly includes Obadiah's charge that Edomites actually entered the gates of Jerusalem, looted the city, and handed over survivors to the Babylonians. Despite the consensus, these passages do not simply confirm Obadiah's claims. Rather, careful attention to detail and literary context reveals that Obadiah is unique in heaping up specific charges against Edom and in casting its crimes as particularly heinous.

Archaeological Evidence

Many nonspecialists think of archaeology as an objective scientific enterprise, more factual than written accounts. But, as those who watch the Discovery or History channels know, not all evidence points in the same direction, and explanations of what lies in the ground can vary greatly. For example, John Bartlett reads the archaeological record to suggest that in the seventh and sixth centuries Edom was an extremely weak and poor state.[13] While Edomite sites show no destruction during the early sixth century when the Jerusalem temple was burned by the Babylonians, destruction layers in the late sixth century suggest that many Edomite cities fell in subsequent Babylonian invasions. Based on this evidence, Bartlett has argued that the Edomites would not have been in a position to exploit—or to aid—Judah in 587. Obadiah's charge that Edom attacked Jerusalem were fabricated, he claims, out of resentment that Edom survived the Babylonian destruction and Judah did not. Bartlett's interpretation of the archaeological record is of an Edom innocent of the crimes of which it is charged, quite the opposite from Beit-Arieh's portrayal of Edomite aggression in the sixth century.

A yet-different scenario is created by Ian Stern in his synthesis and interpretation of the archaeology of Edom in the Persian period.[14] During the sixth to fourth centuries, he explains, both Judah and Edom suffered sharp declines in population, likely as the result of Babylonian invasions. In these "postcollapse societies," some Judeans moved to Edom and some Edomites (also called Idumeans) moved into southern Judah. Personal names in Edomite inscriptions reveal how ethnically diverse the areas became. According to Stern, however, in the second half of the fifth century (after 450), the leadership of Yehud (the Persian name for the area once called Judah) resisted such diversity and sought to establish a clearer ethnic identity for the community. Ezra and Nehemiah led the effort to make Yehud more monolithic, perhaps to bolster the power of those who had returned from exile in Babylon, having maintained their Jewish identity there. While Stern does not explicitly link his study with Obadiah, his scenario suggests that the situation that gave rise to Obadiah's anger might not be Edomite treachery but rather the mixing of populations and the loss of well-established land claims.

I have not done justice to this complex archaeological material. My modest goal in sharing some of these debates, however, has been to establish that the "evidence" used to back up Obadiah's claims against Edom is not as "hard" as it is usually presented. Even the language used to present the evidence often relies on speculation. For example, Raabe suggests,

> This evidence [from the Negev] shows that Edomites resided in the southern parts of Judah during the upheavals of the early sixth century. Thus they *could very well have* engaged in the activities that Obadiah and the other texts mention (my italics).[15]

Beit-Arieh states that the Edomite shrines "*may* mark the path of the Edomite expansion into Judah,"[16] and he also offers as a "*plausible* explanation" (my italics) that at the end of the First Temple period Edom attempted to

> exploit the weakness of the Judaean kingdom at the very time that the latter was engaged in a life or death struggle against the Babylonian army. By seizing certain Judahite-controlled areas in the eastern Negev, Edom at last was able to *satisfy its generations-old ambition* to expand its territory westwards.[17]

Both Raabe and Beit-Arieh suggest what is theoretically possible, but neither provide clear evidence that Edom did indeed seize territory—much less what that nation's dreams and desires were. Both attempt to establish the means and motive for a crime without proving that a crime was committed.

What, Then, Can we Say?

This comparison between Obadiah and other sources, biblical and archaeological, points to several important conclusions about this book and its description of Edom as a bad brother:

1. *Obadiah's identification of Edom as Judah's brother is ideologically driven.* As I have tried to show, such an identification is not a "given." The Genesis narratives regarding Jacob and Esau do not provide objective biological

information, and they may not be any older than Obadiah itself. Moreover, as we have seen, not all of the prophetic tirades identify Edom as a brother. Especially striking in this regard is Obadiah's so-called parallel in Jer. 49. Missing from Jeremiah are not only the specific charges that Obadiah levels against Edom, but, importantly, any appeal to brotherhood as a basis for how Edom should have acted: Obadiah's litany of brotherly duties in verses 10–15 has no parallel in Jer. 49. The author of Jeremiah apparently was aware of the tradition linking Esau with Edom, since it mentions the "calamity of Esau" in 49:8; but, even with this tradition available, the author does not mention brotherhood as a factor in Edom's punishment.

2. *Brother language serves a specific purpose in Obadiah.* Even though Obadiah is not unique in linking Edom's role of brother with an anti-Edomite sentiment, it is unique in the specific way that it connects the two. This becomes clear by comparing Obadiah with Malachi, the only other Prophetic Book to stress the fraternal ties between Edom and Judah. In Malachi, the brotherhood of Judah and Edom establishes the commonality between the two nations. Even though Jacob and Esau are brothers and presumedly equally deserving of honor and favor, Yahweh has chosen to destroy Edom and preserve Israel. Malachi appeals to the brotherhood of Edom in order to underscore Yahweh's (undeserved?) graciousness to Judah. In contrast, Obadiah appeals to Edom's status as brother in order to underscore Edom's obligations: everyone knows that brothers should not treat one another in the way that Edom treated Judah. Malachi and Obadiah are not the same in the rhetorical use of brother language.

3. *Obadiah's use of brother language, as well as its particular recounting of charges against Edom, reflects a self-interest, particularly regarding land.* While comparing Obadiah to other biblical passages reveals the uniqueness of its rhetoric about Edom's fraternal obligations, the comparison also highlights a feature that Obadiah shares with other anti-Edomite material in the Prophetic Books: an assertion of Judah's own claim to land. Many of the passages listed earlier as evidence of the "consensus" concern the resettlement and even enlargement of Judean territory. Ezekiel 36, which claims that the Edomites confiscated land, goes to great lengths to describe how Israel/Judah will be rebuilt, restored, and repopulated. The text repeatedly described the land as "desolate," implying that it is empty—not possessed by Edom, as 36:5 claims. Amos 9 envisions Judah's claim to Edomite land, even though the book nowhere charges Edom with taking Judean land.

> On that day I will raise up
> the booth of David that is fallen,

and repair its breaches,
>   and raise up its ruins,
>   and rebuild it as in the days of old;
> in order that they may possess the remnant of Edom
>   and all the nations who are called by my name,
>   says the LORD who does this.

(9:11–12)

Land is also important to Obadiah. Verses 19–21 not only promise that Judah will reclaim the Negev but also envision the enlargement of Judah's borders in every direction: west to the land of the Philistines; north to Ephraim and Samaria; northeast to Gilead and Phoenicia; and, of course, south to Edom/Mt. Esau itself. Obadiah is not just interested in reclaiming land lost to the Edomites but in expanding Judah beyond its original borders.

The archaeology that we have reviewed may explain why Judah saw itself as needing—even deserving—land and status. The devastation of cities and the loss of population after the Babylonian destruction would have left Judah in a much-diminished state and, if Stern is right, the mixing of populations would have left little clear identity to a self-contained Judah. But, significantly, Obadiah only criticizes Edom—not Babylon or its other neighbors (as does Ezek. 25). Moreover, Obadiah extends its concern beyond that of Edomite land to its own further expansion.

Obadiah's use of the "brotherhood-of-nations" metaphor is not value neutral. The metaphor denies Edom's right to self-defense and/or expansion, even while it grants this prerogative to Judah. While Obadiah claims that brotherly obligations should have prevented Edom from acting against Judah, they clearly do not prevent Obadiah from envisioning a time in which Judah rules over Mt. Esau—just as the bonds of brotherhood did not prevent Jacob from stealing Esau's claim to his birthright. Hosea 12:2–3 condemns Jacob for his usurper role:

> The LORD has an indictment against Judah,
>   and will punish Jacob according to his ways,
>   and repay him according to his deeds.
> In the womb he tried to supplant his brother,
>   and in his manhood he strove with God.

But Obadiah does not. In Obadiah, the brotherhood of Esau and Jacob benefits Judah in a way it does not benefit Edom.

As rhetoric, the book of Obadiah seeks to convince its reader that harm has been done to Judah; that Edomites are to blame; that their treachery is inexcusable because they are "brother"; and that this act of betrayal is worthy of punishment and Judah's taking of Edomite land. But in the final verses of the book the larger goal of this rhetoric is revealed: Judah deserves more than revenge on Edom; it deserves land.

The Ideology of "Brothering" in the Ancient World

As have seen in other chapters, the most common prophetic treatment of the nations is to "other" them—to create disdain through difference and distance. Elsewhere, the Prophetic Books call the superpowers Assyria and Babylon "whore," that woman who stands outside of proper society, outside of accepted norms of social intercourse. When Nineveh suffers punishment as a whore in Nahum, for example, she becomes a spectacle for others, cut off from any comforter.

In Obadiah, the accusation of another nation comes through "brothering," creating a mental picture of a norm of closeness, commonality, sameness. The brother metaphor implies that Judah and Edom are two parties of relatively equal abilities, obligated by a permanent relationship to mutual defense. Edom is not envisioned as a hostile or even as an independent state, with rights to its own national security, but rather one for whom Judah's welfare should be a primary value. Unlike Malachi, which focuses strongly on the father-son metaphor for Yahweh and Israel in order to establish the people's subordinate role to their Deity, Obadiah envisions a family—and a political climate—in which there is no protective father, only a band of brothers.

Other biblical documents reflect many of these same dynamics. For example, the apostle Paul of New Testament fame uses "brother" language frequently to refer to fellow believers, though scholars debate the social and political impact of Paul's rhetoric. Karl Sandnes suggests that when Paul uses "brother" language in his letter to Philemon, "a new relationship based on equality is in the making" even though Paul himself fell short of imagining how that equality could play out in society.[18] Lone Fatum, however, argues that Paul appealed to early Christian believers as his "sons" and "brothers" as a means of asserting power over them:

> Though the Christian brotherhood is a voluntary group based on voluntary commitment, Paul seems intent on pressing upon it a binding commitment characteristic of the kinship group, defined as a non-voluntary association; he strives in fact to organise the brothers according to the social and moral institution of the patriarchal family. . . . The brothers are . . . to form and uphold a tightly organized community of hierarchic interdependence

inwardly, with weaker brothers giving their respect and loyal adherence to stronger ones, and the strong in turn their lenient guidance and support to the weaker, so that all of them together will put forth the image of a well-defined and honourable association.[19]

Fatum reminds readers, too, that while gender-inclusive translations of the New Testament often suggest that Paul addressed "brothers and sisters," the Greek term mentions "brothers" only. Paul's language is male.

> Encouraging, exhorting and instructing his sons and brothers, Paul deliberately employs a man-to-man language stage setting in order to institutionalize a social pattern of fellowship and reciprocity.[20]... the gender ideology and patriarchal social order of Paul's' universe illustrate a pattern of values and virtues according to which male means general or universal.[21]

Brother language, then, can function in egalitarian and/or hierarchical ways. Language that seems universal and inclusive can exclude women and others who remain invisible within the metaphor.

Reflecting on the Brother Metaphor and its Critique

I hope that readers leave this chapter challenged in at least two ways. First, I hope they are encouraged to read Obadiah and the Bible as a whole with some critical distance, not simply assuming that Obadiah's version of sixth-century politics reveals "the way it was." Biblical writers were not simply reporters of events; they were gifted writers who used the skills of rhetoric to persuade their readers. Their skillfulness should be acknowledged, not denied.

But more important, I hope that studying a topic as remote as Obadiah in its historical and literary contexts invites readers to deeper reflection on the power of metaphors in the contemporary world. Just as Obadiah's "brother" rhetoric had real-life implications for Judeans and Edomites, so too modern rhetoric has real-life implications for individuals and for groups. Language matters, because it reflects and creates patterns of thought and assumptions of what is normal and right.

Brother Language and Social Control

As I have tried to show with Obadiah and with other examples from the ancient world, the language of equality can prove coercive as well as egalitarian. In the contemporary world, extending the image of family to those not biologically related can, on the one hand, serve the goals of equality and foster a sense of mutual responsibility and accountability. The rhetoric of brotherhood has advanced the work of the Nobel Peace Prize, the United Nations, and numerous humanitarian movements. The aspirations of brotherhood are expressed in a 2004 address by United Nations Secretary-General Kofi Annan:

> Living together is the fundamental human project—not just in towns and villages from Scotland to South Africa, but also as a single human family facing common threats and opportunities.[22]

On the other hand, the language of brotherhood can also exert power over opponents. As Ann Burlein has demonstrated, the Aryan Brotherhood, a white supremacist group that falls under the umbrella of the Christian Identity movement, promotes hatred against women, gays, African Americans, and others by encouraging the sense of brotherhood and solidarity between white males.[23] "We" are not "them," it says.

More mainstream examples also suggest the way in which brother language can control those within a group. My husband, who spent many years in leadership roles in his labor union, reports that a common tactic for persuading members to accept union decisions was to remind them that "brothers stick together." Those who challenged the leadership were accused of being "in bed with the company," of "breaking rank," and of "violating the brotherhood."

The modern world offers not only these general parallels to Obadiah's rhetoric of brotherhood but also more-focused examples of the political usage of "brother" language.

As introduced in the previous chapter, George Lakoff's analysis of the rhetoric used during the 1990–1991 Gulf War underscores the crucial role played by metaphor. While the United States depicted (and reacted to) Kuwait as "the defenseless maiden to be rescued in the fairy tale," Arab states viewed Kuwait as a member of a larger Arab and Islamic "brotherhood." In this brotherhood, all brothers should share equally:

> To see Arabs metaphorically as one big family is to suggest that oil wealth should belong to all Arabs. To many Arabs, the national boundaries drawn by colonial powers are illegitimate, violating the conception of Arabs as a single "brotherhood" and impoverishing millions.[24]

Since "economic inequities between poor brothers and rich brothers challenge familial harmony,"[25] Iraq saw itself as merely forcing Kuwait to share its wealth with its brothers. Because Kuwait had violated this brotherhood, Iraq saw itself as merely restoring family equilibrium.

Lakoff's analysis underscores the vital importance of understanding the frames in which individuals and nations think and how those frames make certain behaviors seem rational, appropriate, and normal. In the case of the Gulf War, it shows how the brother metaphor can demand conformity to a single vision, even when, from a perspective such as that of the United States, the actions taken to enforce it seem self-serving and authoritarian. As noted previously, Lakoff also points to what all metaphors hide. In the case of "brotherhood," he explains,

> the metaphors used to conceptualize the Gulf crisis hide the most powerful political ideas in the Arab world: Arab nationalism and Islamic fundamentalism. The first seeks to form a racially-based all-Arab nation, the second, a theocratic all-Islamic state. Though bitterly opposed to one another, they share a great deal. Both are conceptualized in family terms, an Arab brotherhood and an Islamic brotherhood. Both see brotherhoods as more legitimate than existing states.[26]

Seeing how these dynamics play out in the rhetoric of the Gulf War and in the rhetoric of Obadiah invites contemporary people to analyze their own rhetoric and that of their leaders. What metaphors do we use for those with whom we disagree? How do our own frames justify our behaviors? How do the frames used by our opponents justify their actions? Does either language mask rather than erase differences in power? Most important, how can such understanding call us to deeper and more meaningful dialogue about our differences and how we might faithfully negotiate them?

"You Can't Pick Your Family"

As we have already seen, the ideology of "brothering" takes the relationship in question as a given. It treats bonds between people and nations as natural and unchangeable rather than intentionally created and fragile. That assumption, I believe, too often absolves those who use such language of the responsibility to work at relationship and to recognize how easily relationship can be broken. The church's use of sibling language runs this risk. Too often Christians appeal to the brotherhood (or even siblinghood) of all believers without having undertaken the hard work of getting to know, understand, and appreciate one another. When people call me "sister" but do not know what matters most to me, or when I avoid necessary conflict by calling a fellow member "brother," sibling language does not serve us well. While the brother/sisterhood of believers indeed may be the goal of the gospel, that relationship must be forged rather than imposed.

This observation holds especially true when, as in Obadiah, "brother" is applied to those outside the community—to other groups, to other nations. The writer of Obadiah portrays the interests of Judah as necessarily shared by one of its closest neighbors: Edom is bound by brotherhood to do what is good for Judah. While a noble goal, this mutuality of political interests is not yet a present reality. Nations must forge alliances and mutual trust rather than appeal to "natural" bonds. Brotherhood must be created. And, unlike in Obadiah, it must be mutual, as binding on the party using the rhetoric as on the one against whom the rhetoric is directed.

Theological Dimensions

On the surface, this metaphor might not seem sufficiently theological to belong in a study devoted to the language that the biblical prophets use for God. After all, Obadiah concerns the relationship between nations, not a relationship that involves Yahweh.[27] A primary goal of this volume, however, has been to erase or at least blur the boundaries between the theological and the political. I have argued throughout that prophetic language for God draws from and influences political and social realities, both in the past and in the present. Picturing God as father or husband or warrior has as much political power as calling Jerusalem daughter or Edom brother, and all have theological implications.

How we think about others, including how we think about other nations, constitutes theology. In the language of theologian Alister McGrath,

> Christian theology is not just a set of ideas; it is about making possible a new way of seeing ourselves, others, and the world, with implications for the way in which we behave.[28]

The same point is made in Luke 10:25–42, which links love of God and love of neighbor:

> "You shall love the Lord your God with all your heart, and with all your soul, and with all your strength, and with all your mind; and your neighbor as yourself." (10:27)

Just as love of God and neighbor go hand in hand, so do mental pictures of God and neighbor.

Rhetoric like Obadiah's ignores the differences between people in terms of money, power, and resources. Rather than challenge inequality, it expects those of unequal means to assume equal responsibility for relationship. Ideological critique of this metaphor, as of others in the Prophetic Books, calls attention to the need to do more than hold hands with other people and call them brothers and sisters. Like the story of the Good Samaritan, which in Luke embodies the true meaning of love of neighbor, ideological critique insists that "neighbor" and "brother" are labels that must be earned.

Conclusion

*T*hroughout this volume, I have insisted that challenging prophetic metaphor ideologically can serve constructive purposes. Bringing into focus the often-invisible assumptions that govern the thinking of ancient authors and modern readers allows a level of reflection on culture and self that other reading strategies do not. It also invites theological engagement beyond simple assent or objection to biblical texts. Theology in this vein becomes not simply learning from the Prophetic Books but also exploring the implications of their explicit and implicit claims about God.

My choice of metaphors has been driven primarily by their popularity in the Prophetic Books: while the prophetic authors were active metaphor makers, they turned most often to the images of husband, father, warrior, daughter, and son. Not just famous but infamous, these metaphors also have polarized commentators and average readers, providing fertile ground for sowing an alternative to "love it or hate it" approaches.

Obviously, all but one of these metaphors derives from the social world of the family. To speak of the divine, prophetic writers turned to the roles of father and husband; to speak of nations, they conjured daughters and brothers. Our discussion of familial roles has highlighted the differences between ancient and modern constructions of the household. The male-female bond described in Hosea diverges significantly from modern understandings of marriage, and an ancient Israelite parenting manual would not sell well in the modern United States. Readers of the Bible need to know these differences in order to speak honestly about the Bible and to avoid replicating its ideologies to the detriment of their own, most deeply held values.

As we have seen, however, ideologies of the family continue to hold sway over contemporary thought and emotion. Modern assumptions about romantic husbands, obedient sons, vulnerable daughters, and loyal brothers fuel readers' reactions to family metaphors in the Prophetic Books. Indeed, readers' investments in their own families often overwrite the actual content of the texts. Their own constructs of family—actual or desired—predispose them to hear prophetic tales of family members as stories about home. Facing squarely our own socialization as well as the actual content of prophetic texts offers the chance to come to terms with both. Seeing painful realities in these passages—violence masked by romance, the dark side of obedience, the paternalism and self-deception lurking in "do it for the children"—may allow us to see the same in ourselves.

The stray nonfamily metaphor, that of God as warrior, reveals something else about the household unit: the family is not always enough. When prophetic texts imagine a savior for daughter Jerusalem, they do not envision a father but a conqueror. Within the prophetic imagination, the most vulnerable must seek help outside the family. Seeing the inadequacy of the father metaphor to answer all of Israel's theological needs may enable modern readers to recognize not only the limits of family metaphors for God but also the limitations of *family*. In her volume *The Unequal Homeless*, anthropologist Joan Passaro recounts story after story of men and women who chose homelessness as an alternative to the confines of the nuclear family. One man explained, "Homelessness was something I had to do for myself."[1] Passaro's research leads her not to fault the family unit itself but rather to complain that American society has little to offer beyond the family. Too much "focus on the family" leaves too few alternatives for those whose families prove unfulfilling, even dangerous.

No simple solution will fix the problems of prophetic metaphors. As I have argued, altering a metaphor changes its meaning, effectively creating a new metaphor with a new set of problems. Yet we cannot avoid speaking metaphorically. Human language—especially human language for the divine—relies on imagery, comparison, mental pictures.

The challenge facing readers of the Prophetic Books is not to *resolve* this dilemma but rather to *engage* it. I envision at least two essential components of that engagement: creativity and continued critique. Rather than rely on a limited set of images for God, readers need creatively to pile them up and let them challenge each other. In *The Writing Life*, Annie Dillard refuses to imagine writing in just one way: writing is like lion taming *and* like sitting up with a dying friend *and* like a runaway mustang *and* like laying out a garden—all these things and more.[2] Each new metaphor points out what the last overlooked and invites another to fill in the gaps left unfilled. The Bible does the same. The Prophets employ multiple metaphors. Paul compares Christians to a body with different but equally important parts. Revelation calls the church the bride of Christ. Each of those metaphors has it own strengths and weaknesses, but none is sufficient.

Imagining the church only as family limits what it can be. When Christians gather at Christ's table, they are not only a family gathered for dinner; they are also friends who have come together to enjoy each other's company and colleagues who share common work. They are partners who come from different backgrounds to commit themselves to one another, and they are the hungry homeless brought together by a common need for nourishment. They are all and none of these things. The church needs poets who will mine the tradition for forgotten treasures and also create new, fresh comparisons. Perhaps in seeing their relationships with one another and with God in new guise, Christians will find new ways of living.

But every metaphor—whether unearthed from the past or manufactured from the resources of the present—will require critique as well. Because every metaphor hides aspects of the truth or leaves someone out, every one will need to be analyzed on the couch, interrogated for information about who it left behind, photographed from different angles.

The church needs poets, but it also needs critics. It needs those who will challenge its metaphors as well as the ideologies that inform them, trusting that critique can bring new life to theological reflection.

Notes

ACKNOWLEGMENTS

1. Annie Dillard, *The Writing Life* (New York: Harper & Row, 1989), 52.

INTRODUCTION

1. Walter Brueggeman, *The Prophetic Imagination,* rev. ed. (Minneapolis: Fortress Press, 2001).

2. Athalya Brenner, "On Prophetic Propaganda and the Politics of 'Love': The Case of Jeremiah," in *Feminist Companion to the Latter Prophets*, ed. Athalya Brenner (Sheffield: Sheffield Academic Press, 1995), 256–74.

3. Julia M. O'Brien, "Nahum-Habakkuk-Zephaniah: Reading the 'Former Prophets' in the Persian Period," *Interpretation* 61 (2007): 168–83.

4. Toni Morrison, *Playing in the Dark* (Cambridge: Cambridge University Press, 1992), 46.

5. Stephen Fowl, "Texts Don't Have Ideologies," *Biblical Interpretation* 3 (1995): 15–34.

6. bell hooks, *The Will to Change: Men, Masculinity, and Love* (New York: Simon & Schuster, 2003).

7. Irving Greenberg, *The Jewish Way: Living the Holidays* (New York: Summit Books, 1988), 253.

8. Tikva Frymer-Kensky, *Studies in the Bible and Feminist Criticism* (Philadelphia: Jewish Publication Society, 2006), 205.

CHAPTER 1: PROPHETIC THEOLOGY:
A BRIEF HISTORY OF INTERPRETATION

1. Richard Hays, *Echoes of Scripture in the Letters of Paul* (New Haven, CT: Yale University Press, 1989).

2. Ibid., 81.

3. Ibid., 35–38.

4. Brevard S. Childs, *The Struggle to Understand Isaiah as Christian Scripture* (Grand Rapids: Wm. B. Eerdmans Publishing Co., 2004), 5.

5. John Sawyer, *The Fifth Gospel: Isaiah in the History of Christianity* (New York: Cambridge University Press, 1996), 43.

6. Cited in Sawyer, *Fifth Gospel*, 48.

7. See Julia M. O'Brien, " Malachi*,"* in *Dictionary of Biblical Interpretation*, ed. John H. Hayes (Nashville: Abingdon Press, 1999), vol. K-Z, 110–13.

8. Childs, *Struggle to Understand Isaiah*, 96.

9. Beryl Smalley, *The Study of the Bible in the Middle Ages,* 3rd ed. (Oxford: Basil Black-well, 1983), 154.

10. Ibid., xi.

11. Ibid, 93.

12. Ibid., 95.

13. Ibid., 157.

14. Ibid., 169.

15. K. Froehlich, "Aquinas, Thomas," in *Historical Handbook of Major Biblical Inter-preters*, ed. Donald K. McKim (Downer's Grove, IL: InterVarsity Press, 1998), 88.

16. Childs, *Struggle to Understand Isaiah*, 157.

17. Ibid., 158.

18. Ibid., 159.

19. Sawyer, *Fifth Gospel*, 32.

20. Childs, *Struggle to Understand Isaiah*, 183.

21. Ibid., 186.

22. Ibid., 211.

23. See O'Brien, "Malachi."

24. Sawyer, *Fifth Gospel*, 128.

25. Childs, *Struggle to Understand Isaiah*, 221.

26. Samuel Macauley Jackson and Clarence Nevin Heller, *Zwingli's Commentary on True and False Religion* (Durham, NC: Labyrinth Press, 1981), 278.

27. Sawyer, *Fifth Gospel*, 135.

28. This quote from Spinoza is printed in Nigel M. de S. Cameron, *Biblical Higher Criti-cism and the Defense of Infallibilism in 19th Century Britain* (Lewiston, NY: Edwin Mellon Press, 1987), 13.

29. Ibid., 15.

30. Quoted in John P. Peters, *The Old Testament and the New Scholarship* (London: Methuen & Co., 1901), 93.

31. For a discussion of Ewald, see Ronald E. Clements, *One Hundred Years of Old Testa-ment Interpretation* (Philadelphia: Westminster Press, 1976), 51.

32. Julius Wellhausen, *Prolegomena to the History of Ancient Israel* (Gloucester, MA: Peter Smith, 1973).

33. Quoted in Clements, *One Hundred Years*, 51–52.

34. See ibid., 57–59.

35. Ibid., 59–63.

36. Michael Dick, "Survey of Israelite Prophecy," in *Introduction to the Hebrew Bible* (Englewood Cliffs, NJ: Prentice Hall, 1988), 187–97.

37. Kyle Yates, *Preaching from the Prophets* (New York: Harper & Brothers, 1942), vii.

38. See Clements, *One Hundred Years*, 63–70.

39. Walther Eichrodt, *Theology of the Old Testament* (Philadelphia: Westminster Press, 1961), vol. 1, 346.

40. Ibid., 351.

41. Ibid., 347.

42. Ibid., 361.

43. Ibid., 331, 334.

44. Ibid., 365.

45. Ibid., 328.

46. Gerhard von Rad, *The Message of the Prophets,* trans. D. M. G. Stalker (New York: Harper & Row, 1967), 34.

47. Gerhard von Rad, *Old Testament Theology,* 2 vols. (New York: Harper, 1962–65).

48. Walter Brueggemann, *Theology of the Old Testament: Testimony, Dispute, Advocacy* (Minneapolis: Fortress Press, 1997), 40.

49. Ibid., 360.

50. "Barmen Declaration," Internet Sacred Text Archive, http://www.sacred-texts.com/chr/barmen.htm (accessed January 14, 2008).

51. Brueggemann, *Theology of the Old Testament,* 33.

52. Brevard S. Childs, *Introduction to the Old Testament as Scripture* (Philadelphia: Fortress Press, 1979), 74.

53. Ibid., 336.

54. Walter Brueggemann, *The Prophetic Imagination,* rev. ed. (Minneapolis: Fortress Press, 2001), 46.

55. Brueggemann, *Theology of the Old Testament,* xvii.

56. Ibid., 223.

57. Ibid., 299.

58. Ibid., 360–62.

59. Ibid., 625.

60. Ibid., 623.

61. Ibid., 745.

62. Ibid, 63.

63. Stephen D. Lowe, "Book Review of Walter Brueggemann, *Theology of the Old Testament,*" *Global Journal of Classical Theology,* http://www.trinitysem.edu/journal/sd_lowe_revu.html (accessed January 25, 2008).

CHAPTER 2: THE CHALLENGE OF FEMINIST CRITICISM OF THE PROPHETS

1. Judith Sanderson, "Amos," in *The Women's Bible Commentary,* ed. Carol A. Newsom and Sharon H. Ringe (Louisville, KY: Westminster John Knox Press, 1992), 206.

2. J. Cheryl Exum, "The Ethics of Biblical Violence against Women," in *The Bible in Ethics: The Second Sheffield Colloquium,* ed. John W. Rogerson, Margaret Davies, and M. Daniel Carroll R. (Sheffield: Sheffield Academic Press, 1995), 252.

3. Ibid.

4. Julia M. O'Brien, "Judah as Wife and Husband: Deconstructing Gender in Malachi," *JBL* 115 (1996): 243–52.

5. Throughout this volume, I refer to English chapter and verse divisions, which occasionally may differ from the Hebrew.

6. United States Department of Agriculture, Safety, Health, and Employee Welfare, *Domestic Violence Awareness Handbook,* http://www.usda.gov/da/shmd/aware.htm (accessed January 26, 2008).

7. Ibid.

8. Drorah Setel, "Prophets and Pornography: Female Sexual Imagery in Hosea," in *Feminist Interpretation of the Bible,* ed. Letty Russell (Philadelphia: Westminster Press, 1985), 87.

9. Ibid., 95.

10. Brenner's argument appears in two slightly different versions: Athalya Brenner, "On Prophetic Propaganda and the Politics of 'Love': The Case of Jeremiah," in *A Feminist*

Companion to the Latter Prophets, ed. Athalya Brenner (Sheffield: Sheffield Academic Press, 1995), 256–74; and Athalya Brenner, "On 'Jeremiah' and The Poetics of (Prophetic?) Pornography," in *On Gendering Texts: Female and Male Voices in the Hebrew Bible*, ed. Athalya Brenner and Fokkelien van Dijk-Hemmes (Leiden: E. J. Brill, 1996), 178–93.

11. Brenner, *A Feminist Companion to the Latter Prophets*; and Athalya Brenner, ed., *Prophets and Daniel: A Feminist Companion to the Bible*, 2nd ser. (Sheffield: Sheffield Academic Press, 2001).

12. Newsom and Ringe, *The Women's Bible Commentary*, 1992.

13. Judith Fetterley, *The Resisting Reader: A Feminist Approach to American Fiction* (Lafayette, IN: Indiana University Press, 1978), xxii.

14. Exum, "Ethics of Biblical Violence," 249–50.

15. Tikva Frymer-Kensky, *Studies in the Bible and Feminist Criticism* (Philadelphia: Jewish Publication Society, 2006).

16. Exum, "Ethics of Biblical Violence," 262.

17. Melissa Raphael, *The Female Face of God at Auschwitz: A Jewish Feminist Theology of the Holocaust* (New York: Routledge, 2003).

18. Judith Sanderson, "Nahum," in Newsom and Ringe, *The Women's Bible Commentary*, 220.

19. Gerlinde Baumann, *Love and Violence: Marriage as Metaphor for the Relationship between YHWH and Israel in the Prophetic Books*, trans. Linda M. Maloney (Collegeville, MD: Liturgical Press, 2003), 230.

20. Ibid., 231.

21. Ibid., 238.

22. Ibid., 235.

23. Ibid., 237.

24. Walter Brueggemann, *Theology of the Old Testament: Testament, Dispute, Advocacy* (Minneapolis: Fortress Press, 1997), 223.

25. Ibid., 361.

26. Ibid., 546–47.

27. Ibid., 223.

28. Ibid., 298.

29. Ibid., 223, n. 13.

30. Ibid., 297, n. 18.

31. Ibid., 299, n 20.

32. Ibid, 299.

33. Ibid., 362.

34. Royce Dickinson Jr. "Heartbroken for the Heartless," in *Preaching the Eighth Century Prophets*, ed. David Fleer and Dale Bland (Abilene, TX: ACU Press, 2004), 22.

35. Ibid., 230.

36. Craig Bowman, "Living in Hosea," in Fleer and Bland, *Preaching the Eighth Century Prophets*, 100.

37. Ibid., 115.

38. Renita Weems, *Battered Love: Marriage, Sex, and Violence in the Hebrew Prophets* (Minneapolis: Augsburg Fortress, 1995).

39. Ibid., 117–19.

40. A popularization of Lakoff's study of metaphor appears in George Lakoff, *Don't Think of an Elephant! Know Your Values and Frame the Debate* (White River Jct., VT: Chelsea Green, 2004).

41. Baumann, *Love and Violence*, 237.

42. While I am committed to using inclusive language for God in the present, I believe readers must recognize that God's masculinity was important to ancient writers.

43. Sallie McFague, *Metaphorical Theology: Models of God in Religious Language* (Philadelphia: Fortress Press, 1982).

44. Gail Yee, *Poor Banished Children of Eve: Women as Evil in the Hebrew Bible* (Minneapolis: Fortress Press, 2003), 166.

45. Renita Weems, *I Asked for Intimacy: Stories of Blessings, Betrayals, and Birthings* (San Diego: LuraMedia, 1993).

CHAPTER 3: ANOTHER WAY OF DOING THEOLOGY

1. hooks claims that "patriarchy is the single most life-threatening social disease assaulting the male body and spirit in our nation." bell hooks, *The Will to Change: Men, Masculinity and Love* (New York: Simon & Schuster 2004), 17.

2. See chap. 2 for a discussion of these authors.

3. Annie Dillard, *The Writing Life* (New York: Harper & Row, 1989), 73.

4. Ibid.

5. Chaim Potok, *My Name Is Asher Lev* (Greenwich, CT: Fawcett Crest, 1972).

6. Martha Nussbaum, *Love's Knowledge: Essays on Philosophy and Literature* (New York: Oxford University Press, 1990).

7. Quoted in ibid., 126.

8. Ibid., 133.

9. Ibid., 138.

10. Richard Kearney, *On Stories* (New York: Routledge, 2002), 13.

11. Martha Nussbaum, *The Therapy of Desire: Theory and Practice in Hellenistic Ethics* (Princeton, NJ: Princeton University Press, 1994).

12. Ibid., 441.

13. Ibid., 471.

14. Lee Smith, *On Agate Hill* (Frederick, MD: Prince Recorded Books, 2006).

15. Serene Jones,"Inhabiting Scripture, Dreaming Bible," in *Engaging Biblical Authority: Perspectives on the Bible as Scripture*, ed. William P. Brown (Louisville, KY: Westminster John Knox Press, 2007), 76.

16. Carol Delaney, *Abraham on Trial: The Social Legacy of Biblical Myth* (Princeton, NJ: Princeton University Press, 1998).

17. David Tracy, *The Analogical Imagination: Christian Theology and the Culture of Pluralism* (New York: Crossroad, 1981), 108.

18. Ibid., 102.

19. Ibid., 99.

20. Ibid., 103.

CHAPTER 4: GOD AS (ABUSING) HUSBAND

1. Tikva Frymer-Kensky, "Deuteronomy," in *The Women's Bible Commentary*, ed. Carol A. Newsom and Sharon H. Ringe (Louisville, KY: Westminster John Knox Press, 1992), 52–62.

2. Carol Meyers, *Discovering Eve: Ancient Israelite Women in Context* (New York: Oxford University Press, 1988).

3. See chap. 2 for a discussion of Bowman.

4. Athalya Brenner, "On Prophetic Propaganda and the Politics of 'Love': The Case of Jeremiah," in *A Feminist Companion to the Latter Prophets*, ed. Athalya Brenner (Sheffield: Sheffield Academic Press, 1995), 274.

5. As in the introduction, I use the language of Toni Morrison (*Playing in the Dark* [Cambridge, MA: Cambridge University Press, 1992], 46).

6. Julia M. O'Brien, "Nahum–Habakkuk–Zephaniah: Reading the 'Former Prophets' in the Persian Period," *Interpretation* 61 (2007): 168–83.

CHAPTER 5: GOD AS (AUTHORITARIAN) FATHER

1. Katheryn Pfisterer Darr, *Isaiah's Vision and the Family of God* (Louisville, KY: Westminster John Knox Press, 1994).

2. Carol Delaney, *Abraham on Trial: The Social Legacy of Biblical Myth* (Princeton, NJ: Princeton University Press, 1998).

3. Delaney, *Abraham on Trial*; Danna Nolan Fewell, *The Children of Israel: Reading the Bible for the Sake of our Children* (Nashville: Abingdon Press, 2003); Donald Capps, *The Child's Song: The Religious Abuse of Children* (Louisville KY: Westminster John Knox Press, 1995).

4. Julia M. O'Brien, "On Saying 'No' to a Prophet," *Semeia* 72 (1997): 111–24.

5. Philip Lancaster, *Family Man, Family Leader* (San Antonio, TX: The Vision Forum, 2003).

6. Ibid., Appendix A: "'Patriarchy'—A Good Word for a Hopeful Trend." 311–13.

7. John P. Bartowski and Christopher G. Ellison, "Divergent Models of Childrearing in Popular Manuals: Conservative Protestants vs. the Mainstream Experts," *Sociology of Religion* 56 (1995): 21.

8. Focus on the Family, http://www.family.org.

9. Alice Miller, *For Your Own Good: Hidden Cruelty in Child-Rearing and the Roots of Violence* (New York: Farrar, Straus, & Giroux, 1983).

10. The quote comes from Alice Miller, "The Crucial Role of an Enlightened Witness, or: Why Must The Existing Law Forbidding Corporal Punishment Absolutely Include Our Own Children?" The Zero: Official Web site of Andrew Vachss, http://vachss.com/guest_dispatches/alice_miller4.html (accessed January 26, 2008).

11. Alice Miller, "Childhood Trauma," The Natural Child Project, October 22, 1998, http://www.naturalchild.org/alice_miller/childhood_trauma.html (accessed January 26, 2008).

12. Capps, *Child's Song*, 60–64.

13. John P. Bartowski and J. Bradford Wilcox,"Conservative Protestant Child Discipline: The Case of Parental Yelling," *Social Forces* 79 (2000): 265–90.

14. Ibid., 279.

15. Philip Greven, *The Protestant Temperament: Patterns of Child-Rearing, Religious Experience, and the Self in Early America* (Chicago: University of Chicago Press, 1977), 25.

16. Ibid., 265.

17. Quoted in ibid., 160.

18. James Dobson, "The New Strong-Willed Child," Focus on the Family, 2004, http://www.family.org/parenting/A000001167.cfm (accessed January 26, 2008).

19. Miller, *For Your Own Good*.

20. Capps, *Child's Song*, 63.

21. John Bradshaw, *Creating Love: The Next Great Stage of Growth* (New York: Bantam Books, 1992), 26.

22. Douglas LeBlanc,"Affectionate Patriarchs: An Interview with W. Bradford Wilcox," *Christianity Today* (August 2004): 46.

23. Ibid.

24. Bartowski and Ellison, "Divergent Models of Childrearing," 21–34.

25. Greven, *Protestant Temperament*, 337.

26. George Lakoff, *Moral Politics: How Liberals and Conservatives Think* (Chicago: University of Chicago Press, 2002).

27. bell hooks, *The Will to Change: Men, Masculinity, and Love* (New York: Simon & Schuster, 2004), 20.

28. Ibid., 21.

29. George Lakoff, *Don't Think of an Elephant! Know Your Values and Frame the Debate* (White River Jct., VT: Chelsea Green, 2004).

30. Greven, *Protestant Temperament*, 330.

31. Ibid., 351.

32. In *Will to Change*, 2, hooks claims, "Because patriarchal culture has already taught girls and boys that God's love is more valuable than mother love, it is unlikely that maternal affection will heal the lack of fatherly love."

33. David Blumenthal, *Facing the Abusing God: A Theology of Protest* (Louisville, KY: Westminster John Knox Press, 1993), 79.

34. Melissa Raphael, *The Female Face of God at Auschwitz: A Jewish Feminist Theology of the Holocaust* (New York: Routledge, 2003), 5.

35. Rosemary Radford Ruether, *Sexism and God-Talk: Toward a Feminist Theology* (Boston: Beacon Press, 1993), 69.

36. "Enlightened Witness" is Alice Miller's term for an adult who remains outside the abusive system and enables a child to understand her own treatment as abuse. See Miller, "The Crucial Role of the Enlightened Witness."

CHAPTER 6: GOD AS (ANGRY) WARRIOR

1. For a good summary, see Theodore Hiebert, "Warrior, Divine," in *Anchor Bible Dictionary*, ed. D. N. Freedman (New York: Doubleday, 1992), vol. 6, 876–80.

2. Ellen van Wolde, "The Language of Sentiment," *Society of Biblical Literature,* 2007, http://www.sbl-site.org/publications/article.aspx?articleId=660 (accessed April 17, 2007).

3. Ibid.

4. F. Rachel Magdalene, "Ancient Near Eastern Treaty Curses and the Ultimate Texts of Terror: A Study of the Language of Divine Sexual Abuse in the Prophetic Corpus," in *A Feminist Companion to the Latter Prophets*, ed. Athalya Brenner (Sheffield: Sheffield Academic Press, 1995), 326–52.

5. Drorah Setel, "Prophets and Pornography: Female Sexual Imagery in Hosea," in *Feminist Interpretation of the Bible*, ed. Letty Russell (Philadelphia: Westminster Press, 1985), 86–95; J. Cheryl Exum, "Prophetic Pornography," in *Plotted, Shot, and Painted: Cultural Representations of Biblical Women* (Sheffield: Sheffield Academic Press, 1996), 101–28; Athalya Brenner, "On Prophetic Propaganda and the Politics of 'Love': The Case of Jeremiah," in *A Feminist Companion to the Latter Prophets*, ed. Athalya Brenner (Sheffield: Sheffield Academic Press, 1995), 256–74; Athalya Brenner, "On 'Jeremiah' and the Poetics of (Prophetic?) Pornography," in *On Gendering Texts: Female and Male Voices in the Hebrew Bible*, ed. Athalya Brenner and Fokkelien van Dijk-Hemmes Brenner (Leiden: E. J. Brill, 1996), 178–93.

6. As elsewhere, biblical chapter and verse citations follow English Bibles.

7. Mary Ellen Chase, *The Bible and the Common Reader,* rev. ed. (New York: Macmillan, 1952), as quoted in A. Preminger and E. L. Greenstein, eds., *The Hebrew Bible in Literary Criticism* (New York: Ungar, 1986), 505–6.

8. Judith Sanderson, "Nahum," in *The Women's Bible Commentary*, ed. Carol A. Newsom and Sharon H. Ringe (Louisville, KY: Westminster John Knox Press, 1992), 220–21.

9. Julia Myers O'Brien, *Nahum* (Sheffield: Sheffield Academic Press, 2002).

10. Van Wolde, "The Language of Sentiment."

11. Peter Craigie, *Twelve Prophets* (Philadelphia: Westminster Press, 1985), vol. 2, 58.

12. Wilhelm Wessels, "Nahum, An Uneasy Expression of Yahweh's Power," *Old Testament Essays* 11 (1998): 625.

13. Abraham Joshua Heschel, *The Prophets* (New York: Harper & Row, 1962), 293.

14. Elizabeth Achtemeier, *Nahum–Malachi* (Atlanta: John Knox Press, 1986), 5–6.

15. Duane Christensen, "Nahum," in *Harper's Bible Commentary*, ed. James L. Mays (San Francisco: Harper & Row, 1988), 736.

16. Susan Brownmiller, *Against Our Will: Men, Women and Rape* (Toronto: Bantam Books, 1975).

17. D. N. Premnath, *Eighth Century Prophets: A Social Analysis* (St. Louis: Chalice Press, 2003), 152.

18. Robert A. F. Thurman, *Anger: The Seven Deadly Sins* (New York: Oxford University Press, 2004).

19. Marge Piercy, "A Just Anger," in *Circles on the Water* (New York: Alfred A. Knopf, 1982), 88.

20. Martha Nussbaum, *Love's Knowledge: Essays on Philosophy and Literature* (New York: Oxford University Press, 1990).

21. Andrew Lester, *The Angry Christian* (Louisville, KY: Westminster John Knox Press, 2003), 89.

22. Melinda Wenner, "Anger Fuels Better Decisions," *Live Science,* June 11, 2007, http://www.livescience.com/health/070611_anger_rational.html (accessed August 13, 2007).

23. Susanna Heschel, "Heschel, Abraham Joshua*,*" in *Dictionary of Biblical Interpretation*, ed. John H. Hayes (Nashville: Abingdon Press, 1999), vol. 1, 503.

CHAPTER 7: JERUSALEM AS (DEFENSELESS) DAUGHTER

1. Katheryn Pfisterer Darr, *Isaiah's Vision and the Family of God* (Louisville, KY: Westminster John Knox Press, 1994).

2. F. W. Dobbs-Allsopp, *Weep, O Daughter of Jerusalem: A Study of the City-Lament Genre in the Hebrew Bible* (Rome: Biblical Institute Press, 1993).

3. Darr, *Isaiah's Vision*, chap. 3.

4. Christl Maier, "'Daughter Zion' as Gendered Space in the Book of Isaiah," Society of Biblical Literature Annual Meeting, Atlanta, GA, November 24, 2003.

5. Antje Labahn, "Metaphor and Intertextuality: 'Daughter of Zion' as a Test Case," *Scandinavian Journal of the Old Testament* 17 (2003): 49–67.

6. Tikva Frymer-Kensky, *In the Wake of the Goddesses: Women, Culture, and the Transformation of Biblical Myth* (New York: Free Press, 1992), 172–73.

7. Cynthia Chapman, *The Gendered Language of Warfare in the Israelite-Assyrian Encounter* (Winona, IN: Eisenbrauns, 2004), 64.

8. Ibid., 82.

9. Kathleen O'Connor, "Speak Tenderly to Jerusalem: Second Isaiah's Reception and Use of Daughter Zion," *Princeton Seminary Bulletin,* n.s., 20 (1999): 184.

10. Chapman, *Gendered Language*, 76–96.

11. Maier, "'Daughter Zion,'" 10.

12. Chapman, *Gendered Language*, 93.

13. Maier, "'Daughter Zion,'" 13.

14. Barbara Kaiser, "Poet as 'Female Impersonator': The Image of Daughter Zion as Speaker in Biblical Poems of Suffering," *JR* 67 (1987): 164–82.

15. Ibid., 166.

16. Dobbs-Allsopp, *Weep, O Daughter*, 51.

17. Hans Walter Wolff, *Micah* (Minneapolis: Augsburg, 1990), 124.

18. Dilbert Hillers, *Micah* (Philadephia: Fortress Press, 1984), 61.

19. James Luther Mays, *Micah* (Philadelphia: Westminster Press, 1976), 108.

20. Ibid., 114.

21. Kathleen O'Connor, "Jeremiah," in *The Women's Bible Commentary*, ed. Carol A. Newsom and Sharon H. Ringe (Louisville, KY: Westminster John Knox Press, 1992), 171.

22. Archie Smith Jr., "'Look and See If There Is Any Sorrow Like My Sorrow': Systemic Metaphors for Pastoral Theology and Care," *Pacific School of Religion,* 2004, http://psr.edu/page.cfm?l=62&id=388 (accessed March 23, 2005).

23. Kaiser, "Poet as 'Female Impersonator,'" 82.

24. Laura Mulvey, "Visual Pleasure and Narrative Cinema," *Screen* 16 (1975): 6–18.

25. Carol Clover, "Her Body, Himself: Gender in the Slasher Film," in *Feminist Film Theory: A Reader*, ed. Sue Thornham (New York: New York University Press, 1999), 234–50.

26. bell hooks, "The Oppositional Gaze: Black Female Spectators," in Thornham, *Feminist Film Theory*, 307–20.

27. Jane Gaines, "White Privilege and Looking Relations: Race and Gender in Feminist Film Theory," in Thornham, *Feminist Film Theory*, 293–306.

28. Mary Collins, *The Essential Daughter: Changing Expectations for Girls at Home, 1797 to Present* (Westport, CT: Praeger, 1992).

29. Joan Jacobs Brumberg, *The Body Project: An Intimate History of American Girls* (New York: Vintage, 1998).

30. Ann Burlein, *Lift High the Cross: Where White Supremacy and the Religious Right Converge* (Durham, NC: Duke University Press, 2002), 3.

31. Ibid, 4.

32. George Lakoff, "Metaphor and War: The Metaphor System Used to Justify War in the Gulf," *Vietnam Generation Journal and Newsletter,* 1991, http://www3.iath.virginia.edu/sixties/HTML_docs/Texts/Scholarly/Lakoff_Gulf_Metaphor_2.html.

33. Diane Superville, "Analogies Made During Iraq War Debate," *USA Today*, February 16, 2007, http://www.usatoday.com/news/washington/2007–02-16-iraq-analogies_x.htm.

34. These authors were discussed in chap. 6.

CHAPTER 8: EDOM AS (SELFISH) BROTHER

1. Richard Kearney, *On Stories (*New York: Routledge, 2002), 37.

2. Paul Raabe, *Obadiah* (New York: Doubleday, 1996), 52.

3. Hans Walter Wolff, *Obadiah and Jonah* (Minneapolis: Augsburg, 1986), 18.

4. Gregory Mobley, "Notes to the Book of the Twelve (except Jonah)," in *The New Oxford Annotated Bible*, ed. Michael Coogan (New York: Oxford University Press, 2001), 1318 HB.

5. Itzhaq Beit-Arieh, *Horvat Qitmit: An Edomite Shrine in the Biblical Negev* (Tel Aviv: Institute of Archaeology of Tel Aviv University, 1995); Itzhaq Beit-Arieh, "Excerpts from the Cover Story of *Biblical Archaeology*, December 1996," *Tel Aviv University News*, 1997, http://www.tau.ac.il/taunews/97spring/edom.html (accessed April 19, 2005).

6. Beit-Arieh, "Excerpts."

7. Beit-Arieh, *Horvat Qitmit*, 314.

8. Raabe, *Obadiah*, 53.

9. Joseph Blenkinsopp, "Notes to Isaiah," in *The New Oxford Annotated Bible*, 3rd ed., ed. Michael Coogan (New York: Oxford University Press, 2001), 1066 HB.

10. John Bartlett, "The Brotherhood of Edom," *JSOT* 4 (1977): 2–27.

11. E. Theodore Mullen Jr., *Ethnic Myths and Pentateuchal Foundations: A New Approach to the Formation of the Pentateuch* (Atlanta: Scholars Press, 1997).

12. Ibid, 17.

13. John Bartlett, *Edom and the Edomites* (Sheffield: JSOT Press, 1989).

14. Ian Stern, "The Population of Persian Period Idumaea according to the Ostraca: A Study of Ethnic Boundaries and Ethnogenesis," paper presented at the Society of Biblical Literature Annual Meeting, Washington, DC, Nov. 19, 2006.

15. Raabe, *Obadiah*, 53.

16. Beit-Arieh, "Excerpts."

17. Beit-Arieh, *Horvat Qitmit*, 314, with my italics.

18. Karl Olav Sandnes, "Equality within Patriarchal Structures: Some New Testament Perspectives on the Christian Fellowship as a Brother- or Sisterhood and a Family," in *Constructing Early Christian Families: Family as Social Reality and Metaphor*, ed. Halvor Moxnes (New York: Routledge, 1997), 163.

19. Lone Fatum, "Brotherhood in Christ: A Gender Hermeneutical Reading of 1 Thessalonians," in Moxnes, *Constructing Early Christian Families*, 189.

20. Ibid., 184.

21. Ibid., 193.

22. Quoted in "Robert Burns at the United Nations," Robert Burns Association of North America. 2004, http://www.rbana.com/burns_un.html (accessed August 13, 2007).

23. Ann Burlein, *Lift High the Cross: Where White Supremacy and the Religious Right Converge* (Durham, NC: Duke University Press, 2002).

24. George Lakoff, "Metaphor and War: The Metaphor System Used to Justify War in the Gulf," *Vietnam Generation Journal and Newsletter*, 1991, http://www3.iath.virginia.edu/sixties/HTML_docs/Texts/Scholarly/Lakoff_Gulf_Metaphor_2.html.

25. Ibid.

26. Ibid.

27. Obadiah does claim that Yahweh is the ultimate author of the oracle and mentions "the day of the Lord" in v. 15 and the rule of Yahweh in v. 15. It does not, however, offer a distinctive metaphor for the Deity.

28. Alister McGrath, *Christian Theology: An Introduction*, 4th ed. (Malden, MA: Blackwell, 2006), 102.

CONCLUSION

1. Joanne Passaro, *The Unequal Homeless: Men on the Streets, Women in Their Place* (New York: Routledge, 1996), 1998.

2. Annie Dillard, *The Writing Life* (New York: Harper & Row, 1989).

Bibliography

Achtemeier, Elizabeth. *Nahum–Malachi.* Atlanta: John Knox Press, 1986.

Bartlett, John. *Edom and the Edomites.* Sheffield: JSOT Press, 1989.

———. "The Brotherhood of Edom." *Journal for the Study of the Old Testament* 41 (1977): 2–27.

Bartowski, John P., and Christopher G. Ellison. "Divergent Models of Childrearing in Popular Manuals: Conservative Protestants vs. the Mainstream Experts." *Sociology of Religion* 56 (1995): 21–34.

Bartowski, John P., and W. Bradford Wilcox. "Conservative Protestant Child Discipline: The Case of Parental Yelling." *Social Forces* 79 (2000): 265–90.

Baumann, Gerlinde. *Love and Violence: Marriage as Metaphor for the Relationship between YHWH and Israel in the Prophetic Books.* Translated by Linda M. Maloney. Collegeville, MN: Liturgical Press, 2003.

Beit-Arieh, Itzhaq. *Horvat Qitmit: An Edomite Shrine in the Biblical Negev.* Tel Aviv: Institute of Archaeology of Tel Aviv University, 1995.

———. "Excerpts from the Cover Story of *Biblical Archaeology*, December 1996." *Tel Aviv University News.* 1997. http://www.tau.ac.il/taunews/97spring/edom.html (accessed April 19, 2005).

Blenkinsopp, Joseph. "Notes to Isaiah." In *The New Oxford Annotated Bible.* Edited by Michael Coogan, 974–1072, HB. New York: Oxford University Press, 2001.

Blumenthal, David. *Facing the Abusing God: A Theology of Protest.* Louisville, KY: Westminster John Knox Press, 1993.

Bowman, Craig. "Living in Hosea." In *Preaching the Eighth Century Prophets.* Edited by David Fleer and Dale Bland, 95–118. Abilene, TX: ACU Press, 2004.

Bradshaw, John. *Creating Love: The Next Great Stage of Growth.* New York: Bantam Books, 1992.

Brenner, Athalya. *A Feminist Companion to the Latter Prophets.* Sheffield: Sheffield Academic Press, 1995.

———. "On 'Jeremiah' and The Poetics of (Prophetic?) Pornography." In *On Gendering Texts: Female and Male Voices in the Hebrew Bible*, by Athalya Brenner and Fokkelien van Dijk-Hemmes Brenner, 178–93. Leiden: E. J. Brill, 1996.

———. "On Prophetic Propaganda and the Politics of 'Love': The Case of Jeremiah." In Brenner, *Feminist Companion to the Latter Prophets*, 256–74.

———. *Prophets and Daniel: A Feminist Companion to the Bible.* 2nd ser. Sheffield: Sheffield Academic Press, 2001.

Brownmiller, Susan. *Against Our Will: Men, Women and Rape.* Toronto: Bantam Books, 1975.

Brueggemann, Walter. *The Prophetic Imagination.* Rev. ed. Minneapolis: Fortress Press, 2001.

———. *Theology of the Old Testament: Testimony, Dispute, Advocacy.* Minneapolis: Fortress Press, 1997.

Brumberg, Joan Jacobs. *The Body Project: An Intimate History of American Girls.* New York: Vintage Books, 1998.

Burlein, Ann. *Lift High the Cross: Where White Supremacy and the Religious Right Converge.* Durham, NC: Duke University Press, 2002.

Cameron, Nigel M. de S. *Biblical Higher Criticism and the Defense of Infallibilism in 19th Century Britain.* Lewiston, NY: Edwin Mellon Press, 1987.

Capps, Donald. *The Child's Song: The Religious Abuse of Children.* Louisville, KY: Westminster John Knox Press, 1995.

Chapman, Cynthia. *The Gendered Language of Warfare in the Israelite-Assyrian Encounter.* Winona, IN: Eisenbrauns, 2004.

Chase, Mary Ellen. *The Bible and the Common Reader.* Rev. ed. New York: Macmillan, 1952.

Childs, Brevard S. *Introduction to the Old Testament as Scripture.* Philadelphia: Fortress Press, 1979.

———. *The Struggle to Understand Isaiah as Christian Scripture.* Grand Rapids: Wm. B. Eerdmans Publishing Co., 2004.

Christensen, Duane. "Nahum." In *Harper's Bible Commentary.* Edited by James L. Mays, 736–38. San Francisco: Harper & Row, 1988.

Clements, Ronald E. *One Hundred Years of Old Testament Interpretation.* Philadelphia: Westminster Press, 1976.

Clover, Carol. "Her Body, Himself: Gender in the Slasher Film." In Thornham, *Feminist Film Theory*, 234–50.

Collins, Mary. *The Essential Daughter: Changing Expectations for Girls at Home, 1797 to Present.* Westport, CT: Praeger, 1992.

Craigie, Peter. *Twelve Prophets.* Vol. 2. Philadelphia: Westminster Press, 1985.

Darr, Katheryn Pfisterer. *Isaiah's Vision and the Family of God.* Louisville: Westminster John Knox Press, 1994.

Delaney, Carol. *Abraham on Trial: The Social Legacy of Biblical Myth.* Princeton, NJ: Princeton University Press, 1998.

Dick, Michael. "Survey of Israelite Prophecy." In *Introduction to the Hebrew Bible*, 187–97. Englewood Cliffs, NJ: Prentice Hall, 1988.

Dickinson, Royce, Jr. "Heartbroken for the Heartless." In *Preaching the Eighth Century Prophets*. Edited by David Fleer and Dale Bland, 227–34. Abilene, TX: ACU Press, 2004.

Dillard, Annie. *The Writing Life.* New York: Harper & Row, 1989.

Dobbs-Allsopp, F. W. *Weep, O Daughter of Zion.* Rome: Biblical Institute Press, 1993.

Dobson, James. "The New Strong-Willed Child." Focus on the Family. 2004. http://www .family.org/parenting/A000001167.cfm (accessed January 26, 2008).

Eichrodt, Walther. *Theology of the Old Testament.* 2 vols. Philadelphia: Westminster Press, 1961–67.

Exum, Cheryl. "The Ethics of Biblical Violence against Women." In *The Bible in Ethics: The Second Sheffield Colloquium*, edited by John W. Rogerson, Margaret Davies, and M. Daniel Carroll R., 252–71. Sheffield: Sheffield Academic Press, 1995.

———. "Prophetic Pornography." In *Plotted, Shot, and Painted: Cultural Representations of Biblical Women*, 101–28. Sheffield: Sheffield Academic Press, 1996.

Fatum, Lone. "Brotherhood in Christ: A Gender Hermeneutical Reading of 1 Thessalonians." In *Constructing Early Christian Families: Family as Social Reality and Metaphor*, edited by Halvor Moxnes, 183–200. New York: Routledge, 1997.

Fewell, Danna Nolan. *The Children of Israel: Reading the Bible for the Sake of our Children*. Nashville: Abingdon Press, 2003.

Fowl, Stephen. "Texts Don't Have Ideologies." *Biblical Interpretation* 3 (1995): 15–34.

Froehlich, K. "Aquinas, Thomas." In *Historical Handbook of Major Biblical Interpreters*, edited by Donald K. McKim, 85–90. Downer's Grove, IL: InterVarsity Press, 1998.

Frymer-Kensky, Tikva. "Deuteronomy." In Newsom and Ringe, *The Women's Bible Commentary*, 52–62.

———. *In the Wake of the Goddesses: Women, Culture, and the Transformation of Biblical Myth*. New York: Free Press, 1992.

———. *Studies in the Bible and Feminist Criticism*. Philadelphia: Jewish Publication Society, 2006.

Gaines, Jane. "White Privilege and Looking Relations: Race and Gender in Feminist Film Theory." In Thornham, *Feminist Film Theory*, 293–306.

Greenberg, Irving. *The Jewish Way: Living the Holidays*. New York: Summit Books, 1988.

Greven, Philip. *The Protestant Temperament: Patterns of Child-Rearing, Religious Experience, and the Self in Early America*. Chicago: University of Chicago Press, 1977.

Hays, John H., ed. *Dictionary of Biblical Interpretation*. Nashville Abingdon Press, 1999.

Hays, Richard. *Echoes of Scripture in the Letters of Paul*. New Haven, CT: Yale University Press, 1989.

Heschel, Abraham Joshua. *The Prophets*. New York: Harper & Row, 1962.

Heschel, Susanna. "Heschel, Abraham Joshua." In Hays, in *Dictionary of Biblical Interpretation*, vol. 1, 503.

Hiebert, Theodore. "Warrior, Divine." In *Anchor Bible Dictionary*, edited by David Noel Freedman, vol. 6, 876–80. New York: Doubleday, 1992.

Hillers, Dilbert. *Micah*. Philadephia: Fortress Press, 1984.

hooks, bell. "The Oppositional Gaze: Black Female Spectators." In Thornham, *Feminist Film Theory*, 307–20.

———. *The Will to Change: Men, Masculinity, and Love*. New York: Simon & Schuster, 2003.

Jackson, Samuel Macauley, and Clarence Nevin Heller. *Zwingli's Commentary on True and False Religion*. Durham, NC: Labyrinth Press, 1981.

Jones, Serene. "Inhabiting Scripture, Dreaming Bible." In *Engaging Biblical Authority: Perspectives on the Bible as Scripture*, edited by William P. Brown, 73–80. Louisville, KY: Westminster John Knox Press, 2007.

Kaiser, Barbara. "Poet as 'Female Impersonator': The Image of Daughter Zion as Speaker in Biblical Poems of Suffering." *Journal of Religion* 67 (1987): 164–82.

Kearney, Richard. *On Stories*. New York: Routledge, 2002.

Labahn, Antje. "Metaphor and Intertextuality: 'Daughter of Zion' as a Test Case." *Scandinavian Journal of the Old Testament* 17 (2003): 49–67.

Lakoff, George. *Don't Think of an Elephant! Know Your Values and Frame the Debate*. White River Jct., VT: Chelsea Green, 2004.

———. "Metaphor and War: The Metaphor System Used to Justify War in the Gulf." *Vietnam Generation Journal and Newsletter*. 1991. http://www3.iath.virginia.edu/sixties/HTML_docs/Texts/Scholarly/Lakoff_Gulf_Metaphor_2.html (accessed April 19, 2005).

————. *Moral Politics: How Liberals and Conservatives Think.* Chicago: University of Chicago Press, 2002.

Lancaster, Phillip, *Family Man, Family Leader.* San Antonio, TX: The Vision Forum, 2003.

LeBlanc, Douglas. "Affectionate Patriarchs: An Interview with W. Bradford Wilcox." *Christianity Today* (August 2004): 44–46.

Lester, Andrew. *The Angry Christian.* Louisville, KY: Westminster John Knox Press, 2003.

Lowe, Stephen D. "Book Review of Walter Brueggemann, *Theology of the Old Testament.*" *Global Journal of Classical Theology.* http://www.trinitysem.edu/journal/sd_lowe_revu.html (accessed January 25, 2008).

Magdalene, F. Rachel. "Ancient Near Eastern Treaty Curses and the Ultimate Texts of Terror: A Study of the Language of Divine Sexual Abuse in the Prophetic Corpus." In Brenner, *Feminist Companion to the Latter Prophets,* 326–52.

Maier, Christl. "'Daughter Zion' as Gendered Space in the Book of Isaiah." Paper presented at the Society of Biblical Literature Annual Meeting, Atlanta, GA, Nov. 24, 2003.

Mays, James Luther. *Micah.* Philadelphia: Westminster Press, 1976.

McFague, Sallie. *Metaphorical Theology: Models of God in Religious Language.* Philadelphia: Fortress Press, 1982.

McGrath, Alister. *Christian Theology: An Introduction.* 4th ed. Malden, MA: Blackwell, 2006.

Meyers, Carol. *Discovering Eve: Ancient Israelite Women in Context.* New York: Oxford University Press, 1988.

Miller, Alice. "Childhood Trauma." The Natural Child Project. October 22, 1998. http://www.naturalchild.org/alice_miller/childhood_trauma.html (accessed January 26, 2008).

————. "The Crucial Role of an Enlightened Witness, or, Why Must the Existing Law Forbidding Corporal Punishment Absolutely Include Our Own Children?" *The Zero: Official Website of Andrew Vachss.* http://vachss.com/guest_dispatches/alice_miller4.html (accessed January 28, 2008).

————. *For Your Own Good: Hidden Cruelty in Child-Rearing and the Roots of Violence.* New York: Farrar, Straus, & Giroux, 1983.

————. "An Open Letter to All Responsible Politicians." The Natural Child Project. February 2000. http://www.naturalchild.org/alice_miller/spanking_open_letter.html (accessed January 26, 2008).

Mobley, Gregory. "Notes to the Book of the Twelve (except Jonah)." In *New Oxford Annotated Bible,* edited by Michael Coogan, 1278–1320, 1325–75, HB. New York: Oxford University Press, 2001.

Morrison, Toni. *Playing in the Dark.* Cambridge, MA: Cambridge University Press, 1992.

Mullen, E. Theodore, Jr. *Ethnic Myths and Pentateuchal Foundations: A New Approach to the Formation of the Pentateuch.* Atlanta: Scholars Press, 1997.

Mulvey, Laura. "Visual Pleasure and Narrative Cinema." *Screen* 16 (1975): 6–18.

Newsom, Carol A., and Sharon H. Ringe, eds. *The Women's Bible Commentary.* Louisville, KY: Westminster John Knox Press, 1992.

Nussbaum, Martha. *Love's Knowledge: Essays on Philosophy and Literature.* New York: Oxford University Press, 1990.

————. *The Therapy of Desire: Theory and Practice in Hellenistic Ethics.* Princeton, NJ: Princeton University Press, 1994.

O'Brien, Julia Myers. "Judah as Wife and Husband: Deconstructing Gender in Malachi." *Journal of Biblical Literature* 115 (1996): 243–252.

———. "Malachi." In Hays, *Dictionary of Biblical Interpretation*, vol. K–Z, 110–13.

———. *Nahum*. Sheffield: Sheffield Academic Press, 2002.

———. "Nahum–Habakkuk–Zephaniah: Reading the 'Former Prophets in the Persian Period." *Interpretation* 61 (2007): 168–83.

———. "On Saying 'No' to Prophet." *Semeia* 72 (1997): 111–24.

O'Connor, Kathleen. "Jeremiah." In Newsom and Ringe, *The Women's Bible Commentary*, 169–77.

———. "Speak Tenderly to Jerusalem: Second Isaiah's Reception and Use of Daughter Zion." *Princeton Seminary Bulletin* n.s. 20 (1999): 281–94.

Passaro, Joanne. *The Unequal Homeless: Men on the Streets, Women in Their Place*. New York: Routledge, 1996.

Peters, John P. *The Old Testament and the New Scholarship*. London: Methuen & Co., 1901.

Piercy, Marge. "A Just Anger." In *Circles on the Water*, 88. New York: Alfred A. Knopf, 1982.

Potok, Chaim. *My Name Is Asher Lev*. Greenwich, CT: Fawcett Crest, 1972.

Premnath, D. N. *Eighth Century Prophets: A Social Analysis*. St. Louis: Chalice Press, 2003.

Raabe, Paul. *Obadiah*. Anchor Bible 24D. New York: Doubleday, 1996.

Raphael, Melissa. *The Female Face of God at Auschwitz: A Jewish Feminist Theology of the Holocaust*. New York: Routledge, 2003.

"Robert Burns at the United Nations." Robert Burns Association of North America. 2004. http://www.rbana.com/burns_un.html (accessed August 13, 2007).

Ruether, Rosemary Radford. *Sexism and God-Talk: Toward a Feminist Theology*. Boston: Beacon Press, 1993.

Sanderson, Judith. "Amos." In Newsom and Ringe, *The Women's Bible Commentary*, 205–9.

———. "Nahum." In Newsom and Ringe, *The Women's Bible Commentary*, 217–21.

Sandnes, Karl Olav. "Equality within Patriarchal Structures: Some New Testament Perspectives on the Christian Fellowship as a Brother- or Sisterhood and a Family." In *Constructing Early Christian Families: Family as Social Reality and Metaphor*, edited by Halvor Moxnes, 150–65. New York: Routledge, 1997.

Sawyer, John A. *The Fifth Gospel: Isaiah in the History of Christianity*. Cambridge: Cambridge University Press, 1996.

Setel, Drorah. "Prophets and Pornography: Female Sexual Imagery in Hosea." In *Feminist Interpretation of the Bible*, edited by Letty Russell, 86–95. Philadelphia: Westminster Press, 1985.

Smalley, Beryl. *The Study of the Bible in the Middle Ages*. 3rd ed. Oxford: Basil Blackwell, 1983.

Smith, Archie, Jr. ""Look and See If There Is Any Sorrow Like My Sorrow": Systemic Metaphors for Pastoral Theology and Care." *Pacific School of Religion*. 2004. http://psr.edu/page.cfm?l=62&id=388 (accessed March 23, 2005).

Smith, Lee. *On Agate Hill*. Frederick, MD: Prince Recorded Books, 2006.

Stern, Ian. "The Population of Persian Period Idumaea according to the Ostraca: A Study of Ethnic Boundaries and Ethnogenesis." Paper presented at the Society of Biblical Literature Annual Meeting, Washington D.C., Nov. 19, 2006.

Superville, Darlene. "Analogies Made during Iraq War Debate." *USA Today*. February 16, 2007.http://www.usatoday.com/news/washington/2007-02-16-iraq-analogies_x.htm.

Thornham, Sue, ed. *Feminist Film Theory: A Reader*. New York: New York University Press, 1999.

Thurman, Robert A. F. *Anger: The Seven Deadly Sins.* New York: Oxford University Press, 2004.

Tracy, David. *The Analogical Imagination: Christian Theology and the Culture of Pluralism.* New York: Crossroad, 1981.

United States Department of Agriculture, Safety, Health, and Employee Welfare. *Domestic Violence Awareness Handbook.* http://www.usda.gov/da/shmd/aware.htm (accessed January 26, 2008).

Van Wolde, Ellen. "The Language of Sentiment." *Society of Biblical Literature.* 2007. http://www.sbl-site.org/publications/article.aspx?articleId=660 (accessed April 17, 2007).

Von Rad, Gerhard. *Old Testament Theology.* 2 vols. New York: Harper, 1962–65.

———. *The Message of the Prophets.* Translated by D. M. G. Stalker. New York: Harper & Row, 1967.

Weems, Renita. *Battered Love: Marriage, Sex, and Violence in the Hebrew Prophets.* Minneapolis: Augsburg Fortress, 1995.

———. *I Asked for Intimacy: Stories of Blessings, Betrayals, and Birthings.* San Diego: Lura-Media, 1993.

Wellhausen, Julius. *Prolegomena to the History of Ancient Israel.* Gloucester, MA: Peter Smith, 1973.

Wenner, Melinda. "Anger Fuels Better Decisions." *Live Science.* June 11, 2007. http://www.livescience.com/health/070611_anger_rational.html (accessed August 13, 2007).

Wessels, Wilhelm. "Nahum, an Uneasy Expression of Yahweh's Power." *Old Testament Essays* 11 (1998): 615–28.

Wolff, Hans Walter. *Micah.* Minneapolis: Augsburg, 1990.

———. *Obadiah and Jonah.* Minneapolis: Augsburg, 1986.

Yates, Kyle. *Preaching from the Prophets.* New York: Harper & Bros., 1942.

Yee, Gale A. *Poor Banished Children of Eve: Women as Evil in the Hebrew Bible.* Minneapolis: Fortress Press, 2003.

Scripture Index

Index of Subjects and Names